HAROLD PINTER AND THE TWILIGHT OF MODERNISM

VARUN BEGLEY

Harold Pinter and the Twilight of Modernism

UNIVERSITY OF TORONTO PRESS
Toronto Buffalo London

© University of Toronto Press Incorporated 2005
Toronto Buffalo London
Printed in Canada

ISBN 0-8020-3887-5

Printed on acid-free paper

Library and Archives Canada Cataloguing in Publication

Begley, Varun
Harold Pinter and the twilight of modernism / Varun Begley.

Includes bibliographical references and index.
ISBN 0-8020-3887-5

1. Pinter, Harold, 1930– – Criticism and interpretation.
I. Title.

PR6066.I53Z54 2005   822'.912   C2005-902193-4

University of Toronto Press acknoweldges the financial assistance to its
publishing program of the Canada Council for the Arts and the Ontario
Arts Council.

Contents

vi   Contents

Acknowledgments

I want to express my thanks to the College of William and Mary, and to the English department in particular, for their generous support of this project. Though I hope it is clear in the text, I would like to acknowledge the influence of Andreas Huyssen's *After the Great Divide: Modernism, Mass Culture, Postmodernism*, one of whose section titles – 'Toward the Postmodern' – is also used in this book. A portion of chapter 2 appeared in *The Pinter Review,* and portions of chapter 3 appeared in the journal *Modern Drama* and in *The Art of Crime: The Plays and Films of Harold Pinter and David Mamet*, published by Routledge and edited by Leslie Kane; I am grateful to the readers and editors for their insights and suggestions and to the editors and publishers for permission to reprint. Special thanks to Jill McConkey, my editor at Toronto, and to the Toronto readers who pushed the book in new and constructive directions.

For comments, ideas, and support at various stages of the project I am especially indebted to David Bathrick, Jutka Devenyi, Scott McMillin, Amy Villarejo, Leslie Kane, Arthur Knight, Elizabeth Barnes, Simon Joyce, and Christopher MacGowan. Thanks also to Valerie Hardy, whose paintings and conversation have helped me to see Pinter's work in a different light. Lastly, I want to express my abiding gratitude for the inestimable support provided by Hope Cooper, to whom this book is dedicated. 'The smallest social unit is not the single person but two people,' as Brecht says.

HAROLD PINTER AND THE TWILIGHT OF MODERNISM

Introduction

... the explosion of modern literature into a host of distinct private styles
and mannerisms has been followed by a linguistic fragmentation of social life
itself ... Modernist styles thereby become postmodernist codes.

Fredric Jameson[1]

A last modernist

This book looks back on the twilight of modernism. It rests on the idea
that the hard edges of modernist debate, considered historically, may
lend some shape to today's more fluid cultural politics. The stark, but
constantly shifting adversarial stances in modernist discourse mapped
a range of aesthetic and political positions that in many ways we still
occupy. Many of modernism's key problems persist in the postmodern
moment, if in increasingly unstable forms. The book is intended as a
contribution to the prehistory of the postmodern – if I can put it this
way – from the perspective of modern drama. As a vehicle for such
investigation, drama has certain advantages. From Ibsen to Beckett,
modern drama provides a ready-made genealogy, a tight and integrated canon that encapsulates the tensions of modern art in a well-
defined form. Moreover, drama is an explicit concern of key contribu-
tors to modernist discourse such as Bertolt Brecht, Georg Lukács, and
T.W. Adorno. Gradually, however, the cultural studies traditions with
which these writers are associated have shifted away from theatre.
Brecht's theories have spread across a number of fields, and the influence of Lukács and Adorno is more evident in areas such as fiction and
music. On a local basis I want to reconnect this influential strain of cul-

tural criticism with its dramatic roots via a late-modern playwright who evokes modernism while anticipating its decline. I will argue that this writer's works collectively traverse the Great Divide (Andreas Huyssen's phrase)[2] between modernism and its historical 'others': popular entertainment, politically committed art, technological mass culture. I take a single author as evidence of a larger crisis, while arguing that the discourses of this crisis can help us to understand his famously enigmatic work. It is vital that neither half of this equation overwhelms the other; I hope that author and context, plays and theory form a balanced conjuncture.

The writer under consideration is Harold Pinter, a singular and imposing figure who is now the subject of almost constant reinterpretation. New monographs and essays on Pinter appear every year – many of the latter in the annual publication, *The Pinter Review* – and two retrospective collections of essays have recently been published.[3] Disturbing political pieces are the focus of festivals; the once scandalously enigmatic early plays are fixtures in classrooms, revivals, and seminars. As this energetic state of flux suggests, Pinter's work has stubbornly resisted domestication. In 2000 the playwright himself (as director) muddied the waters by pairing his first play, *The Room* (1957), with his most recent, *Celebration* (2000). Whether this was intended as a subversive juxtaposition or as an assertion of authorial continuity is unclear, but in a certain sense the question itself makes a point. Pinter presents unusual challenges to literary history, challenges that make him a significant figure for the historiography of modern drama, political art, and modernism more generally. This is the career of a cultural provocateur battling definitive judgments and the aura of mastery they create. Pinter's works and public acts attempt to break the circuit of semantic power and control whose authoritarian political implications are the subject of his 1980s plays. Pinter remains to a curious degree vital and intransigent when confronted with generalizations.

This quality of present-ness, of resistance to detached perspective, is reflected in the flourishing critical literature. I am joining a lively conversation; the expanding field of Pinter studies indicates that his writings and authorship continue to strike a nerve. In various ways criticism has drawn energy from Pinter's recalcitrance. The sheer diversity of the career has fostered salutary self-awareness, encouraging a critical practice mindful of the complexity of authorship and author-study in general. Michael Billington's monumental *The Life and Work of Harold Pinter*, for example, functions as an avant-garde work, one that makes a contribution to the genre of literary biography. Judging from the collected essays in *Pinter at Seventy* and *The Cambridge Companion to Harold Pinter*, the career has become a kind of meta-narrative, an authorial picaresque, which increasingly shapes responses to the primary works. Recondite absurdist, admirer of Beckett, adapter of Proust and Kafka, and apolitical littérateur, but also political firebrand, adapter of middlebrow fiction, screenwriter for florid filmmaker Joseph Losey, toast of the West End – all of these tags could be justly applied. Criticism of Pinter is almost forced to acknowledge the plurality of the subject and (beneficially) the local, provisional nature of the interpretive process.

I would suggest that liminal figures like Pinter can also contribute to cultural studies discourse. Pinter's late-modern authorship blurs the adversarial simplicity of the Great Divide and complicates clear-cut distinctions between the modern and postmodern. One wonders what writers like Lukács, Brecht, and Adorno might think of a writer arguably political and apolitical, modernist and populist, culturally high and low. It is this sort of question that initially inspired this project. Modern drama, cultural studies, Harold Pinter – the book seeks to align these three fields of force. What is needed is an account of Pinter's *modernity*, a reading that takes his work as a response, in a British context, to the political and aesthetic problems of modernism generally. Should an artist engage political realities or withdraw from them? How does mass culture affect the aesthetics of drama, and what does it mean for a serious dramatist to work in television and film? Can entertainment also be art, and vice-versa? Read against the grain, Pinter's complex, contradictory career throws these questions into sharp relief. To counter literary conceptions of authorship, I explore Pinter's connections to the mass media; his absurdism is assessed as entertainment; I read the political plays through the lens of modernism and the modernist plays politically.

I want to return Pinter's work to the historical kiln in which it was first fired, the crisis of art and popular culture, aesthetics and politics, that marks the late stages of modernity. I will argue that Pinter embodies a transition, that his career spans a cultural divide both aesthetically and politically. On the one hand, he can be (and has been) read in relation to canonical modernists like Kafka, Beckett, and Ionesco. Yet his commercial success and multi-media forays continually complicate his literary status. Politically, Pinter moves from professed disinterest to fierce engagement, both on- and offstage. In exploring these tensions I am trying to trace a historical boundary, a late instance of modernism in which the emerging surfaces of the postmodern are already visible. For this reason, the scope of the book is limited to the central arc of Pinter's career as it bears on the culture and politics of modernity, the period between 1958 and 1991, which encompasses the early works that made him famous, his ongoing experiments in radio and film, the introverted memory plays of the 1970s, and the turn to political drama in the 1980s. For purposes of contrast, the book begins and ends with two postmodern plays. The book concludes with *Ashes to Ashes* (1996), a postmodern coda to the cycle of political drama outlined in the last chapter. This introduction concludes with *Moonlight* (1993), which I take as a kind of elegy on the theme of modernity. *Moonlight* provides a rearview mirror that frames the book's look back at modernity. Throughout I argue that Pinter's career, considered holistically, can function as a cultural microcosm, that he is an exemplary figure who can tell us something essential about the late stages of modernism. Anthony Cronin's biography of Samuel Beckett is subtitled *The Last Modernist*,[4] but in a certain way the title better suits Pinter, especially if one could add 'and an early postmodern.'

'someone called Pinter'

Even a brief survey of Pinter's résumé suggests an unusual author – modern and postmodern, asocial and committed, culturally 'high' and 'low.' The narrative of his career embraces historically distinct models of authorship and is therefore well suited to illuminate the erosion of the Great Divide. Pinter's authorship emerges as a transitional phenomenon, one that hangs as a backdrop to the discussion of individual works. Provisionally, one could position his authorship between the poles of the Pinteresque – an adjective that, like Kafkaesque or Beckettian, announces a monolithic structure of feeling[5] – and the postmodern. In hindsight we see an unresolved struggle between the forces of coherent, integrated authorship and the pressures of an encroaching postmodernism. As suggested in the opening epigraph, the postmodern moment works to fragment authorship by reifying and codifying moods and styles and undermining the idea of unmediated expression.

In this aspect Pinter can be linked to other late-modern playwrights such as his younger American contemporaries Sam Shepard and David Mamet. Each of these writers has one foot in a kind of modernist orthodoxy; their origins can be traced to familiar movements and influences. Yet each has worked through and beyond his formative aesthetics, emerging as much more fluid and polyvalent authors. For example, in a recent study, Stephen J. Bottoms has suggested that there are 'three Sam Shepards vying for ascendancy in his writing: the "high" or "romantic" modernist, the "late" modernist, and what I will call the reluctant postmodernist.' Bottoms sees Shepard exhibiting a crisis in expression: avant-garde utopian optimism mixes with absurdist scepticism and eventually with postmodernist resignation to the ubiquity of a 'flashy, violent, and spiritually bankrupt society.'[6] As I will maintain, Pinter has also traversed the modern and postmodern, albeit on a different trajectory and terrain.

A closer analogy might be with David Mamet. One senses that Mamet's public persona, like Pinter's, has been orchestrated (played, almost) with irony, savvy, and often cynicism about media society. Also, Mamet, like Pinter and Shepard, has worked extensively in film. (As Bottoms points out, Shepard's career as an actor further complicates assessment of his authorship and iconicity.) More fundamentally, the brand names Mamet and Pinter evoke tight, invariant combinations of aesthetic world, attitude, and style, even as both writers have played with and against this tendency. Pinter might in this sense be called a 'dialectical author,' a term I have elsewhere applied to Mamet.[7]

Perhaps the best shorthand for Pinter's authorship comes from discussions of the auteur in film. Like the film director, the authorial agency of the playwright is necessarily decentralized and contingent. In both cases, verifying the bona fides of the author requires some active detection and decipherment. The vexing but suggestive debates over auteur theory provide an object lesson in the problem of mediated authorship. In the chapter on auteur theory in his influential book *Signs and Meaning in the Cinema*, Peter Wollen argues that lesser directors leave obvious fingerprints. The authorship of such directors is reducible to a set of repeated, constant motifs, whereas great directors 'must be defined in terms of shifting relations, in their singularity as well as their uniformity.' Wollen is quick to point out that this is not to apply a high cultural model of unmediated artistic expression to commercial film directors, whose 'visions' are modified by a number of factors. Film authorship is heavily mediated, and as a result a film is 'a network of different statements, crossing and contradicting each other, elaborated into a final "coherent" vision.' What one looks for is not the obvious authorial touch, not an evident world view or self-given meaning, but 'a structure which underlies the film and shapes it, gives it a certain pattern of energy cathexis.'[8] Pinter's authorship is likewise highly mediated. It is an authorship contingent on his evolving public persona, subject to varying realizations in stage and film productions, that oscillates between theatre and mass media, entertainment and art. Wollen's provocative suggestion leads us to look not for a unified 'Pinter' but for a complex, shifting structure.

The complexity of this structure poses significant challenges for a study devoted to a single writer. Such a study generally suggests a unified vision on the part of the writer and a unified argument on the part of the critic, to the critic's tactical benefit. Considerable power accrues to a project organized under the aegis of a single author. The rubric 'Harold Pinter' links disparate works to an individual life, embedding textual analysis in commonsensical narratives of personal and artistic development. At the same time, comparing themes or techniques across an author's career may lead inadvertently to a circular and opaque suggestion of self-identity. To say that Jean Renoir is interested in deep-focus cinematography or David Mamet writes about American capitalism or Harold Pinter is concerned with power and language can smother the particularities of the films or plays. The reified author resists historical or ideological differentiation. The danger lies in succumbing to the mystique of originality, in judging diverse works as ancillary to a larger authorial unity.

The danger is compounded in Pinter's case. On the one hand, viewed with a postmodern eye, his career appears to be that of a plural, multivocal author who resists reification. At the same time, there persists an unyielding, total quality that invites generalization. I believe Pinter's authorship is fundamentally marked by this tension between self-identity and difference. His works solicit and mobilize a desire for the univocal Author (the notion of the Pinteresque is an expression of this desire) even as the variety of his works undercuts any easy recourse to unified authority. One could argue – following Peter Raby's assertion of the 'strong coherence' of Pinter's work[9] – that a unified, if complex, authorial identity hovers over or is latent within the surface plurality. For a variety of reasons we like Authors, and the name Pinter has functioned as a double-edged sword. Since the bewilderment surrounding the premiere of *The Birthday Party*, Pinter's plays have been shrouded by his persona. Soon, the initially reticent writer was transformed into an icon – the 'someone called Pinter' that Pinter has ruefully described.[10] This reification affects reception. The familiar Pinter brand name and its variants can serve to evoke but also distance the felt experience of his work. For spectators and critics alike, the plays' strangeness may be softened by the author's familiar garb.

The dialectic of self-identity and difference is observable in the history of Pinter criticism. Earlier I suggested that the continuing vitality of Pinter studies signals complex authorship. In a beneficial sense, those writing in the field are obliged to reflect on questions of unity and coherence in relation to authorial voice, and thus Pinter criticism has much to add, directly and indirectly, to discourse on authorship. Pinter studies, I believe, can serve as a paradigmatic instance of late-modern author study. I will be particularly concerned with the history of critical explanation as it evolved during the earlier phrases of Pinter's career. I consider this history to be part and parcel of the Pinter phenomenon – an evolving discourse that shaped the works' intelligibility in relation to changing cultural conditions. The point is not to invalidate earlier interpretations but to examine the hermeneutic crisis surrounding Pinter as evidence of something fundamental at an aesthetic level.

While loosely unified around 'someone called Pinter,' the vastness of the critical discourse also creates a sense of authorial entropy. A book-length meta-survey of various approaches, trends, and paradigms within Pinter studies appeared as early as 1990.[11] The resistance offered by the works reflexively makes the critic's position more visible and self-aware, and the discourse brings into relief an array of critical methods, theories, and agendas. Indeed, in interesting ways, the history of Pinter studies mirrors the tensions between the modern and postmodern aspects of the primary works. Key early studies by Martin Esslin (1961), Raymond Williams (1968), and Austin Quigley (1975) help to construct Pinter's modernism. Compared with the conspicuous pluralism of recent collections, such as *Pinter at Seventy* and *The Cambridge Companion to Harold Pinter*, these early works have a totalizing, all-or-nothing rhetorical flavour consistent with modernist conceptions of singular authorial vision and style. The earlier criticism is premised on acceptance of a fully formed aesthetic world willed into being by the artist. The coherence of this world is established by monolithic abstractions. Esslin's frame of reference for Pinter is the Absurd, writ large; Quigley's seminal study is starkly titled *The Pinter Problem*; Williams's comparisons are with high modernism: he writes in 1968 that Pinter's plays 'are strange only in the absence of a tradition in European literature of the last fifty years.'[12]

Peter Raby, by contrast, in his introduction to *The Cambridge Compan-*

ion to Harold Pinter (2001), concludes that while the diverse essays collectively convey that Pinter's writing has a 'sense of continuity and evolution,' it is also true that his work 'invites constant re-evaluation' and that the collection represents only one 'set of perspectives.'[13] The essay, rather than the book, seems the privileged form for these postmodern interventions, since the essay is self-consciously provisional and fragmentary. *The Pinter Problem* is monolithic in both topic and argument, whereas the coherence of *The Cambridge Companion to Harold Pinter* is only tenuously guaranteed by 'Harold Pinter.' In the collection as a whole, the presumptive unity of the author is in practice undercut by the multiple voices and perspectives. Relatively speaking, the first book is about a modern Pinter, the second about a postmodern one.

A contemporary book-length study of Pinter is obliged to mirror the dialectical author, to incorporate the competing pulls of identity and difference, coherence and fragmentation into the structure of its argument. Particularly now, as the postmodern Pinter solicits local, provisional interpretive acts, a book about Pinter must try to remain faithful to the ethics of the essay even as it seeks a composite view. Part of what makes Pinter a provocative topic is that his liminality necessarily affects the critical form. By virtue of its status as a book and its focus on Pinter's modernist moment, this study is partly a totalizing response to a totalizing aesthetic. But it also reflects a process of pluralization as its subject and its argument move towards the postmodern.

Resistance

The playwright Terence Rattigan once confronted Pinter with an allegorical reading of *The Caretaker*: 'It's the Old Testament God and the New Testament God, with the Caretaker as humanity – that's what it's about, isn't it?' Pinter disagreed: 'It's about two brothers and a caretaker.'[14] Something essential emerges from this anecdote; Pinter's plays hum with Significance but combat its articulation. Commentators phrase this predicament in various ways, but I consider it the result of systematic *resistance* to meaning-making, a formal quality that pervades both local details and larger structures. This quality is one of the book's central motifs. Resistance strikes a dissonant chord that sounds over many of Pinter's works. To forestall the Sisyphean prospect of perpetual interpretive frustration, it is useful to step back and examine resistance as a constitutive formal feature. Pinter's work is

obviously not alone in creating an aura of aesthetic density that interrupts conventional cognitive processes and habits of perception.
Indeed, this has long been identified as a characteristic feature of modern art. As early as 1917, the formalist critic Victor Shklovsky argued:
'The purpose of art is to impart the sensation of things as they are perceived and not as they are known. The technique of art is to make
objects "unfamiliar," to make forms difficult, to increase the difficulty
and length of perception because the process of perception is an aesthetic end in itself and must be prolonged.'[15] Though inhabiting a
much different context, one could say that Pinter shows a latter-day
affinity for Shklovsky's early-modern sensibility. Again, it is reciprocally useful to link Pinter's aesthetics to other strains of modernist
discourse.

The paradigm of formal intransigence and perceptual strain allows
us to relate widely disparate responses to Pinter's work. Indeed, this
disparateness is a logical outcome of an aesthetic based on difficult
forms. Seen in this light, the vicissitudes of Pinter criticism are not
solely matters of academic interest, but rather reflect a fundamental
recalcitrance that all spectators are forced to confront. Implicitly and
explicitly, the critical literature on Pinter has much to say about the
nature and function of interpretative processes. Beyond the aesthetic
value that Shklovsky terms 'defamiliarization,'[16] Pinter's resistance
acts as a prism that refracts and exposes the analyst's expectations
and perceptions. Often, the plays' open hostility to abstract interpretation shifts emphasis to the troubling materiality of language, objects,
and gestures. This shift undermines detached perspectives, underscoring a crisis in meaning that can be referred back to modernism
generally.

Through close analysis, one can locate interpretive obstacles that
compel new tactics of reading. Typically, Pinter's works dangle a
mirage of deep meaning, inviting and then discouraging hermeneutic
interpretation. Early in *The Homecoming*, the ageing patriarch Max
advises his son Joey, an aspiring boxer: 'What you've got to do is
you've got to learn how to defend yourself, and you've got to learn
how to attack. That's your only trouble as a boxer. You don't know
how to defend yourself, and you don't know how to attack.'[17] This
image appears self-consciously metaphorical, but it is also nearly
unreadable. Is Max describing bad boxing or existential paralysis? In
either case, the speech is a jab to the solar plexus, generating an immediate affective response while knocking the wind from articulate

exegesis. Beyond or before critical reading, what survives a Pinter performance is a kind of guilty pleasure: uneasy laughter, an abiding sense of disquiet, and a perception of having been, however strangely, entertained. To an unusual degree, his work remains immanent in the encounter, as if it were used up in a complex visceral experience that is subsequently difficult to explain.

Affective excess is an enemy of interpretation, insofar as it defines a negative space in the architecture of explanatory systems. Abstract interpretations often strive to master the strangeness and excess of Pinter's works by postulating an Archimedean distance. But does critical 'distance' constitute a solution or an evasion? Indeed, post hoc hermeneutical posturing was already taken as evidence of the titular dilemma in Austin Quigley's seminal *The Pinter Problem* (1975). In revolutionary fashion, Quigley exposes a persistent movement towards second-order abstractions in Pinter criticism, and his study remains an indispensable critique of metaphysical tendencies. In the secondary literature, Quigley discerns recurrences of allegorical hermeneutics, 'symbol hunting,' linguistic naïveté, and other vestigial errors of mimetic criticism. Conventional approaches fostered dualistic treatments of language; particular speech-acts were subordinated to hidden networks of meaning felt to be present beyond, above, or below the surface of the scene. He suggests that such dualisms displace significance to imaginary poetical and aesthetic realms while implicitly denigrating Pinter's specific uses of language on stage.

Quigley's own anti-hermeneutical structuralism provides a countering explanatory model of Pinter's recalcitrance, one that seeks to return to the plays' immediacy in performance. 'It seems to be in retrospect rather than in performance that the problem of relating technical virtuosity to something felt to be more substantial occurs,' he writes; 'somehow an understanding sufficient for a memorable performance is not sufficient to provide an adequate basis for accounting for the success of that performance.' I would go further and say that this basic disjuncture between performance and memory is heightened by the forbidding insularity of Pinter's dramatic world. The plays' execution leaves an impression of craftsmanship and skill, but this sensation is severed from referential significance. Presentation is privileged above representation, and the works appear better suited to engagement than reflection. In this context, Quigley's alternative is systematically to explore how individual enunciations and speech-acts function to assert, challenge, and structure the various identities, relationships, and contexts operative in a given situation. The result is a kind of rhetoric of Pinter, a refreshingly social conception of the 'functional plurality of language'[18] in his plays.

It is interesting, however, that Quigley's study also sometimes invokes extrinsic yardsticks by which the particularities of the 'memorable performance' are measured. On the subject of characters, for example, he remarks that 'their linguistic battles are not the product of an arbitrary desire for dominance but crucial battles for control of the means by which personality is created in the social systems to which they belong. As they struggle to cope, their misunderstandings and miscalculations provide a great deal of amusement for any audience, but invariably desperation and terror are eventually revealed as the linguistic warfare becomes increasingly crucial.' Quigley's view of language is performative and relational, but his conception of performance is occasionally mimetic. Here, he posits a representational correspondence between the world of the play and 'social systems' whose 'crucial' status for the audience presumably derives from their verisimilitude. Quigley thereby lays claim to a realist aesthetic that tends to convert the pleasures and resistances of performance into a kind of pedagogical value. His admirable impatience with those who hypostatize Pinter as a transcendent poet ('Unless the evidence deceives us all, Pinter is a dramatist')[19] is periodically offset by a willingness to universalize the theatre as a privileged, neutral site for the production of social knowledge. The complexities of audience response are implicitly reduced, as an apparently superficial 'amusement' yields to 'crucial' understanding. In writing about Pinter, it is admittedly almost impossible to escape such teleological moments. But this double bind is precisely at issue; at the most general level, what Pinter's work resists is the teleology of criticism. In modelling this resistance, it is crucial to preserve one of Quigley's core insights, namely, the fact that Pinter's work derives power from its capacity to subvert critical hierarchies by engaging perception and intuition as well as rational cognition.

Negation, autonomy, commitment

Resistance also points down another path, one that runs through a different precinct of modernism. In an idiom with which Pinter is not normally associated, resistance might be rephrased as *negation*. The term links formal difficulty to an influential paradigm of aesthetic autonomy, one that rests on political assumptions that prove surprisingly germane to Pinter's career. I am borrowing the idea of negation from the cultural criticism of Frankfurt School figures such as Max Hork-heimer, Herbert Marcuse, and, most centrally, T.W. Adorno. Pinter and Adorno: strange bedfellows, one would think. Indeed, it is true that Adorno's key points of reference were canonical modernists such as Kafka and Beckett and that, at the other end, British dramatic criticism has, in the main, steered clear of the modernist discourse arising from the Frankfurt School. But I would suggest that Pinter's transitional career provides an exemplary case study for the critical theory associated with the Frankfurt School, and, reciprocally, that the idea of negation can serve as a bridge linking the aesthetic and political poles of Pinter's work.

Negation is a way of phrasing art's social force, though this force paradoxically derives from rigorously refusing society's reality principle. Negation is the formal incarnation of protest against reality and the wish that it were otherwise. The philosophy underlying this idea is best understood dialectically, as one pole in a significant historical debate about commitment, autonomy, and the nature of political art. It is useful to summarize the competing positions, which emerged in stark contrast after the publication of Jean-Paul Sartre's *What Is Literature?* in 1947. The committed work of art is conceived as a social intervention, an act that seeks to shatter the reactionary aura of culture by emphasizing art's materiality, its productive force. The committed work takes a position, not only in relation to social reality, but within it. Such works are telic, in Adorno's account – oriented towards the 'end' of the public sphere, directed towards the purpose of social transformation.

The autonomous or 'atelic'[20] tendency suggests that the work that succumbs to ideological debate becomes part of the culture it sought to criticize. In his 1958 exchange with Kenneth Tynan, for example, Eugene Ionesco argued: 'An ideological play can be no more than the vulgarization of an ideology.'[21] Committed art is invariably reductive, politically and aesthetically degraded: 'Bad politics becomes bad art, and vice versa,' according to Adorno. The utopian potential of art lies in its distance from the world, its uselessness. As Adorno suggests, art must resist 'by its form alone.'[22] The weapons of the autonomous work are expressly formal: resistance, estrangement, alienation. This 'negative' aesthetic becomes affirmative when artworks refuse the means and ends of administered society and embody alternative desire, however faintly. In Adorno's words, '[autonomous] art criticizes society just by being there.'[23]

As various moments in his career, Pinter has seemed to embody and occasionally fuse the two extremes. Collectively, his works testify to a crisis confronting political art as it begins to encounter postmodern problems associated with commercial culture, popular audiences, and fragmented public spheres. In his plays, committed and autonomous impulses circulate and merge in complex, sometimes contradictory hybrids. This trend signals the onset of one of Adorno's chief fears, namely, the waning in contemporary society of the tension by which art had traditionally constituted itself. Like Herbert Marcuse's diagnosis of a 'one-dimensional' society marked by repressive 'happy consciousness,'[24] the erosion of art's autonomy is linked to a general ebbing of the critical power of negation. In a society of presumptive hyper-abundance, it is increasingly difficult to register what is precluded and repressed. In effect, society says, 'Whatever could be already is,' and art struggles to say otherwise. In this sense, Adorno might be considered a philosopher of the end of art. In his eyes, historical crisis was everywhere manifest in lax and undifferentiated cultural life. Even well–intentioned artworks emerged as leaky compromises, uneasily seeking to estrange and engage society simultaneously. In late modernity, these gestures grow more equivocal and anticipate the symptomatic postmodern conflation of aesthetics and politics.

If Pinter's early plays generally embrace an autonomous aesthetic based on negation, his later works begin to document the vicissitudes and paradoxes of commitment. Indeed, the difficulty and interest of his political plays are reminiscent of committed writers such as Sartre and Brecht, about whom Adorno wrote with particular edge. Despite their formidable intelligence and conviction, Adorno suggests that both writers' works come to embody the opposite of their intentions. This is not a particular failing, in his view, but rather a reflection of a fundamental aporia. Against a perceived disenchantment of language, culture, and experience, Sartre's doctrine of *engagement* seeks to awaken the authentic, reciprocal 'deep choice' of the author and his or her readers by stressing the possibilities of human freedom and agency in opposition to a world of passivity and alienation. One privileged mechanism for furthering this goal was what Sartre famously termed the 'theatre of situations,' in which dramas are constructed to highlight the exercise of free, authentic choice – individuals acting as subjects rather than objects, making choices – often through the dramatic device of the 'limit situation,' where the existential stakes are raised because one choice leads to death. Aesthetically, then, the drama of situations requires a kind of mimetic innocence, a belief in the theatre's capacity to reproduce reality, as well as faith in language as a medium of rational thought and transparent communication. Sartre's commitment implicitly rejects modernist scepticism about language and its love of ambiguity. 'If words are sick,' he writes, 'it is up to us to cure them. Instead of that, many writers live off this sickness ... I distrust the incommunicable; it is the source of all violence.'[25]

For Adorno, however, Sartre's plays break faith with his philosophy. Any theatre of ideas, any representation of rational agency, omits the transformations necessary to art. Art becomes another discourse, a kind of social program or pseudo-philosophy. As readers of *No Exit* can attest, Sartre's drama is marked by conventional plotting and characterization. There is a tension between the representation of individual moral choice – necessarily particularized in terms of character psychology – and Sartre's intention that characters illustrate the larger problem of human freedom, that is, communicate his philosophy. Respect for the specificity and integrity of individual existence does not mesh comfortably with a manipulated illusion of individuality designed to prove a universal principle. Adorno writes, 'Sartre's plays are vehicles for the author's ideas ... They operate with traditional plots, exalted by an unshaken faith in meanings which can be transferred from art to reality. But the theses they illustrate, or where possible state, misuse the emotions which Sartre's own drama aims to express, by making them examples. They thereby disavow themselves. When one of his most famous plays ends with the dictum, "Hell is other people," it sounds like a quotation from *Being and Nothingness*.'[26]

In Adorno's account, Brecht's Epic theatre was also fatally split, in this case by what we might call a negative and a positive tendency. The negative tendency, exemplified by Brecht's notion of alienation, sought to estrange perceptions and to attack conventions. The positive tendency, by contrast, was didactic and rationalist, busily attempting to teach pragmatic lessons and to analyse real historical situations. The contradiction between these two tendencies leads Adorno to allege two faults in Brecht's political dramas. The first, exemplified by plays like *Saint Joan* and *Mother Courage*, is the transposition of present social problems to imaginary contexts (mythic Chicago, the Thirty Years War) and the embodiment of these problems in individual characters. Through such tactics, Brecht tries to express socio-economic facts about a modern society that can no longer be represented directly or grasped in individual terms. The aesthetic displacement and reduction invalidates the social analysis; realist and anti-realist impulses cancel each other. What lessons, Adorno wonders, does *Mother Courage* actually teach about the nature of modern war? The second conflict, in many ways a reaction to the first, is extreme aesthetic immersion in character and situation as a means of authenticating political messages; the danger is that the aesthetic garb may mask and reverse the political intent. Thus, the violence of *The Measures Taken* or the motherly lyricism of *The Caucasian Chalk Circle* are aestheticized and effectively become ends in themselves. Against Brecht's stated goals, the plays can be (and have been) read as odes to violence and motherhood, respectively.

In Pinter's political plays, there are echoes of both Sartre and Brecht. Commitment alters the aesthetic basis, generating tensions that recall Adorno's argument. When Nicolas in *One for the Road* (1984) says, 'Do you think waving fingers in front of people's eyes is silly? ... But would you take the same view if it was my boot – or my penis?' or, 'One has to be so scrupulous about language,' these statements sound a bit like Sartrian epigrams.[27] In *Mountain Language* (1988), alienating details and episodes – such as the talking dogs and silent conversation – are uncomfortably fused with what seems to be a didactic realist critique of authoritarian power. Likewise, in *Party Time* (1991) and *Ashes to Ashes* (1996), A-effects (the victim Jimmy's ultimate arrival in blinding light; Rebecca's final, echoed monologue) mix with apparently straightforward attacks on bourgeois decadence and complicity. What lessons, we might polemically wonder, do these plays actually teach about existing political injustices? Complicating matters, however, is the fact that the late political plays share with their predecessors a movement towards negation, accomplished in this case by powerfully estranging the realist frame of reference. Offsetting the plays' crypto-realism is an impulse towards abstraction that carries considerable negative force. In this sense, the political plays critique their own conditions of possibility.

Here, Pinter's career incarnates a late version of a paradox that Adorno associates with Beckett, whose works, he feels, fundamentally preserve and record the truth of contemporary reality by registering this reality in abstracted, mutilated form. Committed art often falls prey to the false consciousness it opposes, while the most rigorous refusal of social utility may allow art to keep faith with the original goals of commitment. Beckett's plays, rather than those of Brecht or Sartre, best fulfil the promise of the committed work of art. In this sense, the impulse towards abstraction in Pinter's political plays harks back to high modernist works such as *The Caretaker* (1960) and *The Homecoming* (1965). Through Adorno's paradoxical lens, we might interpret the earlier plays as political acts, albeit ones more closely aligned with autonomous aesthetics. As Adorno said of Beckett, autonomous art resists reality by refusing it: 'Here every commitment to the world must be abandoned to satisfy the ideal of the committed work of art.'[28]

Politics

Beckettian modernism constitutes one frontier of Pinter's theatre, but there is much more to the story. His drama is also formally and ideologically bounded by self-conscious politics, as we have seen, and also by popular culture – both of which Adorno considered adversaries of autonomous modernism. Politics and popular culture are perhaps the liveliest areas of current Pinter research, and in subsequent chapters I explore these topics using the analytic framework just described. With growing hindsight Pinter's multiple voices invite us to sort his work into periods and categories, and nowhere is this temptation greater than with the cycle of political plays beginning in the 1980s. It is only a mild exaggeration to say that Pinter's career began (at least) twice: the disastrous premiere of *The Birthday Party* in 1958 and the opening of *One for the Road*, which Pinter himself directed in 1984. The latter play, about a functionary supervising the torture of a family, inaugurated a political turn that has forced a reinterpretation of everything before and established new interpretive parameters for everything after. With varying degrees of explicitness, the subsequent plays – *Mountain Language* (1988), *Party Time* (1991), *The New World Order* (1991), and *Ashes to Ashes* (1996) – grapple with openly political themes. The turn was especially surprising for a writer who, in the words of D. Keith Peacock, 'had consistently repudiated any social or political intent, whether expressed in terms of the commitment expected of the New Wave dramatists of the late 1950s and early 1960s or the political agit-prop of the 1970s.'[29]

The shift in subject matter coincided with an increasingly loud public voice on political matters. The later revisionist Pinter[30] claimed that his plays had always been political and that he had long harboured the kind of quasi-Leftist positions he began to espouse in the 1980s (worldwide human rights abuses, American foreign policy, Thatcherism, and nuclear proliferation were favoured targets). This reassessment con-flicts, however, with many statements made in the 1960s and 1970s (as late as 1981 Pinter asserted that his political views 'do not come into my work as far as I can see').[31] The provocateur thus unhelpfully stirred an already bewildering broth of terms, concepts, and -isms – a broth based, at bottom, on incompatible understandings of political art.[32]

On a positive note, however, the political turn has led a number of commentators to revisit holistically both the aesthetics of Pinter's poli-tics and the politics of his aesthetics. As Mireia Aragay succinctly states, the 1980s plays have 'led critics to speculate as to whether they embody a fresh departure by which the playwright's oeuvre has become openly, ostensibly political as opposed to his earlier, more met-aphorical explorations of power games, or whether, on the contrary, it has been political through and through from the very start.'[33] As I have suggested, this tension, this problem, itself is the crucial element; it should be emphasized rather than resolved. Pinter is a significant historical figure in part because his work fuses two competing approaches to political art. The committed art championed (in different ways) by Brecht and Sartre collides with the hermetic high modernism advocated by Adorno and practised by Beckett, all in the space of a sin-gle career. Pinter links the two impulses in a manner consistent with the late stages of modernism.

In recent essays Aragay and Austin Quigley have examined the problem from the other side, using the conceptual language of post-modernism to construct political narratives. Aragay – following Marc Silverstein[34] – sees the early works as embodying a postmodernist pol-itics. These works are treated as explorations of the micro-physics of power (Foucault's term),[35] of the ways in which the language, codes, and conventions of the dominant order work to regulate identities and relations in the private sphere. Aragay qualifies Silverstein (who sees all of Pinter's work as 'political' in the sense described) by suggesting that later, self-consciously political works like *Ashes to Ashes* express a desire to overcome the 'political quietism' of the postmodern drama, which is unable to conceptualize resistance or an 'outside' to the hege-mony it details.[36]

But one could also plausibly argue the reverse. From a different per-spective, the early works embrace a rigorously autonomous modern-ism in comparison with which the uneasy hybridity of a play like *Ashes to Ashes* suggests disintegration and postmodernist political quietism.

It is a question not of which model is more politically effective, in a tangible sense, but rather of whether the tension between the two is symptomatic of the crumbling of the Great Divide and the complex transition to what comes after (to modify the title of Huyssen's book). Moreover, postmodernist political readings of the early works sometimes seem to incorporate an oddly mimetic manoeuvre. Such readings can leave the impression that the plays are in some direct way 'about' theoretical notions like the Other, as if Pinter had archaeologically unearthed the skeletal truth of the grim struggle of life as it is lived within ideology. The dramas are then read as a kind of theory or ideology critique, like companion pieces to the work of writers such as Lacan, Foucault, and Althusser. What Austin Quigley calls the 'irreducible singularity' of the plays, their wealth of 'complex and diverse local detail,'[37] is thereby devalued. In such theoretical accounts, one senses that specifics and particulars are often used to confirm the existence of abstract systems: cultural codes, symbolic orders, subject positions. Details become examples.

Quigley makes the idea of the 'local' the linchpin of his reading of Pinter's politics. For Quigley, the political value of Pinter's plays resides in their insistence on small-scale personal encounters, contracts, and relations that defy the forces of large-scale authority and integration. Taken together, both early and late plays depict complex, plural experiences in which individuals negotiate the demands of 'social living,'[38] resisting the oppressively global while striving – provisionally and at the level of a 'small community' – to engage the claims of 'larger collective life.' According to this postmodern micropolitics, the irreducible individual demarcates a last line of battle against the inscriptions and reductions of the 'political' (authority, power, hegemony), which leads Quigley to invert and remake an old slogan into a maxim for a postmodern neoliberalism: 'the political is, among other things, the personal.' This political model is mapped on a particular conception of the aesthetics of modernism and postmodernism. Following Ihab Hasan, Quigley distinguishes three (overlapping, recurring) 'voices' in modernism: avant-garde modernism (radical, interventionist); high modernism (solipsistic, utopian); and postmodernism ('a voice of eclectic mingling').[39] While he acknowledges that Pinter has at various times operated in all three registers, Quigley privileges the postmodern – aesthetically and politically.

While I find Quigley's defence of the 'local' eloquent and persuasive, my discussions of Pinter's politics shift the emphasis and terminology.

As Adorno and other theorists of the Great Divide have argued, 'high' modernism also has a politics, and Pinter's resistant particularity is consistent with this paradigm. Quigley provides a concise description of high modernism: 'art as aesthetic object, as cultural artifact, as difficult, abstract, reflexive, ironic, distanced, [and] autonomous.'[40] The possibilities for such art are not limited to solipsism or utopianism; there are strains of critical modernism (Kafka, Beckett) premised on negation, on producing elaborate photographic negatives of what Adorno called 'damaged life,'[41] versions of something felt to be essential about the world rendered in a form that the world can't easily digest or use. I will first try to analyse the politics of Pinter's work as so many local aesthetic gestures towards a common purpose, what Adorno called (in relation to Beckett) the 'determinate negation of meaning.'[42] This modernist undertaking might be described as the systematic accumulation of small resistances and singularities – episodes in which conventional circuits of meaning-making are disrupted – that add up to a dystopian counter-totality, an evocation of the world's guilt, its debris, victims, and violence.

In chapter 1, 'The Politics of Negation,' I develop this approach synchronically, arguing that the politics of Pinter's early masterworks – *The Birthday Party* (1958), *The Caretaker* (1960), and *The Homecoming* (1965) – are legible in terms of modernist aesthetics. In chapter 3, 'Towards the Postmodern,' this synchronic analysis is first extended to the 1970s by a juxtaposition of two of Pinter's apparently apolitical memory plays – *Old Times* (1971) and *No Man's Land* (1975) – with British socialist theatre of the period. Finally, in chapter 3 I conclude with a diachronic assessment of Pinter's politics from the modern to the postmodern, from *The Birthday Party* through the political cycle of 1984–91 to *Ashes to Ashes* (1996), by tracing transformations in the psychopathology of Pinter's thugs.

Popular culture

In chapter 2, 'The Modernist as Populist,' the focus is on questions of popular culture. Over time, this topic has proved as complex as Pinter's politics. Even at first glance, Pinter's popularity is perplexing. He is an established figure in the high cultural canon, yet he has had at least eight plays on television, seven on BBC radio, five adapted as feature films, numerous long runs in the West End and Broadway, and uncounted regional, local, and university performances around the world.[43] At a conservative estimate, millions have seen his work in some form. Moreover, Pinter has shown little sentiment for literary authority. In addition to his involvement in television, he has written at least thirteen screenplays. One could argue that his work has been influenced by Kafka and Beckett but also by film noir, melodrama, and vaudeville. This pedigree seems to me more subtle and interesting because of the lack of any pure genealogy. An elegant and sustained tension between high and low cultural traditions is one of Pinter's most provocative achievements.

Kimball King and Marti Greene point out that 'film' – second only to 'language' – is the most common keyword in recent Pinter scholarship.[44] Thus, one way that Pinter's career has encouraged attention to popular culture is via the question of medium. Steven H. Gale, among others, has written extensively on Pinter's screenwriting and the processes of film adaptation.[45] My approach to Pinter's popularity is somewhat different. I begin by suggesting that the aesthetics of popular culture pervades Pinter's theatrical work. In chapter 2 I first argue that 'low' cultural elements are integral to the Pinter universe, using what is arguably his lightest play, The Dumb Waiter (1959). I then focus on two examples that incarnate medium difference. The first, A Slight Ache (1959), was written for radio but later performed on stage, and the second, Betrayal (1978), is a play whose content and structure anticipate its own film adaptation and that looks sideways, aesthetically, at melodrama, soap opera, and television. I am interested in how such works reflect the erosion of the Great Divide by undermining one kind of absolutist, purist thinking about medium encountered in modernism and modern drama.[46] Across the chapter, the popular emerges as shorthand for questions of pleasure, form, entertainment, suspense, humour, and reception (difficulty vs ease, contemplation vs consumption) – an ensemble of forces that have collectively shadowed modernist practice as an indispensable adversary until the advent of postmodernism's Great Integration.

Consider the adventures of the adjective Pinteresque; Pinter's transitional modernism is accompanied by a struggle to name this unnameable quality. Pinteresque is a distinctively modern feeling-tone: dread swathed in bleak humour, controlled by an overriding sense of complicity. The term signals both aggression and fear, evoking a tenuous truce between self and other, self and object-world – a truce that barely masks an inarticulate but palpable hostility. It is a regressive feeling, which both envies and resents the hegemony of language from which it is excluded, unthinkable without the idea of an unconscious and a theory of fantasy. Fans recognize the singular affect linked to Pinter's work, something between hilarity, expectancy, and nausea.

This feeling-tone is helpful in understanding both Pinter's popularity and his modernism. On the one hand, the Pinteresque seems consistent with the notion of 'body' genres (melodrama, horror, and pornography, in Linda Williams's influential account),[47] sensational forms that work to produce ecstatic responses in spectators' bodies. Culturally, such forms have been branded 'low' because they aim at body rather than mind, because they fuse irrationality and affective power. Surely Pinter's calling card has also been resistance to rational interpretation coupled with visceral potency. At the same time, the Pinteresque is a by-product of an insular aesthetic world forged through hostility to abstract interpretation and easy meaningfulness. This could be considered a modernist gesture, one that zealously guards the singularity of the particular from the tyranny of the general. Pinter's drama short-circuits semiosis while bristling with a kind of phenomenological electricity. This tendency is linked to the strain of autonomous modernism exemplified by Beckett, which internalizes, derides, and resists philosophical system-building, making the problem of meaning-making self-conscious ('We're not beginning to ... to ... mean something?' Hamm wonders, alarmed, in *Endgame*).[48]

Here, something should be said about the question of aesthetic value. To take Pinter seriously as an entertainer is to consider the possibility that he may be, in effect, a popularizer of modernism. At the level of common sense, most would probably agree that his work is more palatable than Beckett's, for example, and one could also argue that the Pinteresque amounts to a domestication of a once unyielding structure of feeling. To consider such matters is not to devalue Pinter as an artist, but again to foreground the transitional nature of his aesthetics. On the one hand, Pinter's very name has become a cultural commodity, a phantom value attending the reception of his individual works. Despite the ambiguity attributed to his writing and the adventurousness of his work in various media, both popular reception and highbrow criticism of Pinter derive from a perception of self-identity. His stage plays, radio dramas, teleplays, and film-scripts seem to emanate from the transcendent 'someone called Pinter.' Notwithstanding the restless experimentation evident in his career, Pinter has, ironically, acquired the feel of a well-worn popular object. For all its variety, the phenomenon of Pinter presents itself as a singular thing. To transpose Marc Vernet's diagnosis of film noir: Pinter's work resists definition, yet in a strange way it has come to stand as a discrete object of beauty. Like a Harley-Davidson motorcycle, you know it when you see it.[49]

A holistic exploration of Pinter's popularity is bound to be traversed by familiar but still pressing debates about high and low cultures. Indeed – in addition to problems of autonomy, commitment, and negation – I consider the high/low divide to be a central axis in plotting Pinter's late modernism. In this sense, the adjective *Pinteresque* implies that Pinter's works can be reduced to an isolable essence, reflecting a consumer's love of the trusted brand name. Pinteresque is an uneasy term, however, which seems aware of its limits. Its usage testifies to a fantasy of continuity and coherence that may or may not be borne out in practice. The term is also suggestive because of its ambivalence with respect to the problem of art and entertainment. On the one hand, Pinteresque implies a unique, profound artistic voice, deserving of its own adjectives. At the same time, the term evokes the kind of manufactured feeling-tone one associates with lowbrow cultural forms (melodrama, thrillers, slapstick comedies, etc.), reducible to a set of techniques or tricks that can be readily imitated.

Much of Pinter uncomfortably resides at the intersection of entertainment and art, and this tension compresses an important paradox. On the one hand, the extent to which it is possible to speak of culture as a reified domain independent of society echoes the fragmentation and estrangement of social life. But the dystopian separation of culture also enables autonomy, which is a precondition of critical aesthetic practice – if art is to have any value apart from unflagging complicity with the status quo. At the same time, modern art can quickly grow dogmatic or morbidly insular if it denies all connections to lived experience and popular culture. Against the absolute claims of modernist partisans, many today would argue that artists, entertainers, critics, and consumers actively negotiate and produce cultural meanings, even if these meanings and this process are subject to ideological constraints and determinations. Looking ahead to the postmodern – the increasingly fine line between ideology and art, the commercial and the cultural – is one way of understanding the transition from modernism to the looser ensemble of texts, readings, and behaviours ranged under the heading of cultural studies. This discourse provides a vital context for Pinter's popularity, and his work in turn sheds light on the waning of the high/low cultural split.

Immanent criticism

I want to say a word about method. Throughout I aim for a particular kind of interpretive practice, one that dovetails with the conception of modernism I have been outlining. Indeed, the critical method could be seen as an extension of a tendency already present in the plays. I will try to work from bottom up rather than top down to build from the 'irreducible singularity' described above. This approach is, in a certain sense, mandated by the preponderance of 'local detail' that refuses to settle into generalization. Anyone writing on Pinter is faced with the immediate problem of what to do with the sheer fleshiness of the various rooms and their inhabitants, the utter tactility of the veritable junk-pile of modernity that litters the plays, the intense specificity of the various toasters, ashtrays, toilets, and toy drums. Critics may empathize with Lenny in *The Homecoming*; Lenny tells Ruth that he has been awakened by a ticking clock, but he is not sure because there are 'all sorts of objects, which, in the day, you wouldn't call anything else but commonplace ... But in the night any given one of them is liable to start letting out a bit of a tick.'[50]

Pinter's work attaches unusual intensity to particular objects and utterances; these material phenomena are invested with psychic energy, cathected. As a result, it can be hard to distinguish the trivial from the significant. The plays also avoid normalizing symbolic, semantic, and narrative patterns, substituting the kind of condensation and displacement associated with dream-work. As in dreams, the centre often shifts to the margins, and a single element can lead to multiple associations. For both characters and spectators, the bric-a-brac of the Pinter universe speaks loudly, to the point that bits of dialogue sound like taunts ('*take* it, *take* a table, but once you've taken it, what are you going to do with it?').[51]

Andreas Huyssen calls T.W. Adorno 'the theorist par excellence of the Great Divide,'[52] and my model of interpretive practice is the immanent criticism Adorno championed. This kind of critique moves from the particular to the general rather than the other way round. It looks for textual ruptures, contradictions, and resistances that can be examined as historical fingerprints; it presupposes that shifts in cultural forms can be referred back to the historical circumstances from which they emerge. Adorno wrote of Kafka: 'he is assimilated to an established trend of thought while little attention is paid to those aspects of his work which resist such assimilation and which, precisely for this reason, require interpretation.'[53] Adorno is transposing to literature a perception he elsewhere attaches to society, namely, the trend in the modern period towards the tyranny of the abstract over the concrete. Immanent criticism tries to work against this tendency.

At the level of criticism, the approach mirrors modernist aesthetics insofar as it privileges recalcitrance, disharmony, and contradiction. In Adorno's words, 'a successful work, according to immanent criticism, is not one which resolves objective contradictions in a spurious harmony, but one which expresses the idea of harmony negatively by embodying the contradictions, pure and uncompromised, in its innermost structure.'[54] The autonomy of art, its radical separation from the world, is the precondition of its power of negation and its capacity for refusal. Autonomous art, in this view, resists what Quigley calls 'large-scale generalization'[55] – fraudulent universality – by mirroring its violence and unreason in an aesthetic form. This is a critical rather than utopian modernism. Not only is it 'about' the struggle between the local and the global at the level of content, but it has also sewn the contradiction into its own fabric at the level of form.

Adorno argues that the essay has historically been the most common vehicle of immanent criticism. The essay does justice to contradiction by 'refraining from any reduction to a principle, in accentuating the fragmentary, the partial rather than the total.' The essay 'shies away from the violence of dogma'; in it 'thought acquires its depth from penetrating deeply into a matter, not from referring it back to something else.' Pinter's drama, I would argue, is faithful to these principles. Its totality is constituted, paradoxically, through its respect for fragments; it magnifies the unavoidable aesthetic struggle between parts and whole. Pinter's work and the variety of criticism it has engendered collectively display a healthy distrust of semantic reduction and fixity. For Adorno, this is also an attribute of the essay: 'For the essay perceives that the longing for strict definitions has long offered, through fixating manipulations of the meanings of concepts, to eliminate the irritating and dangerous elements of things that live within concepts.'[56] Pinter's is a drama of 'irritating and dangerous' things.

An immanent critic of Pinter is obliged to respect the local irritations of his work by incorporating the ethics of the essay into the monographic form. A balance between the local and the global requires that thematic and theoretical narratives emerge from concrete readings rather than the other way round. As examples, I want to begin two interpretations that will be developed later in the book. First, as the anecdote above suggests, one should be careful in approaching *The Caretaker* abstractly, as Terence Rattigan did. Pinter bluntly rebuffed the proposal that the play was an allegory of humanity and the Old and New Testaments. Rather, one might begin with the more immediate and taxing matters of shoes that do not fit or the monk with the reputedly extensive collection of charity footwear who tells Davies in no uncertain terms to 'piss off.' The question of the shoes – and the screws, nuts, lumber, and gas stove that clutter the stage – summons in one stroke the grim object-world of early-modern peasants and proletarians and with it a pathos of labour and misery that, since Van Gogh's peasant boots, modern art has sought to redeem. As Fredric Jameson suggests, Van Gogh's transformational modernism refigures these tokens of brute existence in their intimate connection to the natural world and to lived experience, as sources of pleasure and aesthetic reward.[57] Yet in this play even the minimal promise of happiness afforded by an earlier modern aesthetic is heckled by a sarcastic late-modern voice that tells this whole utopian enterprise to 'piss off,' leaving the early-modern bric-a-brac of *The Caretaker* subject to a post–Second World War estrangement, as lifeless and disconnected as the monolithic gas stove.

Or one could consider the newspaper in Pinter as iconographic linchpin of an entire social system implied by the figure of the man reading at the dinner table, ruminating at leisure on the affairs of men, pleasingly centred in his household even as the larger bourgeois world is emblematically centred on him. While it might seem that the political plays of 1984–91 represented an abrupt left turn for Pinter, one could argue that the outwardly peaceful domestic tableaus at the beginnings of many early plays (*The Room* [1957]; *A Slight Ache* [1958]; *The Homecoming* [1965]) begin to arouse a proto-political terror, whose intensity matches the more evident horrors of plays like *One for the Road*. In these opening scenes the newspaper recalls not only the solitary pleasures of a more orderly world but also the violent separation from which modern ideas of privacy and solitude were born. The trauma of estrangement from others haunts individualism, stalking its lonely pleasures. The newspaper harks back to an emergent mass cultural populism but also to the atomized, private consumption that is the guilty face of cultural modernization. These plays take the ostensibly tranquil image of domestic stasis and dwell on it like a disease. What in melodrama or farce might lead to adulterous revelations or forgotten relatives is instead autopsied.

Against the claim that a play like *A Slight Ache* is not political, one could invoke what Adorno and Max Horkheimer wrote in the 1940s: 'The bourgeois whose existence is split into a business and a private life, whose private life is split into keeping up his public image and intimacy, whose intimacy is split into the surly partnership of marriage and the bitter comfort of being quite alone, at odds with himself and everybody else, is already virtually a Nazi, replete both with enthusiasm and abuse.'[58] Pinter's newspaper tableau serves as a metonym for this entire scheme. In this way, fragments in Pinter spawn unexpected ideological narratives. As Lenny might say, details begin to tick.

Cultural studies

The case for Pinter as a transitional figure, which I have advanced throughout this introduction, expresses in positive form the perception that his work is slightly out of step, at odds with its historical place and time. Had he been French, one speculates, or at least a Parisian émigré, born twenty years earlier (Beckett's generation) or ten years later (nearer Caryl Churchill, Howard Brenton, and David Hare), we might be confronted with a different kind of oeuvre. At the same time, of course, liminality can be as a source of aesthetic strength. Within the confines of his own particular situation, Pinter's predicament resembles that of the late modernists described by Fredric Jameson, writers such as Nabokov, Borges, and Beckett, 'who had the misfortune to span two eras and the luck to find a time capsule of isolation or exile in which to spin out unseasonable forms.'[59]

Put another way: Pinter has been popular but seldom, save for his coming-out period (1958–65), fashionable. Even the Swinging London evoked in the second half of the Joseph Losey film *The Servant* (1963) – from Pinter's adaptation of Robin Maugham's novel – becomes visible only in jarring contrast to anachronistic class struggles and absurdist role reversals, through a veil of mannerist eroticism. In the progressively postmodern cultural glare of the 1970s, 1980s, and 1990s Pinter's sensibility and the modernist aesthetics from which it derived grow more incongruous and defiant even as his celebrity and canonic stature increase. This trajectory is linked to the decline of a certain strain of modern European theatre, the end of an Ibsen-Beckett line with its total aesthetic beliefs and emphatically white male connotations. Moreover, Pinter's ascendancy coincides with the late stages of the post-1956 British theatrical renaissance, and his energetic self-renewals after 1980 take place as this renaissance begins to wane. As time goes on, Pinter's work is located nearer the exact centre of a cultural blind spot, and in a truly postmodern denouement, the grouchy modernist is absorbed by the middlebrow. A singular vision – a unique, disturbing style – becomes a familiar code, an available signifier.

In his article 'The Good, the Bad, and the Indifferent: Defending Pop-. ular Culture from the Populists,' British critic Simon Frith wryly notes an evolution in taste among academic critics. In the wake of the Frank-furt School's withering critique of the culture industry, academics tended towards the straightforward position 'if it's popular it must be bad.' Accepting that mass culture was hopelessly commodified, enter-prising sociologists then began to look for instances in which consumer behaviour seemed particularly active, participatory, and resistant. This led to the modified view, 'if it's popular it must be bad, unless it's pop-ular with the right people.' In cultural studies circles, where textual rather than empirical approaches were prevalent, distinguishing resis-tance from stupefaction often boiled down to seemingly arbitrary choices made by individual critics. Punk rock or soap opera might be privileged as authentic examples of youth culture or non-phallic desire, respectively, but the experiences of other groups were then implicitly devalued, reduced to conformity or false consciousness.

Reactions against the selective elitism of the second position in turn fuelled the final, postmodernist response, 'if it's popular it must be good!' Here the de-centred and chaotic spaces, forms, and iconogra-phies of contemporary culture – shopping malls, tattooing, horror films, MTV – are taken to create libidinous, nearly schizophrenic pockets of transgression independent of the intentions of particular consumers. To avoid disparaging particular niche audiences or micro-publics this final approach sees the meanings and values of cultural experiences as largely determined by the popular text, now celebrated as vehemently as it was once condemned. Frith considers this postmodernist populism condescending, an eerie mirror of the Frankfurt School elitism that second-wave cultural studies initially opposed: 'It is hard to avoid the conclusion that the more celebratory the populist study, the more pa-tronizing its tone.'[60]

Indeed, the ostensible all-embracing populism of this last post-modern utopia in fact remains highly selective and exclusionary. A persistent, symptomatic gap in the methodology emerges around con-stituencies neither high nor low enough to warrant special attention, namely, partisans of so-called middlebrow culture, members of the

Book of the Month Club or its equivalents, what Frith calls 'the easy listener and light reader and Andrew Lloyd Webber fan.'[61] I would argue that over the course of Pinter's career mainstream theatre increasingly occupies this cultural space, a middlebrow domain that partly defines Pinter as well. For example, given the poetics and politics of Pinter's work, one would expect points of intersection with British cultural studies. The tensions originally underlying British cultural studies – high and low cultures, populism and the politics of reception, the need to engage present realities – would seem germane to the early Pinter. At the level of coincidence, both Raymond Williams's seminal *Culture and Society* and Pinter's *The Birthday Party* appeared in 1958.

Indeed, relations between the New Left and the theatrical New Wave in the 1950s were close and complex (not surprising, given the demographics of British intellectual life). In his lively counter-history, *1956 and All That*, Dan Rebellato describes the many contributions made by New Left figures such as Raymond Williams and Stuart Hall to the radical theatre journal *Encore* during the heady days of the late 1950s and early 1960s,[62] and John Stokes has shown that, on the whole, *Encore* reacted perceptively and favourably to the politics of Pinter's early works.[63] There seems to have been a moment when Pinter was part of this aesthetic and social conjuncture. As time went on, however, his career began to zigzag against the prevailing theatrical and political current. As the new British drama was radicalized in the 1960s and 1970s, Pinter's work drifted towards the antisocial inwardness of the memory plays; he turned to Leftist politics in his drama only after Thatcher. This contrariness has tended to reduce points of contact between Pinter and lager social movements.

In any case, the methods and concerns of British cultural studies began to shift in directions unfavourable to the analysis of mainstream theatre in general and idiosyncratic modernists like Pinter in particular. After its founding in 1964, much of work emerging from the Centre for Contemporary Cultural Studies at the University of Birmingham (the Birmingham School) was directed against institutional middle-class art and towards culturalist recovery of lived social experience, including working-class culture, folk art, leisure activities, domestic life, popular music, and sport. From this perspective, the commercial confines of the West End, the various subsidized British theatres, and even the avant-garde Fringe might seem politically and culturally problematic, despite the largely leftist overtones of British drama in the 1960s and 1970s. Moreover, this intellectual and cultural rift has deepened over time. The arrival of European structuralism and post-Marxism during the 1960s and 1970s complicated the culturalist methodology of first-generation cultural studies and its recourse to lived experience, placing a new emphasis on questions of ideology and false consciousness.[64] The construction of subjects through cultural discourses and practices became a theoretical and political focus, coupled with energetic debates about struggle and resistance. Not surprisingly, institutional theatre takes on a drowsy, middlebrow air in the rush to new ideological battlefields centred on film, television, advertising, journalism, tourism, shopping, medicine, and law.

Meanwhile, in academic theatre studies, the influence of cultural studies has been felt in ethnographic work on multicultural performance, studies of avant-garde performances said to engage or resist ideological determinations, postmodernist encounters between media, technology, and theatre, and the performance studies explosion into sub-fields like stand-up comedy and an entire arena of 'restored' or 'twice-behaved' behaviours not previously considered performative. In this context, Pinter's work is neither sufficiently new nor sufficiently old to find a comfortable home among the avant-garde of theatre theory or the museum guards of theatre history, and it is neither radical nor popular enough to be of particular interest to recent cultural studies methodologies.

Moonlight and modernity

I would associate these theoretical and social developments with the twilight of modernism, a shift that leaves transitional writers like Pinter in a culturally ambiguous position. Against this backdrop I want to end the introduction at a kind of vanishing point, with a Pinter play that suggests the completion of a modernist narrative and the beginning of a new, postmodern stage of his career. Moreover, this play incorporates elements of an earlier aesthetic but fragments and reprocesses them in what is no longer an expression of unified style but an amalgam of outdated codes. The play then functions as a coda, a postscript, with one foot in an old sensibility and one foot in a new. A focus of this book's chapter on popular culture is the question of pleasure, and in this spirit I will conclude the introduction by contrasting the old and new sensibilities via a comparison of two jokes.

The play in question is *Moonlight* (1993), which, given the fifteen-year interval since Pinter's previous full-length play, *Betrayal* (1978), reads like a return of the repressed. In *Moonlight*, Pinter, well into his sixties, produced a work that in many respects proceeded as if little had changed since 1965. Of course this is the same writer who would later playfully and provocatively pair his most recent play, *Celebration* (2000), with his first, *The Room* (1957), so the undermining of historicity can perhaps be examined as a trend in Pinter's late phase. For, while the cannibalizing of one's own earlier works and preoccupations may signal a devious and still vital creativity, it is also the gesture of an older writer struggling against obsolescence in a period defined by a waning of historicity, by increasingly violent juxtapositions of histori-cally distinct styles and tones. At the same time, the grouchy and total-izing modernism of Pinter's high style (1958–65) could hardly be less in sync with the cultural and aesthetic climate of the 1990s, so one route to postmodern chic was to hearken back as if history did not exist and rewrite the high style in pastiche.

This postmodern return of the repressed underscores the fact that the meanings of cultural phenomena change, and this is especially true of theatre, whose sociality is always bounded by the horizon of a present tense. What *The Homecoming* 'meant' in England in 1965 is inevitably not identical with what it would mean in a New York revival today, and when Pinter abruptly began writing full-length plays again with *Moonlight* in 1993, the terrain had shifted, as had his place in the cultural imagination. In many ways *Moonlight* looks back directly to Pinter's masterpiece period of 1958–65, but it is also a frag-mented, composite work filtered through an older consciousness. The play includes both a decaying patriarch (cf. *The Homecoming*) and two men bantering in a disconnected room (cf. *The Dumb Waiter*), but the governing mood has shifted. *Moonlight* features a ghost, for example – unthinkable in earlier works. Here, death seems a legitimate, unironic, philosophical and aesthetic concern.

In this sense *Moonlight* functions as an elegy on Pinter's modernist phase, looking back at discarded sensibilities as if the decade of politi-cal drama had not intervened. The tenor here is nostalgic and some-what sentimental; *Moonlight* is a kind of tone poem on the theme of modernity – Pinter's own modernity, in particular – which is decom-posing as it rubs up against both mortality and a new sensibility anchored to the contemporary. The violence of this process is im-printed on the play's structures and forms. The plot centres on a dying man, Andy, and his wife, Bel, who banter and dissect their relationship and children while Andy lies on his deathbed. These conversations alternate with scenes of the couple's two sons, Jake and Fred, who in a spatially disconnected bedroom improvise vengeful Oedipal routines and exchange obscure reflections about their damaged lives, while in a separate space in 'faint light' Bel and Andy's dead daughter, Bridget, drifts, delivering the play's opening and closing monologues.

The stage thus fractures into three distinct spaces, as if the unitary, claustrophobic room of the early Pinter could no longer contain an ongoing disintegration. Moreover, each space retains its own linguistic register – cryptic recrimination in Andy's well-furnished bedroom, dysfunctional burlesque in Fred's 'shabby' bedroom, and poetic lament in Bridget's nebulous 'area.' Each register loses some measure of authenticity by existing in this uneasy combination; the wrenching languages and styles of modernism congeal into glib, appropriable postmodernist codes. This is especially true of Fred and Jake, who use a deranged idiom cobbled from commercial speech and the rhetoric of the upper classes. The unsettling humour of their exchanges likewise fuses competing sensibilities, one a digestible, reassuring wit and the other a regressive incongruousness that recalls Pinter's earlier works. The first example comes from one of Jake's disquisitions on his father: 'He was not in it for pleasure or glory. Let me make that quite clear. Applause came not his way. Nor did he seek it. Gratitude came not his way. Nor did he seek it. Masturbation came not his way. Nor did he seek it. I'm sorry – I meant approbation came not his way.'[65]

Later, Bel calls her sons to inform them their father is very ill. Inexplicably, Jake answers the phone, 'Chinese laundry?' The following three-way conversation ensues.

BEL: Your father is very ill.
JAKE: Can I pass you to my colleague?
FRED *takes the phone.*
FRED: Chinese laundry?
Pause.
BEL: It doesn't matter.
FRED: Oh my dear madam. Absolutely everything matters when it comes
    down to laundry.
BEL: No. It doesn't matter. It doesn't matter.
Silence.
JAKE *takes the phone, looks at it, puts it to his ear.*
BEL *holds the phone.*
FRED *grabs the phone.*

FRED: If you have any serious complaint can we refer you to our head office?

BEL: Do you do dry cleaning?

FRED *is still. He then passes the phone to* JAKE.

JAKE: Hullo. Can I help you?

BEL: Do you do dry cleaning?

JAKE *is still.*

BEL *puts the phone down. Dialing tone.*

JAKE *replaces phone.*

JAKE: Of course we do dry cleaning! Of course we do dry cleaning! What kind of fucking laundry are you if you don't do dry cleaning?[66]

Jake's remarks about his father embody a kind of theatrical wit rare in Pinter. The humour stems from a slip in the first two syllables of the final nouns, dispelling the Latinate grandeur of 'approbation' with mild adolescent scatology and draining the Periclean aura of the speech like air from a balloon. One could debate whether Jake or Pinter is ultimately responsible for the slip; for the two brothers are prone to verbal gymnastics and ironies of this kind, but in any case the appearance of 'masturbation' calls attention to a self-conscious intelligence behind the utterance and encourages pleasurable recognition in the traditional mode of dramatic irony. This Pinter joke resembles the theatrical style of that radically different but equally famous other pillar of British drama, the champion wit, Tom Stoppard. Stoppard's humour often depends on dawning awareness of an authorial Grand Design that rewards one's ability to recognize and appreciate abstract patterns in plot, situation, character, and *mise en scène*. The result is a kind of competitive irony sweepstakes, a guessing game in which the audience seeks to catch up and identify with the cerebral machinations of the author.

Humour of this type is ultimately exhilarating and reassuring even when the solution lingers momentarily out of reach; for Stoppard usually provides a cumulative payoff, creating a final distanced perspective where one can admire the full inventory of ironies, analogies, parallels, and metaphors. Pinter's masturbation joke engages this method on a small scale. The second exchange concerning the Chinese laundry seems to me quite different. There is no available frame of reference in which the laundry image might make sense, but neither does its appearance in the play seem a gratuitous gesture towards absurdity. With a little ingenuity one might interpret the conversation as the sublimated enactment of ancient family quarrels, but this, too, does not fully complete the picture. The humor depends on a delicate, balanced movement; the scene begins with the ludicrous 'Chinese laundry?' but proceeds to a studied juxtaposition between the mother's melancholy pronouncements ('Your father is very ill'; 'It doesn't matter') and the orientalized formality of the brothers ('Oh my dear madam'; 'Can I pass you to my colleague?'). In the unwieldy analytic terminology of humour we may write this off as something like incongruousness, which would then fall under the umbrella of irony. Indeed, if the sequence ended with the mother's 'Do you do dry cleaning?' the feeling would be one of complete reversal, symmetrical denouement, and full closure to the exchange.

However, Jake's final outburst, which closes the scene, orients the humour differently. The indignation addressed to the dead telephone is so deep that his question, 'What kind of fucking laundry are you if you don't do dry cleaning?' seems ontological rather than rhetorical. This misguided earnestness is probably aesthetically legible as slapstick, but the manoeuvre is regressive and immanent to the extent that the joke returns to the radical uncertainty of its concrete object rather than proceeding to a safe interpretive distance. In their debased, misanthropic idiom the brothers try to use the racialist signifier 'Chinese laundry' as a kind of verbal bludgeon, a weapon of opaque otherness to repulse their mother, but she turns the tables and the signifier circles back on them. The dialogue taps the energy of this verbal double-cross, awakening also the intractable mysteries of 'dry cleaning' (the phrase itself sounds like a contradiction). Finally, Jake's burst of outrage and dismay, after the initial confidence of his impersonation, unexpectedly resurrects an ontological crisis, a disconnection from origin, a literal and figurative dial tone after mother hangs up on son.

The Chinese laundry begets an ache, while masturbation and approbation yield a satisfying one-liner. In response to a reporter's ingratiating joke about his omnipotence, Al Capone's first line in *The Untouchables* (written by David Mamet) is 'Like a lot of things in life, we laugh because it's funny and we laugh because it's true.' The Chinese laundry is neither. Clearly, there is an element of perverse recognition (who understands dry cleaning?), but on the whole, the scene occasions as much guilt as pleasure. Jake's question to the dead telephone compels, rather than asserts, the suspicion of the world retreating under the phenomenal thumb and of the dead air between mother and son, signifying not only estrangement but something worse.

In what follows I will argue that regressive gestures of this kind in Pinter's work crystallize a particular affect linked to modern society, a variant of an earlier noir sensibility that insinuates guilt and degradation into even the most complacent mechanisms of amusement. The legacy of American film noir in Pinter's work is a debated subject, often in relation to Pinter's supposed ironic use of the clichés of the genre. In my view, however, the question is not primarily one of influence, as if noir could be digested and processed as a more-or-less stable and coherent set of conventions. Both forms, after all, bear the fingerprints of historical determination; their characteristic neuroses and perversions belong not only to aesthetics but to society. Like film noir, Pinter's distinctive style has begun to ossify into codes and clichés, a process ironically hastened by the author in his postmodern phase. One hopes the modernist works will survive to darken sunny, amnesic dreams of cultural utopias and new world orders like a chronicle of modernity's bad faith.

Despite age, these works retain much of their recalcitrance; one is surprised to find they still bite. In their famous diatribe against the culture of modernity, 'The Culture Industry' chapter of *Dialectic of Enlightenment*, Horkheimer and Adorno look back approvingly on the liberating power of the detail in great art. Single notes, vibrant colours, eccentric characters, arresting objects – all could embody a kind of healthy insubordination of part against whole. (Such insubordination, they felt, had been systematically crushed by the culture industry.) 'When the detail won its freedom, it became rebellious,' they write. It 'asserted itself as free expression, as a vehicle of protest against the organization.'[67] As many of those writing on Pinter suggest in different ways, his drama reflects an ongoing struggle for the integrity and voice of the individual part – indeed, for its very existence – in the face of constraining organization. It is to such details that this book is dedicated.

CHAPTER ONE

The Politics of Negation

Art remains marked by unfreedom; in contradicting it, art achieves its autonomy. The *nomos* which art obeys is not that of the established reality principle
but of its negation.

Herbert Marcuse[1]

In hindsight, the politics of Pinter's early plays has emerged as a central critical concern, and the goal of this chapter is a political assessment of three formative masterworks: *The Birthday Party* (1958), *The
Caretaker* (1960), and *The Homecoming* (1965). The task is complicated,
however, because these plays don't immediately suit the category, if
what we mean by political art is the sympathetic depiction of working-
class life, dramas about factory takeovers, or biting critiques of totalitarianism. The last is actually a fair description of the short plays Pinter
began writing in the 1980s, and in provocative ways they have tended
to politicize thinking about the earlier work. But the politics of the anti-
authoritarian cycle are also complex, which muddies the waters further. In writing about the plays of the 1980s and 1990s, one encounters
a basic tension between content and form. Because they make mention
of authoritarian violence and (apparently) take place in repressive
states, the later plays solicit a new kind of content-based analysis; at
the same time, one sees clear formal similarities with the 'non-political'
works. The fact that the precise locations of the later plays remain
unspecified, for example, signals a familiar kind of Pinteresque equivocation. Indeed, the 'political' plays derive much of their power from
this quasi-realism, from conveying a sense of both fact and metaphor.[2]
But is this the same kind of ambiguity one finds in earlier works?

It is evident that early and late plays alike traverse a spectrum of realism and modernism, with the frequency of the real continually modulated by various degrees of modernist estrangement. Social realities certainly grow more audible, but political signifiers can also be detected in the early masterworks. In various ways, the latter aesthetic extends from and depends on a former aesthetic, and a complete assessment of the anti-authoritarian plays is impossible without first sorting through the social implications of their predecessors. But it is soon clear that this task requires a different language, one that frames the relation between aesthetics and politics in terms of formal resistance and negation rather than simply content. Here, Pinter can tell us something about modernism, and modernist discourse can shed light on Pinter. Walter Benjamin wrote that 'Kafka's work is an ellipse with foci that lie far apart and are determined on the one hand by mystical experience ... and on the other by the experience of the modern city dweller.'[3] Though mystical experience is clearly not a focus, I would argue that Pinter's early work might also be thought of as an ellipse – that is, as art whose palpable relationship to social reality is powerfully mediated and estranged by a competing aesthetic sensibility. The opening stage directions of *The Homecoming* state: 'The back wall, which contained the door, has been removed. A square arch shape remains.'[4] In symptomatic fashion, *The Homecoming* defines a liminal space, somewhere between the 'real' Hackney of Pinter's youth and an abstracted social world marked by primal relations and archetypal shapes.

Mediation is a good word to describe the relations between Pinter's full-length high modernist plays and their social contexts. There is a critique of authoritarianism embedded in *The Birthday Party*; *The Caretaker* radiates tensions around class, race, and modern life; *The Homecoming* explores the underpinnings of patriarchal society. Yet these plays refuse to be exhausted by referential meaning. Instead, they forge autonomous aesthetic spaces that resist the governing reality principle. I will argue that Pinter's high modernist works can be understood as a particular mode of committed writing, albeit one more closely aligned with aesthetic autonomy than with direct political engagement. In this Pinter partakes of the ethos of modernism, and the political implications of his early work are clearer when examined in relation to post-war debates about artistic commitment. In 1958 Kenneth Tynan, Eugene Ionesco, and others engaged in a very public dispute in the *Observer* over art and politics. The dispute was occasioned by a London revival of two Ionesco plays, which Tynan castigated for retreating from social reality. Ionesco countered that ideological art degrades both art and ideology, and that engaged writers, such as Brecht, Miller, and Sartre, were merely 'conformists' of a left-wing sort.[5]

Yet Ionesco's *The Lesson* concludes with the suggested introduction of a Nazi armband, and his *Rhinoceros* is often interpreted as a political allegory. Their polemics aside, it would seem that Ionesco partially concurs with Tynan's commonsensical point that art is part of social life, though Ionesco seeks to resist incorporation by the social through reflecting reality in a distorted, estranged form. The armband signifies differently in *The Lesson* than it would in a realist play, just as the interrogations in *The Birthday Party* cannot be interpreted narrowly as a critique of fascism. The vicissitudes of the idea of commitment amplify this tension. It should be said that that term may now have a musty, anachronistic quality. To a contemporary ear, commitment may infelicitously summon overtones of outdated political formations and early-century mass movements. From the perspective of the present there is perhaps good reason to be wary of both extremes in Walter Benjamin's suggestion in 1936 that fascism renders politics aesthetic and communism responds by politicizing art.[6] At the same time, Benjamin's proposition still usefully preserves the violent, global nature of a problem that postmodernism has reconfigured in much more microcosmic, local terms. Commitment can serve as a reminder of the modernist configuration of aesthetics and politics when Pinter began his career in the late 1950s.

The idea of commitment modifies what has been a prevailing understanding of art since Kant, namely, the idea of the aesthetic as a realm of purposefulness without purpose. Commitment assigns to art an explicit social purpose – an end or goal – devaluing aesthetic autonomy and negating the essence of art's anti-economic stance: its radical separation and uselessness. One instinctive position taken against commitment is to question whether art is the appropriate venue for social struggle or whether politics is better left to the sphere of the political. A counter-argument might then make the obvious point that works of art are also social commodities, and that aesthetic autonomy is at least a fiction and at worst a damaging and profoundly ideological delusion, one that has enabled ideology to cloak itself in the apparent apolitical naturalness of the aesthetic and thus do its work all the more efficiently. The first line of reasoning against commitment can also be extended, however, until we reach a kind of aporia in which opposed positions erode and begin to bleed into each other. Perhaps committed works of art, by imposing social criteria upon themselves, only hasten their assimilation to the unwanted reality. Thus, paradoxically, radically autonomous works can be seen as keeping faith with the impulses of the committed, by protecting the limited but crucial promise of freedom embedded in the idea of art as a separate realm. Commitment to an aesthetic world displaces and fulfils commitment to the real one.

The last position belongs to T.W. Adorno, who held out Beckett as an example of rigorous aesthetic commitment. I would argue that through the complex mediations of his early works, Pinter strives towards a similar negation of the reality principle. They partially conform to Adorno's position, which serves as a grimly sceptical answer to Sartre's question 'Why write?' Pinter would seem to share with Adorno a fundamental and defining reaction to fascism, which made the question of art, politics, and violence an ethical matter. For Adorno, the nature of modernity was inextricably linked to the intellectual and social regression of fascism and the Holocaust, which called into question the right of art to exist. His vision of committed literature oscillates between the potential of art to provide voice and memory to victims and the contrary tendency of art to exploit suffering as imagery, to capitulate to universals, or worse, to accommodate forgetting or even enjoyment. Critics of Adorno have often accused him of championing elitist art and forsaking the public sphere and mass audiences. Some have argued that the idealization of intellectual and imaginative freedom in Adorno's autonomous art represents a reactionary withdrawal from a world marked by real struggles and matters of life and death. Yet for Adorno the perilous, attenuated position of art itself was symptomatic of historical crisis. In its complex, mediated relation to authoritarianism, *The Birthday Party* can likewise be interpreted as a response to this crisis.

Reading *The Birthday Party*

The apolitical tenor of many early interpretations of Pinter now seems odd, given the clear authoritarian overtones in *The Birthday Party*, whose plot can be briefly summarized as follows. The solitary lodger in a seaside boarding house run by a late-middle-aged couple – the quiet Petey and his ebullient wife, Meg – is Stanley, a bespectacled pianist with an ambiguous reputation. On the morning of Stanley's birthday, two strangers appear, asking unsettling questions. These well-heeled thugs, Goldberg and McCann, interrogate Stanley before his evening birthday party, reducing him to mute abjection. The morning after the party – an odd affair, to put it mildly – Goldberg and McCann examine the silent Stanley again, then abduct him. In the last moments of the play, Petey avoids telling Meg, who is slightly cross with Stanley for sleeping so late, though this does not dampen her giddiness after the party.

Apart from any political significance one may attach to Stanley's abduction, the virulence of critical responses to the play's first run (which helped to ensure its quick failure) already suggests a desire to censor something felt to be challenging or radical. In a vitriolic *Financial Times* review, Derek Granger wrote: 'Harold Pinter's first play comes in the school of random dottiness deriving from Beckett and Ionesco and before the flourishing continuance of which one quails in slack-jawed dismay. The interest of such pieces as an accepted genre is hardly more than that of some ill-repressed young dauber who feels he can outdo the *école de Paris* by throwing his paint on with a trowel and a bathmat; and indeed – to come back to the terms of the playmaking – as good if not a better result might have been achieved by summoning a get-together of the critics' circle or the vegetarians' unions [and] offering each member a notebook and pencil.' Granger continues: 'The fact that Mr. Pinter has stolen a march on his predecessors by lacing his own mad, wearying and inconsequential gabble with an odd strain of Jewish banter must merely be put down to a question of time-lag.'[7]

In one venemous outburst, Pinter is criticized for his artiness, his amateurism, his pretension, his use of low comedy, and his Semitism. It is interesting that even at this early moment the *Financial Times* finds Pinter guilty of decadent Continental formalism as well as a kind of low, unwanted, ethnically coded realism, here condescendingly expressed as 'Jewish banter.' Given the telling appearance of this last grievance at the end of a long laundry list, it appears that what perplexes Granger is not only the play's indebtedness to the 'school of random dottiness' but the mixture of this sensibility with another, anchored in some sector of the real. Indeed, on closer examination, the play is a disturbing hybrid; from the outset, *The Birthday Party* centres on radical twists and transformations imposed on the banal. The opening announces naturalism of a pointedly mundane variety. The set is simply a living room, complete with dining table and kitchen hatch, 'prodigally furnished with packets of cornflakes and detergent.'[8] Furthermore, the seaside locale initially suggests the kind of symbolically charged environment one associates with late naturalism – a transitional space between nature and civilization, perhaps reminiscent of Ibsen's poisoned baths (*An Enemy of the People*) or Chekhov's cherry orchard. Quickly, however, naturalist expectations are displaced. Using generic shorthand, Pinter sketches a caricature of lower-class married life drawn from conventional middle-class English comedy. This is familiar terrain in the British cultural imagination, and the initial transformation of naturalistic convention via comedy alters our response to the malevolence of Goldberg and McCann. These menacing strangers are also coded as stock comedic gangsters, Jewish and Irish, respectively, and between interrogations they comically ruminate on tradition, modernity, and the travails of working life.

Yet it is difficult to read *The Birthday Party* as parody. The ritualized humiliation of Stanley, coupled with Meg's strange epiphany at the end of the play, introduce a genuine disturbance with no point of cultural reference, deprived of any closing gesture of restoration. These tensions – between naturalism and stock comedy on the one hand, comedy and catastrophe on the other – are prefigured in the first scene. The action begins innocuously at the breakfast table as Petey eats cornflakes and Meg darns a pair of socks. Petey has returned from his early duties as a deckchair attendant, and Meg enquires about the weather.

MEG: Is it nice out?
PETEY: Very nice.
MEG: Is Stanley up yet?
PETEY: I don't know. Is he?
MEG: I don't know. I haven't seen him down yet.
PETEY: Well then, he can't be up.
MEG: Haven't you seen him down?
PETEY: I've only just come in.
MEG: He must be still asleep. What time did you go out this morning, Petey?
PETEY: Same time as usual.
MEG: Was it dark?
PETEY: No, it was light.
MEG: But sometimes you go out in the morning and it's dark.
PETEY: That's in the winter.
MEG: Oh, in winter.

PETEY: Yes, it gets light later in winter.
MEG: Oh.[9]

This is distilled speech typical of comedy, relying on rhythmical disagreements about more-or-less obvious phenomena. But in an extreme form, this kind of dialogue betrays a double-edged crisis in naturalistic representation. The formal proclivities of the revue sketch unexpectedly merge with the mimesis of everyday speech. This union discloses a kind of social truth in the comic sensibility and a chilling, mechanical hilarity in the rhythms of everyday life. I mean that by 1958 naturalism often verged on self-parody and, simultaneously, that the skeleton of banal conversation in this outwardly comic interplay also intimates damage to the real, a dangerously frayed connection to the world that is perhaps the modern destiny of the ordinary life naturalism sought to represent. Pinter narrows the gap between realism and absurd comedy; the mechanical, formalized speech of vaudeville finds itself thirty years later a very credible imitation of married life. Whether this is ultimately regarded as funny depends on one's view of marriage, but any sentimental attachment to ordinary relationships that survives in Pinter's portrait of this couple is further disturbed by a series of harsh, fundamental oppositions more violent than the disputes of traditional comedy. 'Who's on First?' for example, depends on a kind of transforming utopian silliness (that a baseball player might be named Who, for instance) played against the sweeping imaginative canvas of the American national pastime. Misunderstandings centre on benign, invented phenomena. Here, on the other hand, problems of identity and non-identity arise around matters of basic human orientation: up and down, light and dark, winter and summer, 'nice' and whatever dark quality one chooses as an antonym.

There is incipient pathos in Meg's line 'Oh, in winter,' which may invite psychological interpretation in the manner of realism. But we seem to be dealing with types rather than fully rounded personalities, and Pinter's emphasis on comic convention suggests that we laugh rather than say, 'Poor Meg,' or something equivalent. At the same time, the linguistic shell is all the characters have and they inhabit it desperately; language functions as skin, as trace evidence of impermanent, translucent identity. In an exemplary account in 1968 Raymond Williams says of the dialogue between Petey and Meg: 'What [it] offers is at once the attachment to ordinary life – the conviction of normality, of the everyday – and a covert valuation, beyond the anxious imitation – of a loss of significance, a loss of reality.' Williams reads the play as an adaptation of a peculiar 'structure of feeling' in modern literature. 'The precarious hold on reality, the failures of communication, the inevitability of violence' are inherited tendencies and conventions internalized and transformed by Pinter. The atmosphere, in Williams's view, is 'the strange world of Kafka, now in an English seaside boarding house.'[10] This reading plausibly situates Pinter in modern cultural history, though it is interesting to note how the sting of the play in its British context is removed by inserting Pinter safely into a pre-existing cultural narrative.

Any attempt to capture the play's structure of feeling is obliged to wrestle with the two interrogations of Stanley. In these exchanges, Pinter mutilates convention, combining barbarity and comedy, torture and burlesque. The result is a disorienting mixture, one that testifies to a crisis in representation. These scenes gesture towards history, towards a 'real' referent, but the real remains invisible and barely perceptible, like a faint signal captured by a dying radio. This signal is then further dampened and estranged by the accompanying generic noise, the pastiche of sensibilities loudly vying for the spectator's attention. The first interrogation begins in the style of film noir, with Goldberg and McCann asking gangsterly questions like 'Why did you betray us?' (58). The interrogation is headed towards Stanley's eventual wordless scream, but along the way his increasing confusion is audible only though a crescendo of conflicting references that form the shifting basis of the unanswerable inquisition. Interspersed with personal attacks on Stanley's sleeping habits and piano playing ('How many fingers do you use?') are intractable political considerations ('What about Ireland?'), a lofty rhetorical denunciation ('you're a traitor to the cloth'), allusions to the history of Catholicism (Oliver Plunkett, 'the Albigensenist heresy'), and mention of an early twentieth-century cricket controversy in Australia (61).

The interrogation provides a compressed expression of the play's dialectic of banality; the frame of reference swings wildly from the historical to the personal, the abstract to the particular. As this is an interrogation, its overarching theme, of course, is guilt, a guilt that stains and implicates the cultural and historical imaginary from which the schizophrenic allusions are drawn. Insensibly, however, the final determinant of the first interrogation is its plain association with sketch comedy ('No society would touch you. Not even a building society' [61]); this link is consonant with the many music-hall elements in the play, and, when performed, the interrogation can be both funny and exhilarating. But this is only act one of a two-act interrogation, and the second half works to complicate and undermine the amusement one might have felt during the first. The tone of the second interrogation is much different; the wordless Stanley has been reduced to infantile sounds, and Goldberg and McCann now speak the language of therapy and cure.

> GOLDBERG: We'll make a man of you.
> MCCANN: And a woman.
> GOLDBERG: You'll be re-orientated.
> MCCANN: You'll be rich.
> GOLDBERG: You'll be adjusted.
> MCCANN: You'll be our pride and joy.
> GOLDBERG: You'll be a mensch.
> MCCANN: You'll be a success.
> GOLDBERG: You'll be integrated.
> MCCANN: You'll give orders.
> GOLDBERG: You'll make decisions.
> MCCANN: You'll be a magnate.
> GOLDBERG: A statesman.
> MCCANN: You'll own yachts.
> GOLDBERG: Animals.
> MCCANN: Animals. (93–4)

These fragments of class fantasy and clichés derived from advertising and popular culture, replete with the dubious high spirits of authoritarian fellowship, are offered as a kind of magical resolution of earlier anxieties, as a cure for the play's disease. When addressed to the catatonic Stanley, this language – with the macabre implications of being reorientated, adjusted, integrated, and owning yachts and animals, while being made both a man and a woman – summons the fragmentary, mechanical adaptations inflicted on the modern personality. This is the residue of the human encounter with progress; it is the world of Chaplin's *Modern Times* reduced to mere echoes or slogans. These slogans function in the play as parody without a governing ironic sensibility. The parodic gesture presupposes a detached, neutral space from which to dissect and evaluate. *The Birthday Party*, by contrast, with one foot in the mundane and one in a cultural phantasmagoria, insistently refuses the consolation of a stable frame of reference or Archimedean point from which to assess its juxtapositions of genre and clashes of sensibility. Like many of Pinter's subsequent plays, this one derives much of its power from the cat-and-mouse game it plays with the hermeneutic impulse.

One crucial difference, however, is that *The Birthday Party* is still desperately clawing its way towards the light of historical reality. One senses that the trio of Goldberg, McCann, and Stanley 'stand for' something; that they embody real types or classes and collectively correspond to a social or political referent; that the play as a whole is tenuously attached to history. Considered in the context of his career, there is irony and pathos in the fact that Pinter's first professionally produced play depicts a fall from reality into representation. The historical signals in *The Birthday Party* are faint, already drowning in competing signifiers. The play testifies to a crisis in historicity, in the capacity to represent and feel authentically connected to historical time. This crisis is Pinter's primal scene; the early plays document a palpable though finally unsustainable impulse towards historical realism, as their political and social energies gradually withdraw into the autonomous spaces of modernism.

The end of *The Birthday Party* signals this movement. The abduction and exit of Stanley – a difficult image to grasp without thinking about politics and history – also announces Pinter's departure from an authoritarian political terrain he will not openly revisit until the 1980s. Consider the play's final lines, after Stanley has been escorted out, gurgling, in his newly 'integrated' coat and tie. Meg, who thinks Stanley is still in bed, is nostalgic after the previous evening's party, and Petey tries not to disturb her rapture.

> MEG: I was the belle of the ball.
> PETEY: Were you?
> MEG: Oh yes. They all said I was.
> PETEY: I bet you were, too.
> MEG: Oh, it's true. I was.
> *Pause.*
> I know I was. (97)

In closing, Pinter resurrects a rhapsodic theatre of memory and delusion reminiscent of *A Streetcar Named Desire*. It is difficult to imagine a linguistic register more opposed to the slogans of Goldberg and McCann. The mirage of melodrama surrounding Meg courts deep emotions and encourages the kind of realist identification that the play otherwise prohibits. In Pinter's first play, the rigorousness of this final gesture – the implacable negativity of the impulse – constitutes a retreat into modernist ambiguity but also signals a form of aesthetic commitment.

Finally, I want to return for a moment to the play's initial reception. Alone among London reviewers in May 1958, Harold Hobson praised Pinter in the *Sunday Times*. It is interesting that in his review he perceives a mediated form of political expression: 'Mr. Pinter has got hold of a primary fact of existence. We live on the verge of disaster. One sunny afternoon, whilst Peter May is making a century at Lord's against Middlesex, and the shadows are creeping along the grass, and the old men are dozing in the Long Room, a hydrogen bomb may explode. That is one sort of threat. But Mr. Pinter's is of a subtler sort. It breathes in the air. It cannot be seen, but it enters the room every time the door is opened.'[11]

Hobson rhetorically evokes and exploits Cold War fears by contrasting the insanity of nuclear annihilation with Britain's idyllic, pastoral self-imagery. Though he distinguishes Pinter's threat as a 'subtler sort,' it remains grounded in the analogy. Here, at least one critic senses *The Birthday Party* is animated by catastrophe, not spiritual or existential but emphatically historical in character. Thirty years later, Harold Bloom claimed that sensitivity to the Holocaust was 'inevitable for a sensitive dramatist, a third of whose people were murdered before he was fifteen. A horror of violence, with an obsessive sense of the open wound, is Pinter's unspoken first principle.'[12] Indeed, for twenty-five years after Stanley's exit visible brutality was largely absent from Pinter's work. He carefully avoided the dangerous intersection of violence and aesthetic realism. But this 1958 play seems stained by fascism – the short distance from Weimar civility to the death camps, the dire implications of a knock at the door. Of course, the problem of political art is not so simple, and *The Birthday Party* insists on complex mediations and displacements that render its categorization as an instance of Holocaust literature deeply problematic. Indeed, the play goes to great lengths to ensure that the ontological status of Goldberg and McCann remains unclear. They simultaneously engage and undermine the meaning-making habits ingrained by the aesthetics of realism. Are they gangsters? Secret police? Psychiatric workers? Clowns?

In a political assessment of early Pinter, this is the heart of the matter. A political reading of Pinter must acknowledge that complex mediations and displacements are the precondition of a certain kind of committed writing, not merely evidence of obscurantism or a love of enigmas. The task would then be to construct the relation between *The Birthday Party*'s interrogations and a modern world that has often sanctioned such practices, while preserving the idea that Pinter's work evokes a particular reality while refusing to be only a representation 'of' it. To say that *The Birthday Party* is 'about' the Holocaust would do an injustice to victims and, in a different sense, to the play.

The aesthetics of resistance: *The Caretaker*

As *The Birthday Party* transmutes fascism, *The Caretaker* transmutes capitalism, though according to a much different aesthetic logic. Both plays might be described as quasi-realism, though I would argue that *The Caretaker* more subtly negates the realities it intermittently signals. The evocation of historical violence in *The Birthday Party* is metaphorical. By virtue of the play's anti-realism, Goldberg, McCann, and Stanley can be associated with a variety of victimizers and victims and consequently with many strains of authoritarianism. In contrast, *The Caretaker*'s connection to historical reality feels metonymic. This 1960 play is, at first glance, more narrowly realistic and particular. It is difficult to argue that the characters metaphorically stand for or embody social abstractions, and the hermetic setting comes across as a lonely corner of an offstage world, a world that can be grasped only through synecdochic inference. Goldberg and McCann arrive from some distinct ontological realm, whereas reality appears to bleed into *The Caretaker* from contiguous social spaces. The broken and malevolent environment on stage signals a dehumanized world heavy with economic and racial animosity. Yet the play subtly undercuts the invitation to read it as topical social realism. *The Caretaker* does not aspire to the kind of indeterminate symbolic pastiche exemplified by *The Birthday Party*; rather, it embraces a principle of modernist negation that encourages and then complicates social interpretation.

This principle can be clarified by way of an example. In a crucial speech, the elder brother, Aston, recalls that he was forced to undergo electroshock treatment in a psychiatric hospital. This anecdote, along with references to other topical matters such as racism and immigration, would seem to point to explicit social commentary. But as the playwright John Arden remarked in 1960, Aston's story 'is highly detailed and circumstantial. But it is true? If it is true, why isn't Mr.

Pinter writing that serious social play to denounce the cruelty prevalent in mental hospitals? And if it is not true, why does it take the crucial place in the text?'[13] This equivocal crypto-realism – which includes recognizable social signifiers but is unable to organize them in a coherent shape – testifies to a defining problem of late-modern art. In different ways, writers from Georg Lukács to Fredric Jameson have suggested that modernism in its advanced stages reflects the growing incommensurability of the local and the global. The isolated artwork must struggle to grasp an increasingly abstract and total socioeconomic reality.

This tension is even more evident with respect to race, an issue that *The Caretaker* pointedly announces at the outset. In the opening moments of the play, Davies complains that 'them Blacks ... Greeks, Poles, the lot of them' have been persecuting him at work, and he concludes that 'all them toe-rags, mate, got the manners of pigs.'[14] On the one hand, it is true that *The Caretaker* was conceived in the aftermath of the Notting Hill riots, and the play appears permeable to the complex racial and class antagonisms that the riots explosively catalysed. At the same time, it must be said that the play comes across as a perplexing political metonym. John Stokes writes: 'None of [Pinter's] allusions to race respect the realist rule that an unquestioning focus on a previously identified – and prejudged – situation is the only starting point ... He neither explains nor excuses, but shows racism in action as a state of mind, as an incidental phenomenon not to be understood in isolation.'[15] But this formulation fails to identify the determining social reality to which racism is 'incidental.' A partisan of realism could well argue that an engaged artist is obliged to prejudge and explain political phenomena, to place actions and behaviours in a meaningful frame.

How adequate is *The Caretaker* as a critique of English racism? Davies is certainly problematic as a vehicle for such a critique because the characterization is strongly overdetermined – an odd mixture of modernist tramp (Chaplin, Beckett) and what Stokes calls an 'authentic ... portrait of a contemporary racism.'[16] Surely this character does not take us far in unearthing root causes. Davies meets no recognizable standard of 'typicality'; he is an unlikely stand-in for any particular constituency central to an understanding of emergent racial tensions. Moreover, like the allusion to mental hospitals, the references to race are fragmentary. After the opening, the issue becomes muted. Ultimately, I would argue, race functions as one more signifier in a tissue of 'political issues' that are grafted on without being fully explored. I am reminded here of Godard's films, in which political, literary, and cultural references are carefully shorn of context. In a film like *Weekend* (1967), allusions to Engels, Brecht, Yves Saint-Laurent, Emily Bronte, and James Bond appear as so many shards, as discontinuous signifiers drawn from appropriable codes. Susan Sontag once remarked that 'ideas are chiefly formal elements in Godard's films, units of sensory and emotional stimulation. They function at least as much to dissociate and fragment as they do to indicate or illuminate the "meaning" of the action.'[17] Something similar could be said of Pinter's filtering of social reality in *The Caretaker*.

Here we return to the question of mediation. With Pinter one is seldom sure where to position the frame of reference; wherever interpretive lines are drawn, one is constantly worried by the peripheral sight of material that doesn't fit. This is especially true of *The Caretaker*. The play is, in certain ways, one of Pinter's most local, topical works, but it has also been successfully performed around the world and has engendered many abstract religious, allegorical, and symbolic interpretations. This broad, ambiguous appeal suggests that *The Caretaker* engages social desire at a fundamental rather than a topical level. From the perspective of mediation, I think that the play's power derives in part from its capacity to mobilize basic fantasies about the nature of alienated labour itself. Focusing on the issue of labour provides a way of grappling with the play's sheer junkiness, its insistent juxtaposition of an oppressive object-world with themes of alienated production and work. Examined closely, *The Caretaker*'s configuration of labour and its objects transcends the frame of reference of Britain in the 1950s and engages the reality principle of capitalism more generally.

The Caretaker probes what we might call the capitalist unconscious, an arena of anxiety, malevolence, and guilt that the sunny storefront of commodity culture strives so hard to conceal. Fredric Jameson suggests that 'in middle-class society, the fact of work and of production – the very key to genuine historical thinking – is also a secret as carefully concealed as anything else in our culture. This is indeed the very meaning of the commodity as a form, to obliterate the signs of work on the product in order to make it easier for us to forget the class structure which is its organizational framework. It would indeed be surprising if such an occultation of work did not leave its mark upon artistic production as well.'[18] *The Caretaker* can be read as a meditation on and critique of the aesthetic 'occultation of work.'

Thematically and formally, *The Caretaker* is focused on alienated labour and its products. It is no coincidence that an occupation gives the play its title, since issues of employment and work pervade the play. A man, Aston, brings an elderly itinerant, Davies, into a room in a run-down London house. Aston invites Davies, who has apparently just been fired, to stay and recuperate. It turns out the house belongs to Aston's brother, Mick – a contractor with his own van – who has entrusted Aston with various home improvements. Aston plans to build a shed, and he spends much of the play trying to repair a broken toaster. During the course of the play, Davies is variously offered and denied the odd position of caretaker of the property. He appears poised to accept, but the offer is finally rescinded when Mick decides that Davies lacks the requisite interior-decorating skills. At the end of the play it appears that Davies will be thrown out. The play's thematic focus on labour is in turn mapped on a very distinctive space, one marked by a profusion of semiotically charged objects. Formally, the stage space mobilizes anxieties about commodity reification, which is the theoretical corollary of the alienation of labour. The opening stage directions immediately convey the play's preoccupation with things: 'An iron bed along the left wall. Above it a small cupboard, paint buckets, boxes containing nuts, screws, etc. More boxes, vases, by the side of the bed. A door, up right. To the right of the window, a mound: a kitchen sink, a step-ladder, a coal bucket, a lawn-mower, a shopping trolley, boxes, sideboard drawers. Under this mound an iron bed. In front of it a gas stove. On the gas stove a statue of Buddha. Down right, a fireplace. Around it a couple of suitcases, a rolled carpet, a blow-lamp, a wooden chair on its side, boxes, a number of ornaments, a clothes horse, a few short planks of wood, a small electric fire and a very old electric toaster' (15).

It is important to note that many of these items are marked as anachronistic or historically liminal. The signifiers 'iron,' 'coal,' and 'gas' lead to the 'electric' fire and toaster, and this progression sketches a sort of pre-history of the electrical age. Many of the things are estranged not only from the historical and social conditions of their production but also from any present use. The sink and stove are disconnected, functionless; Davies is scared of the electric fire; the toaster doesn't work. This object-world is menacing and recalcitrant; it is heavy with the pathos of a denatured, inhumane society, a sense reinforced by the menacing allusions to racial and class animus. Moreover, in a manner reminiscent of Beckett's *Endgame* (1957), the object-world of *The Caretaker* serves as a negation of the commodity culture of the 1950s. Fragmented, temporally alienated, and riddled with incongruities, Pinter's ensemble of objects refuses to settle into naturalistic illusion. In 1936 in his seminal essay 'Narrate or Describe?' the Marxist theorist Georg Lukács argues that as a representational style, naturalism passively ratifies the object-world of capitalism by mechanically describing dead decorative details and interchangeable things. Naturalism indiscriminately embraces the 'second nature' of capitalism. Pinter works against this tendency by introducing discarded, broken things, creating a veritable junkshop of modernity. What is largely missing is the strain of 1950s electrical commodities exemplified by the television set. This studied absence confers special importance on the sudden activation of the electrolux, a 1950s commodity par excellence, which Mick uses to menace Davies in Act 2. Taken together, the electrolux and the junk define a spectrum without a happy medium. Objects are either wildly incongruous – like the Buddha statue that Mick demolishes – or terrifying and hyper-modern.

This emphasis on objects interlocks with a virtual laundry list of references to work. Davies has just been fired from a cafe, and much of the play is devoted to his negotiations for the caretaker job. Mick, for his part, underscores the fact that he is a contractor with his own van. At least in theory, Aston has his two ongoing projects, namely, the building of a backyard shed and the fixing of the electric toaster, which has a defective plug. The question of productivity is explicitly thematized, as Mick worries about his brother's fitness as a caretaker: 'I'm coming to the conclusion he's a slow worker' (58). Finally, the play makes jarring reference to a signally postmodern profession. Davies is desperately confused when Mick changes the caretaker's original job description and makes it clear that he expects a professional interior decorator. Incongruously, Mick asks, 'You mean you wouldn't know how to fit teal-blue, copper and parchment linoleum squares and have those colors re-echoed in the walls?' (81).

The abrupt shift in register recalls misplaced signifiers such as the Albigensenist heresy and Oliver Plunkett in *The Birthday Party*, though the effect is somewhat different here. The interrogations estrange the already jumbled aesthetics of *The Birthday Party*, with its uncertain fusion of naturalism, comedy, and melodrama. Interior design, by contrast, dispels the aura of working-class realism – an aesthetic with a long history and one undergoing a revival in the late 1950s. Instead, we get a discordant glimpse of a knowing consumerism with a much different class basis. Interior design signals a neo-bourgeois sensibility presumably in tune with art, fashion, music, and other aspects of the breathless modernization that would come to define Sixties Swinging London. Mick continues: 'You wouldn't be able to decorate out a table in afromosia teak veneer, an armchair in oatmeal tweed and a beech frame settee with a woven sea-grass seat?' (81). Mick's tangential speeches begin to seem central in the light of Davies's stammering responses and the fact that he is subsequently accused of being a duplicitous imposter. Like the electrolux, the references to interior design are formally destabilizing. The play enacts class violence but negates the conventional form for dramatizing this violence – social realism – by introducing an incommensurable cultural register. Such intricate gestures of textual resistance suggest that the play is orchestrating deep-seated social fantasies beneath a realistic veneer.

In thinking about how the play engages such fantasies, it is significant to note that with one or two minor exceptions, no work is ever performed. Ultimately, *The Caretaker* sketches a spectrum of different kinds of work. It creates a pastiche of labour, a jolly, insensible classified ad that stands in stark contrast to the depicted crisis in human production and self-production. The centrepiece of this conflict is Aston's ongoing attempt to fix the very old electric toaster. Here, the play furnishes a bit of textual evidence that evokes the kind of deep angst and existential horror that Fredric Jameson famously associates with modernism. One possible reason for Aston's 'slowness,' as he recounts, is that as a young man he was taken to a mental hospital where a doctor told him, 'we're going to do something to your brain' (64). Against his will, they did so, using 'big pincers, with wires on, the wires were attached to a little machine. It was electric' (65). This horrifying image organizes much of the foregoing material into an ideological shape. The toaster, then, can be read as figure for Aston himself. The fetishistic spell it casts expresses a desire to disavow – through repetition – the moment when his body was treated as an appliance, when he was literally electrified. Following the motif of electricity, we are authorized, I think, to read this trauma as also containing an anxious fantasy about modern industry and labour. The notion of an electrified labourer, a pure circuit of production, seems a powerful modern image for a kind of absolute reification of labour power. Moreover, via the postmodern notion of interior design, so at odds with the play's early-modern junkiness, we are reminded of the perpetual newness of a consumer culture that perpetually discards older forms and products of human work.

This is perhaps the moment to reflect on Pinter's early full-length plays in general. After an examination of *The Birthday Party* and *The Caretaker*, it becomes clear that the early works partake in what has been a feature of modernizing art since Schiller famously identified the 'sentimental,' namely, self-consciousness about the problem of aesthetic expression itself. Of course, this problem reaches crisis proportions in the modern period, and there is a sense in which Pinter's early plays – despite their gestures toward history – are centrally concerned with form rather than content. To put it somewhat differently: it would not be far off to say that these plays, whatever their specific content, are engaged in the negation of conventional meaning-making. A defining feature is *resistance* to interpretation, though for a variety of social and institutional reasons interpretation and its discontents has long been a key issue in relation to Pinter's work.

Indeed, resistance to interpretation is not the same thing as meaninglessness, and Pinter's early reception documents a lively struggle for the cultural capital inherent in fixing the meaning of the plays. In interesting ways, Pinter's high modernist moment is also a liminal moment, insofar as the force of aesthetic autonomy in the plays is partially offset by their overdetermined place within competing cultural discourses. These plays simultaneously incite and disable conventional economies of meaning-making, and in hindsight Pinter's early reception appears to map an entire cultural spectrum. Simply stated, Pinter is polarizing. For audiences, his work has long flickered between opaque modernism and accessible populism; for critics, the same plays have paradoxically seemed to validate radically different conceptions of the work of art. Politically, the early plays engendered both progressive and reactionary interpretations. John Stokes claims that Pinter was judged 'politically apposite' by critics writing in the radical theatre journal *Encore* in the late 1950s and early 1960s. These critics felt that Pinter's plays reflected a Sartrian committed style that 'strove above all else to grasp the present.'[19] At the same time, for many critics Pinter's appeal resided precisely in his apparent distance from the growing politicization of British theatre. As Drew Milne succinctly phrases it, 'Pinter's reputation was fostered in opposition to the forms of political theatre which emerged in the 1950s and persisted into the 1970s.'[20]

Plainly the cultural sphere in which the early Pinter surfaced was marked by wide political divergences and accompanying ambivalence about the politicization of the new British drama. If, as Stokes suggests, Pinter could be incorporated into a narrative of this politicization by left-wing critics, it is also true, as Milne indicates, that Pinter's appeal in other quarters derived precisely from his perceived distance from political theatre. This ambiguous reception appears more complicated when we overlay a broader ambivalence concerning English vs Continental literature, interpretation and meaningfulness, and indeed modernism itself. Some critics, such as Derek Granger, felt that the early Pinter had misguidedly appropriated the 'dottiness'[21] of absurdism, while a few reviewers, according to Yael Zarhy-Levo, 'present[ed] Pinter's dramatic style as a source of pride and a turning point in British drama.'[22] In hindsight, it seems that responses to Pinter reflect larger political positions and feelings about the state of British culture. This tendency in Pinter's reception – its symptomatic quality – snowballed as his name and reputation grew more familiar. Over time, the reception of individual works has been intimately bound up in a broader appraisal of Pinter's meaning as icon and as writer – an intuitive sense of what he was up to and whether it represented an advance or a decline. In Britain, by the mid-1960s if not before, it would have been difficult to innocently take in a Pinter play. An opinion about Pinter might entail a number of far-reaching cultural positions.

Insofar as Pinter became associated with known absurdist writers, his reception reflects various feelings about European modernism and its relation to British drama. Among other things, the early full-length plays allow for a kind of domestication of a strange and unyielding aesthetic; as Raymond Williams remarks above, *The Birthday Party* can be taken as Kafka transplanted in an English seaside boarding-house. In her essay 'Pinter and the critics,' Yael Zarhy-Levo traces a two-stage process by which Pinter was first compared to recognized modernists (such as Kafka, Beckett, and Ionesco) and in effect naturalized by insertion into an accepted genealogy. Pinter's originality was then stressed, creating a contradictory sense that he was simultaneously familiar and novel, known and unknown. Over time, she argues, 'the inexplicable quality of Pinter's style, used by the critics to justify their initial rejection, serves consequently as their means for selling him to the public, and eventually becomes his trademark.'[23] Moreover, this critical bait-and-switch can be interpreted as a culturally conservative phenomenon. If Pinter's 'inexplicable quality' could be converted into a meaningful aesthetic virtue, then by extension forbidding modernism might be made more palatable. If Pinter could be redeemed from his obscurity by critics, this redemption might yield fringe benefits: assimilation of the work to aesthetic and ethical conventions; promulgation of an ideology linking aesthetic value with deep meanings, intense appreciation, and elaborate interpretations (thereby requiring critics); and an elevated perception of English drama, gained by assigning Pinter a place in a liberalized literary canon.

Indeed, the second-stage defences described by Zarhy-Levo establish Pinter's 'greatness'[24] by emphasizing the aesthetic depth of his work and the consequent necessity of interpretation. A latent, deep meaning is alleged, which then requires professional decoding. Here, something also needs to be said about the 'full-length' nature of *The Birthday Party*, *The Caretaker*, and *The Homecoming*. What I have been calling Pinter's high modernist moment appears in hindsight remarkably insular and circumscribed. While Pinter did write many shorter pieces during the period and a variety of works since, for many his reputation rests with these three full-length masterworks produced during the relatively brief period of 1958–65. In this period Pinter is most fully invested in the paradigm of autonomous art – the willed creation of a fully formed aesthetic world that exists in negative, critical relation to the real. It is interesting to note that the more fragmentary nature of later works conveys an implicit distrust of this totalizing moment, as if it came to represent a reactionary acceptability that he grew restless to transcend. For one of the novel features of Pinter's liminal career is that it begins with an oddly domesticated modernism. In their popularity and openness to elaborate interpretations, Pinter's early masterworks could be thought of as a reassuring cultural reservoir – strange, yes, but deep, English, and reliable.

For many, the masterworks embody a complete artistic vision only partially expressed in other pieces; as Kimball King and Marti Greene point out, they are by one measure Pinter's most widely studied plays.[25] The aura of the masterwork contributes to the domestication of modernism. The masterwork reconciles a modernist ideology of total, transforming artistic vision and the perfection of individual style with humanist beliefs in self-expression and the social value of great literature. But one thing to distrust about masterworks is that this reconciliation amounts to a mystification, since the two positions it embraces are incompatible. Is the social function of the work of art to reclaim deep meanings, evoke shared experiences, and minister to society, or is it to create resistant, autonomous structures that symbolically transform and negate reality? There are the outlines here of two distinct aesthetic philosophies, the first centred on redemptive meaningfulness and the second on negation. In the context of modern drama, the first position is especially associated with Martin Esslin, whose seminal study *The Theatre of the Absurd* (1961) and its later editions worked to integrate Pinter into an absurdist canon. Consider the following excerpts from Esslin's book: 'Concerned as it is with the ultimate realities of the human condition, the relatively few fundamental problems of life and death, isolation and communication, the Theatre of the Absurd ... represents a return to the original, religious function of the theatre'; and somewhat later: 'There are enormous pressures in our world that seek to induce mankind to bear the loss of faith and moral certainties by being drugged into oblivion – by mass entertainments, shallow material satisfactions, pseudo-explanations of reality, and cheap ideologies ... the need to confront man with the reality of his situation is greater than ever.'[26]

The movement of this argument is towards universality. Ancient drama is held up as a timeless paradigm, while the 'cheap' sphere of contemporary mass culture is viewed as a narcotizing distraction from 'fundamental problems.' The Theatre of the Absurd is judged the legitimate descendant of ancient drama and is considered capable of supplying a mirror of 'ultimate realities.' Esslin's construction of the absurd depends on a total composite image of the human condition: the degradation of language, the disappearance of god, the absurdity of contemporary existence. This paradigm became a highly influential context for the reception and understanding of Pinter's early works. Absurdism, I would argue, itself is a strategic domestication of modernism. The category subsumes a heterogeneous body of intensely specific works under a series of unequivocal generalizations. With its user-friendly philosophical precepts, absurdism allows a reassuring aura of meaningfulness to emerge from recalcitrant works. But the positive pull of this interpretive strategy is nearly the opposite of a view of modernism premised on negation.

Absurdism and other similarly universalizing approaches may struggle with local details whose power often depends on a very particular, critical relation to the real. To return to the toaster in *The Caretaker*: Esslin writes, 'In a world that is increasingly deprived of meaning, we seek refuge in being experts in some narrow field of irrelevant knowledge or expertise. In trying to become master of some electrical appliance, Aston is seeking to get a foothold on reality.'[27] Before it comes to stand for inaccessible reality or a world without meaning, I would suggest that a toaster first must be confronted as a toaster, and here an intensely cathected one, as we have seen. By mobilizing potent fantasies about reification and work, the toaster subtly negates the reality principle of alienated labour. Even more fundamentally, this strange artefact of early modernity, coded as vestigial and outdated, could be taken to signal a violent struggle between industrial technology and the more primitive organic sensibility signified by the slice of bread. The toaster is irrelevant only from a detached perspective, and Aston, at any rate, approaches the junk pile of his object-world with so much phenomenological alarm that resignation to a world 'deprived of meaning' might be a consolation.

In hindsight, Pinter's early masterworks are situated on a cultural fault line. The polarized responses to these plays document a variety of conflicting social attitudes and philosophical positions. What is astonishing is the degree to which the plays seem very precisely to anticipate and exacerbate this hermeneutical crisis. They both solicit and confound the interpretive impulse, creating discursive mushroom clouds as evidence of violent conflicts in meaning-making. Ultimately, the plays' power of negation rests in this dialectic. The intimation of depth and the apparent invitation to explore it are characteristic of the masterworks; in this respect, Esslin's universal toaster is not surprising. I would argue, however, that the presentation of the object-world in plays like *The Caretaker* suggests symbolism and a meaningful aesthetic vision but finally punctures and retracts this appearance by returning to the opacity of the object, by reaffirming its recalcitrance and materiality. The semblance of depth proves to be a mirage. Moreover, this process is not limited to Pinter's treatment of objects but extends to other apparent symbolisms as well.

That said, I want to underscore the complexity of this gesture, which is not merely a negative one that frustrates any attempt at interpretation and refuses all symbolic or metaphorical meanings, creating what T.W. Adorno called a 'bad positivism of meaninglessness.'[28] Rather, the gesture depends for its power on harnessing an ineradicable impulse to make meaning, to meet the world halfway – an impulse, however, that never quite obtains its object. In this sense, characters and critics are confronted by similar predicaments. For both, the repudiation of meaning would mean less if meaning did not seem, at moments, so tantalizingly near. The difference is between the sublimation of interpretive desire and its mere repression. The feeling-tone of Pinter's plays is seldom one of resignation; instead, we see the intricate, devious paths taken by desire when there is no possibility of simple fulfilment. Similarly, for critics, the mirage of deep existential or social significance in *The Caretaker* and other Pinter plays fuels the manufacture of an elaborate web of sublimated interpretations. *The Caretaker* frustrates and organizes the hermeneutic gesture in a way that signals a historical impasse confronting modernism.

In the introduction to his well-known book on postmodernism, Fredric Jameson outlines the transition from Van Gogh's celebrated painting *A Pair of Boots* to Andy Warhol's *Diamond Dust Shoes*. Following Heidegger, Jameson suggests that Van Gogh's painting first may be read as a restoration of the objective world of peasant toil and agrarian misery from which the boots were concretely derived. This first stage we might call a realist gesture. In Van Gogh's painting, however, the lived context is miraculously sublimated as 'the most glorious materialization of pure color in oil paint,' a grand utopian affirmation of visual pleasure as compensation for the brute existence against which it recoils. These twin displacements, which Jameson takes as emblematic of modernism, position the viewer simultaneously to recover and redeem the boots and their original lived situation. I would suggest that this modernist paradigm is, among other things, a vindication of hermeneutical operations by which 'the work in its inert, objectal form is taken as a clue or a symptom for some vaster reality which replaces it as its ultimate truth.'[29] The ideal spectator re-enacts the work's displacements, discerning a gap between the crude banality of the boots and Van Gogh's stylistic variation, resurrecting their dismal origin alongside the painting's material, utopian transformation.

One detects some initial similarity to Pinter here. There is perhaps no dramatist so concerned with social detritus and bric-a-brac, with the painstaking transformation of banality, the minute presentation of a life-world that both invites and frustrates comparisons with our own. This predilection might lead us to revisit the peculiar ontological debates about theatre in general – whether a newspaper on stage (for example) is presented or represented, existent or performed, displayed in unmediated fashion or 'used' as an exemplar of 'newspaperness.' Such questions, in turn, can be applied to many different kinds of stage phenomena. In Pinter's case, at least, the object world is skewed and bipolar; toasters and toy drums sometimes appear opaque and recalcitrant, sometimes meaningful and symbolic. The question, then, is primarily hermeneutical: does Pinter's work organize or display its raw materials to highlight stylistic variations, to open a space between post-war British 'reality' and its transformation so that the audience can perceive the discrepancy?

The other end of Jameson's spectrum is Warhol's *Diamond Dust Shoes*, 'hanging together on the canvas like so many turnips, as shorn of their earlier life world as the pile of shoes left over from Auschwitz.' Warhol's shoes, Jameson contends, no longer address the spectator with the promise of shared, secret knowledge or interpretive give-and-take. There is no way to restore context or 'complete the hermeneutic gesture.' Jameson famously uses Warhol to begin to assess the new 'cultural logic' of postmodernism, the ubiquitous postmodernist coding of modernist styles and variations that cites or reproduces the old transforming depth of modernist experiment as glossy commodity spectacle. In Jameson's enlarged account, postmodernism is further marked by what he calls a 'waning of affect' in spectators and audiences. Aesthetic experience is now characterized by quasi-schizophrenic spasms of psychological intensity rather than the deep emotions associated with high modernism. As he writes of *Diamond Dust Shoes*, 'Nothing in this painting organizes even a minimal place for the viewer, who confronts it at the turning of a museum corridor or gallery with all the contingency of some inexplicable natural object.'[30]

As a third term on the footwear spectrum, compare the use of shoes in *The Caretaker*. When he first arrives in the cluttered junk-pile that serves as sleeping quarters, Davies has only a pair of sandals, inadequate to the dank weather and his endless walks around London. During the first fifteen minutes of the play his main motivation is to procure a more serviceable pair of shoes from Aston. Eventually, Aston offers him a pair one size too small, which occasions the following rant by Davies against a monastery that had advertised free footwear; it is worth quoting in its entirety.

> Can't wear shoes that don't fit. Nothing worse. I said to this monk, here, I said, look here, mister, he opened the door, big door, he opened it, look here, mister, I said, I come all the way down here, look, I said, I showed him these, I said, you haven't got a pair of shoes, have you, a pair of shoes, I said, enough to keep me on my way. Look at these, they're nearly out, I said, they're no good to me. I heard you got a stock of shoes here. Piss off, he said to me. Now look here, I said, I'm an old man, you can't talk to me like that, I don't care who you are. If you don't piss off, he says, I'll kick you all the way to the gate. Now look here, I said, now wait a minute, all I'm asking for is a pair of shoes, you don't want to start taking liberties with me, it's taken me three days to get here, I said, three days without a bite, I'm worth a bite to eat, en I? Get round the corner to the

kitchen, he says, get round the corner, and when you've had your meal, piss off out of it. I went round to this kitchen, see? Meal they give me! A bird, I tell you, a little bird, a tiny little bird, he could have ate it in under two minutes. Right, they said to me, you've had your meal, get off out of it. Meal? I said, what do you think I am, a dog? What do you think I am, a wild animal? What about them shoes I come all the way here to get I heard you was giving away? I've a good mind to report you to your mother superior. One of them, an Irish hooligan, come at me. I cleared out. I took a short cut to Watford and picked up a pair there. Got onto the North Circular, just past Hendon, the sole comes off, right where I was walking. Lucky I had my old ones wrapped up, still carrying them, otherwise I'd have been finished, man. So I've had to stay with these, you see, they're gone, they're no good, all the good's gone out of them. (14–15)

The first thing to notice, I think, is the painterly sensibility at work in this long speech. The heightened, rambling vernacular is marked by backtracking, repetition, and overlapping ('here, I said, look here, mister, he opened the door, big door, he opened it, look here, mister, I said, I come all the way down here, look, I said'). This technique seals and papers over any potential gaps or silences; the result is very nearly a wall of sound or the verbal concreteness of prose poetry. Enhancing this sensation is the almost purely digressive character of the monologue, which interrupts Davies's testing of the available footwear. Indeed Aston's only response is to hand him a second pair of shoes, with the laconic remark, 'Try these.' In this context, the long digression hangs suspended like a speech balloon. Pinter is working in a painterly mode of non-dialogic, fixed verbal evocation; he is using the monologue, almost graphically, to paint a picture. However unlikely it might be, one can picture the three-day march, the long walkway leading from the monastery gate, the enormous door, the humiliating shuffle around the corner to the kitchen, the measly portion of food that a bird could eat in 'under two minutes.' On balance, we may be tempted to interpret the anecdote as outright falsehood or at least an old man's bellowing exaggeration. At other moments in the play, Davies certainly comes across as an inveterate liar (he uses the assumed name 'Bernard Jenkins' for no good reason). At war with the wild implausibility of what is recounted, however, is the authentic indignation and puzzlement emanating from the speech. The stuttering detail has something of the erratic intensity of a real memory, and the tortured specificity of the description grants the escapade a momentary, imagistic truth, whatever its factual basis.

Indeed, the desire to reconstruct a factual basis is only the most obvious source of hermeneutic frustration here. Pinter goes to lengths to evoke a grim and particular life-world, a human history, punctuated by this one glaring injustice. The broken-down shoes are in some obvious way tokens of a terrifying elderly dispossession and homelessness: days without food, wandering the expressways near Hendon in search of forgotten friends, employment, and sustenance. The familiarity of the humanist iconography surrounding old shoes is partly the result of painters like Van Gogh, and traditional values concerning poverty and degradation are forcefully recalled in Davies's retorts: 'What do you think I am, a dog? What do you think I am, a wild animal?' Like Van Gogh, Pinter seems to be marshalling the potent force of modernist synecdoche – using the shoes as markers of a long-lived experience of suffering – to more fully flesh out a grimy instance of post-war British realism. At this point, when one stops to think about it, the hermeneutic gesture begins to encounter resistance. A realism of old men walking Hendon expressways? Of discourteous monks? Of old tramps invited into cluttered rooms only to be mistreated by dysfunctional siblings?

The army of incongruities arrayed against interpretation is led by the monk who tells Davies to 'piss off out of it.' 'If you don't piss off,' he reportedly says, 'I'll kick you all the way to the gate.' The inappropriateness (to say the least) of this response, its clipped, sceptical diction, posits an elemental doubt about the *value* of the anecdote – indeed, the value of the whole modernist gesture and its interpretation – *within* the anecdote. We may imagine elaborate scenarios: a monk in a crisis of faith, feeling unwanted stirrings of non-celibate desire, questioning the efficacy of institutional charity, when an unfortunate tramp knocks on the door. But in Davies's account, the first monk was not alone; indeed the entire monastery appears to be a hotbed of hooliganism. Like Davies, the spectator is incredulous and defensive. The anecdote is a momentary, imagistic representation of a crisis in criticism and interpretation: a breaking of the hermeneutic circle, with the larger play, in some fashion, containing this crisis while being implicated in it.

Pinter's shoes are somewhere between Van Gogh and Warhol. We have not yet come to what Jameson calls the 'deathly quality' of the Warhol image, 'as though the external and colored surface of things – debased and contaminated in advance by their assimilation to glossy advertising images – has been stripped away to reveal the deathly black-and-white substratum of the photographic negative which subtends them.'[31] In fact, one of the most distinctive modernist tendencies in the early Pinter – here reminiscent of Beckett – is the exclusion of a contemporary commodity world that is often either the target or the means of postmodernist intervention. Pinter's object-world is populated by holdovers, hand-me-downs, junk; his typical objects are one generation late. By contrast, the toasters and television sets in Sam Shepard's plays, for example, are coded as American consumer kitsch in a manner much more attuned to late-capitalist culture than are any of Pinter's mechanisms or appliances. The epistemology of objects – their ontological strangeness, their sheer resistance – is profound and harrowing in Pinter's works, in contrast to the superficial 'intensities' Jameson identifies in postmodern consumption. At the same time, Pinter's shoes reject both the conventional correspondences of realist iconography and the aesthetics of modernist transformation. Davies's last line sounds a note of elegy. About his sandals, he says 'they're gone, they're no good, all the good's gone out of them.'

We have here, I think, the outlines of a poetics of resistance: incitement to deep emotion without the restoration of meaningful context, interruption of the hermeneutic circle, refusal of safe ironic distance, juxtaposition of violently opposed sensibilities. These characteristics begin to delineate a rhetorical approach to the problem of committed writing by modelling commitment to a particular world – one lodged between the aesthetic and the real – that cannot be easily processed or exhausted by interpretation.

Anti-Oedipus: *The Homecoming*

The cluttered specificity of *The Caretaker* furnishes the ground for its subtle exploration of the capitalist unconscious. The play is less about the surface realities of capitalism than about what capitalism *feels like* – to transpose a famous phrase of Richard Dyer.[32] *The Caretaker* works against the social grain by summoning a primal experience of alienation amid a junk shop of unredeemable things. By contrast, *The Homecoming* (1965) centres on psychoanalytic rather than economic reality, though the psychoanalytic terrain it explores is gendered in politically significant ways. If *The Caretaker* transmutes capitalism, *The Homecoming* transmutes patriarchy. Again, we are dealing less with visible naturalism than with the evocation of unconscious structures: what patriarchy feels like and how it reproduces itself. *The Homecoming* introduces a new form of negation, however, by deconstructing not only the patriarchal family, but also conventional family drama as an ideological structure. The play provides a point-by-point meta-critique of the ideological underpinnings of such drama, suggesting that conventional cultural forms are an important medium for the political regulation of gender.

In an important essay on realist drama and feminism, Jeanie Forte cites Catherine Belsey's enumeration of the characteristics of 'classic realism.' They include illusionism, closure, the creation and dissolution of enigmas, the re-establishment of order, and a 'hierarchy of discourses' that posits the ultimate 'truth' of the story. She goes on to discuss the Oedipal scenario and its relation to narrative in general. Paraphrasing Teresa de Lauretis, Forte writes that, in the logic of the Oedipus complex, 'Woman functions both as a sign (representation) and a value (object) ... woman's role constitutes the fulfillment of the narrative promise (made, in the Freudian model, to the little boy), the reward at the end of the Oedipal journey; a representation which supports the male status of the mythical, culturally constructed subject.'[33]

Narrative is thus gendered, the argument goes, and conventional realist narrative is particularly suspect because it works so powerfully (and stealthily) to reinforce the dominant patriarchal order. The ostensibly timeless epistemology of narrative – journeys, goals, enigmas, payoffs, resolutions – in fact represents an ideological way of ordering the world. Realist narrative works covertly to naturalize a highly constructed version of reality, thereby mystifying the status quo. Forte continues: 'a refusal to perpetuate the conventions of realism/narrative would presumably not only thwart the illusion of "real" life, but also would function to threaten the patriarchal ideology imbedded in "story" ... A subversive text would not provide the detached viewpoint, the illusion of seamlessness, the narrative closure, but would instead open up the negotiation of meaning'[34] The negation of realism as an ideological mode, however, is a complex undertaking. In her essay, Forte examines a range of dramatic models from a feminist perspective, from Marsha Norman's crypto-feminist play *'night, Mother* to the radically non-narrative work of Adrienne Kennedy. In reflecting on distinctions between anti-realist forms, I would identify a difference between abstract and determinate negations of realism. The former is marked by the creation of new formal languages and non-narrative structures, whereas the latter remains bounded by its object, deconstructing realism according to its own conditions of possibility.

In these terms, I would argue that Pinter's *The Homecoming* (1965) can be read as a determinate negation of conventional family drama. As Michael Billington points out, there have been attempts to interpret the play autobiographically as an earnest variant of East End Jewish melodrama,[35] but I will treat *The Homecoming* as a meta-commentary on the formal conventions of this kind of drama. Even a preliminary look reveals that *The Homecoming* runs counter to the attributes of classic realism described above. In the introduction to this chapter I alluded to the opening stage directions, which call for a semi-realistic rendering of a large room in a London house. Tellingly, however, the back wall has been removed, leaving only an arch shape that once enclosed a door. We might describe this setting as a determinate negation of illusionism. Later in the play, when Teddy and Ruth arrive, Teddy provides a cryptic explanation for the remodelling: 'Actually there was a wall, across there ... with a door. We knocked it down ... years ago ... to make an open living area. The structure wasn't affected, you see. My mother was dead.'[36] In his book *Harold Pinter and the Language of Cultural Power*, Marc Silverstein borrows 'The structure wasn't affected' for the title of his psychoanalytically oriented chapter on *The Homecoming*, and it does seem a key phrase. The ambiguous use of the word 'structure' – simultaneously architectural and familial – suggests that we are dealing not with an illusionistic depiction of a 'real' family, but rather with the deconstruction of an ideological formation. The audience stumbles, as it were, upon family drama in a process of remodelling and, as a result, sees ideological forms typically covered by realistic drywall.

Likewise, in several ways *The Homecoming* frustrates expectations of a 'hierarchy of discourses' that discloses the narrative's ultimate 'truth.' Conventionally, dramatic narratives achieve closure and establish truth in a number of ways, including the climactic revelation of a secret, a well-timed death, and sometimes both. *The Homecoming* compresses these conventions in an alienating fusion that mocks dramatic resolution. Near the end of the play, Sam reveals that 'MacGregor had Jessie in the back of cab,' upon which he *'croaks and collapses.'* Max is utterly unperturbed to learn of this liaison between his wife and his best friend and instead is irate that Sam has not fulfilled his dramatic responsibilities. When informed that the prostrate Sam is still alive, Max says in disgust, 'He's not even dead!' (94). The related idea of a 'hierarchy of discourses' can be further clarified by comparison with a prior canonical example of family realism, namely, Lorraine Hansberry's *A Raisin in the Sun* (1959). 'Hierarchy of discourses' suggests that classic realism is authoritarian rather than pluralistic; that is, the form cannot tolerate the coexistence of competing voices and values, and instead yearns for restitution of ideological order. Thus, from a feminist perspective, Hansberry's play – justly famous for its complex and compelling female characters – can also be seen as profoundly Oedipal. The voices of the African-American women and the values of love and community they embody seem much more mature and engaging than the voice of the lone adult male, Walter, who spends most of the play driven by compulsion and self-pity. But the progressive power of the women's voices is bounded by the play's narrative structure. Formally, the action is bracketed by the death of one patriarch and the birth of a new one. The disordering impetus of the dramatic journey is the death of Big Walter, and the restorative close of the journey occurs when Walter (Jr) takes his place as head of the family. This ideological shape is underscored by Mama's description of Walter at the end of the play: 'He finally come into his manhood today, didn't he? Kind of like a rainbow after the rain.'[37]

The hierarchy ultimately installed by this and other realist plays emanates from a patriarchal logos that tolerates competing voices only insofar as they pay obeisance to the sign of the father. Compare the conclusion of *The Homecoming*, in which several incommensurable discourses remain in flux. We are ultimately confronted with the family-secret narrative, whose dubiousness has already been described; the divorce narrative, in which Teddy inexplicably leaves his wife, who inexplicably calls him 'Eddie' as he departs; the prostitution narrative, in which the pimp Lenny is able to facilitate a desired sexual scenario for himself and his father and brother; and, finally, the Ruth narrative, in which she apparently seizes control by driving a hard bargain. The jumbled nature of these discourses is finally inscribed by the pointed failure of Oedipal restoration. At the end of the play the sexually dysfunctional Lenny is detached, an impotent voyeur; Joey regresses, his head in Ruth's maternal lap; and, most significantly, the patriarch Max *'begins to groan, clutches his stick, falls on his knees by the side of her. His body sags ... He looks at [Ruth], still kneeling'* (97). The patriarch, whose 'stick' normally guarantees narrative coherence, is here unable to bind the various discourses in a hierarchical arrangement.

In these local ways, *The Homecoming* shorts the conventional circuits through which realist drama normally flows. If the play went no further it might remain a slight, amusing parody. *The Homecoming* goes deeper, however, by hyperbolizing the fantasies and psychic fixations of family drama and refusing to sublimate them in a reassuring narrative structure. One could say that *The Homecoming* is about the unconscious of family drama – its ideological underpinnings and patterns of cathexis. This psychoanalytic, subtextual dimension has been reflected in the critical literature, since many critics have refused to take the play at face value. As early as 1965 Stuart Hall contended that *The Homecoming* advanced a thesis about families, though 'its roots lie in the fantasies, rather than the social relationships, which seem to Pinter to underpin these families. His purpose is to expose the machinery of fantasy.'[38] More recently, Marc Silverstein has persuasively argued that the play exposes the family as 'a site for producing appropriate gendered subjects, ready to assume their place in the system of social relations that supports the perpetuation of patriarchy.' In an intricate theoretical account indebted to Lacan, Silverstein finds in *The Homecoming* a crisis in normative family structure, one that stems from the fact that the actual father and mother do not coincide with social constructions of 'symbolic father' and 'symbolic mother.'[39] Patriarchy depends on the mother's recognizing the father's symbolic power and her own 'lack' and mistakenly associating the father with the ideological trappings of the father: law, language, the phallus. Silverstein suggests that *The Homecoming* radically destabilizes these roles.

Yet if the family is an ideological institution, it is one whose reproduction is also cultural, and family drama can be grasped as a site in which a particular ideology of 'family' has been propagated. *The Homecoming* functions as a critique of family drama, but in a manner consistent with modernism, the critique is immanent rather than analytic. As we have seen, the play does not comment on conventions from a distance, but instead inhabits and deconstructs familiar tropes, negating ideological closure by denaturalizing what is represented. *The Homecoming* accomplishes this subtle negation by rendering its dialogue and iconography heavy with regressive anxiety and fantasy and, like *The Birthday Party*, by rapidly shifting the frame of reference from the banal to the barbaric. For example, the play's first line – delivered by the irascible patriarch Max to his hostile, unresponsive son – is 'What have you done with the scissors?' The menacing thrust of the question alerts us to a powerful process of cathexis, and, more specifically, the scissors announce a castration threat that looms over the play. *The Homecoming* centres on a father, Max, his two sons, Lenny and Joey, and his brother Sam: a family unit that has been disarranged by the death of Jessie, the late wife and mother. The play is replete with sexual tensions exacerbated by the arrival of Max's expatriate son, Teddy, and Teddy's wife, Ruth. The wife is both a threat and an object of desire, and this dialectical ambivalence is underscored by the play's famously enigmatic ending, in which Ruth has negotiated a position as a prostitute and new matriarch of the family. As described above, the play concludes with the patriarch Max symbolically castrated: on his knees, gurgling like a baby, pleading for a kiss.

Through the scissors, the play marks the quiescent object-world of realistic family drama with troubling associations. In conventional drama, the neutrality of this object-world is crucial in grounding and naturalizing the ideological depiction of family life. The estrangement of objects thus violates the seamless, illusionistic realist text. Moreover, the association of scissors with castration is part of a larger pattern of fantasy at work in the play. Here, it is helpful to turn to Freud, since *The Homecoming* taps those anxious psychic energies that crystallize in 'primal phantasies,' as he calls them. Freud traces the outlines of these fantasies through elements 'which continually recur in the story of a neurotic's childhood.' He concludes that the archetypal vignettes of a neurotic's childhood may derive from real experiences or may be fantasized 'on the basis of hints and allusions.'[40] The three primal fantasies on which he concentrates are 'observation of parental intercourse, seduction by an adult, and the threat of castration' (322). In this light, I would identify Lenny as the focal point of the play's neurosis. The role of Lenny anchors the deployment of primal fantasies, and, as the play progresses, he encounters fantasy material in increasingly raw, unsublimated forms.

We might approach Lenny's castration anxiety from the perspective of Max's cane, an object that emerges as a kind of linchpin. The cane signifies both power and infirmity. Throughout the play, the rather desperate phallic ambitions that the cane suggests are undercut by fears of impotence, culminating in Max's childish crawl at the conclusion. Early on, Lenny appears to win an Oedipal war of words with his father when he says, mockingly, 'Oh, Daddy, you're not going to use your stick on me, are you? Eh? Don't use your stick on me Daddy' (27). At the same time, however, this masquerade of submission proves uneasy for Lenny, whose aggression is noticeably tinged with sexual ambivalence and obsessive anxiety. At a growing distance from the phallic cane, Lenny, in his combative relations with others, becomes associated with objects such as a water glass and a cheese roll in arguments with Ruth and Teddy. It is interesting that both cheese roll and water glass are quasi-phallic in shape, and compared with Max's cane, the items are to some degree feminized by their association with domesticity. Either might be taken as a fetish-object, which, as Freud tells us, 'is a substitute for the woman's (mother's) penis which the little boy once believed in and ... does not wish to forgo.'[41] The fetish is an inherently unstable structure that entwines knowledge and disavowal, desire and anxiety. Thus, when Lenny initially meets the cool, sexually confident Ruth, he becomes fussily preoccupied with removing her water glass. In panic, he invests in an ostensibly asexual object, and the inadequacy of this defensive displacement is revealed when Ruth says, 'If you take the glass ... I'll take you.' All Lenny can manage by way of retort is the anemic line, 'How about me taking the glass without you taking me?' (50).

Lenny's interaction with Ruth begins to suggest the Freudian fantasy of seduction by an adult. For the neurotic, this fantasy may hark back to an attempt 'to cover the childhood period of auto-erotic activity; the child evades feelings of shame about onanism by retrospectively attributing in phantasy a desired object to the earliest period.'[42] Lenny's sexuality has a similarly contrived, regressed quality, as if he were scripting events to deflect the terror and shame of sexuality by attributing it to others. Thus, when Ruth suggestively offers to 'pour [water] down your throat' – inviting Lenny to assume a childish, supine position – he responds with neurotic apprehension: 'What are you doing, making me some kind of proposal?' (50). Seduction fantasy is more graphically evident in one of Lenny's earlier stories to Ruth, in which a woman 'falling apart with the pox' (46) supposedly accosted him by the docks. This woman, he claims, 'started taking liberties ... which by any criterion I couldn't be expected to tolerate' (47). This improbable, suggestive vignette begins with Lenny's 'watching all the men jibbing the boom, out in the harbor, and playing about with a yardarm' (46). The auto- and homoerotic associations of these activities are desperately disavowed by the concoction of a heterosexual seduction, which Lenny can likewise conceive only with horror. Tellingly, the anecdote concludes with Lenny punching and kicking the woman in response to her advances, evoking a regressed state in which erotic and aggressive energies are relatively undifferentiated.

What ultimately anchors *The Homecoming* – and much family drama generally – is the fantasy of the primal scene. The primal scene is a privileged locus of sexual and Oedipal anxiety; it is an unseen, unspoken, unconscious field of force that shapes the family romance and its

dramatic representation. Real or imagined, the image of parental intercourse irrevocably conjoins sexuality and trauma; as it assumes different forms in later life, the fantasy harks back to a child's perception of
intercourse as violence. Seen in Oedipal terms, the aura of menace
attached to the image is further compounded by the fact that the child
is excluded from its *mise en scène*. Moreover, the castration anxiety
occasioned by the primal scene is doubly amplified: the image is a
threatening, simultaneous revelation of the mother's castration and the
father's potency. Freud's elaborately hermeneutical analysis in the
'Wolf Man' case also reminds us that the repression of the primal scene
fuels its recurrence as a psychic structure in a variety of forms. As an
unconscious structure – a setting for desire, as Jean Laplanche and
Jean-Bertrand Pontalis define fantasy[43] – the primal scene emerges
through the mediations of dreams, symptoms, and other kinds of displacement. It is, I would suggest, an invisible locus of considerable
energy in family drama, and a central component of *The Homecoming*'s
negation is to make the primal scene disarmingly evident and literal.
Again, our resident neurotic, Lenny, attempts to rebuff his father
through a clever, though psychically hazardous misdirection: 'I'll tell
you what, Dad, since you're in the mood for a bit of a ... chat, I'll ask
you a question. It's a question I've been meaning to ask you for some
time. That ... you know ... the night you got me ... that night with Mum,
what was it like? Eh? When I was just a glint in your eye. What was it
like? What was the background to it?' (52).

It is a commonplace that societies regulate normality through taboo,
and from Michel Foucault we know that socially enforced repression
is marked not by silence but by 'a veritable discursive explosion.'[44]
In other words, power does not merely forbid; it also investigates,
depicts, and ritualizes. It might be said that one function of family dramas – however edgy or unsentimental – is to ask edgy, unsentimental
questions that stop short of Lenny's ontological inquiry. The family is
ritually policed through representation, but this discourse of the family
itself is a mechanism of ideological power. Looking back on the history
of dramatic realism, one gets the impression that any aspect of the family can be interrogated except its fundamental basis. Despite its humor-
ous overtones, Lenny's question retains a capacity to shock because
there are no cultural circumstances under which it might legitimately
be asked. Knowledge of parental sexuality and one's immediate origin
feels socially obscene. In *Totem and Taboo*, Freud argues that civilization
begins with two fundamental prohibitions – against incest and patri-

cide – and that these two prohibitions correspond to the structure of the Oedipus complex. Ontogeny recapitulates phylogeny; macrocosm and microcosm appear concentric. In Oedipal patriarchy, preoccupation with the primal scene represents a regressive incestuous fixation, one that defies the father's proprietary authority and interferes with the 'civilizing' deferral and displacement of desire. It is not surprising, then, that Max responds to Lenny's question as if it were an act of primal insurrection. In an interesting image that harks back to the womb, Max retorts: 'You'll drown in your own blood' (52).

In a fanciful, provocative passage, Freud argues that primal fantasies have a collective historical basis: 'It seems to me quite possible that all that today is narrated in analysis in the form of phantasy, seduction in childhood, stimulation of sexual excitement upon observation of parental coitus, the threat of castration – or rather, castration itself – was in prehistoric periods of the human family a reality.'[45] Primal fantasies are the necessary after-image of life in the 'primal horde,' as Freud elsewhere calls it. Or, more accurately, they negatively represent the rationale for civilizing prohibitions against incest and murder, but they also testify to the trauma of individual repression that the new law of civilization compels. The structure of these fantasies is thus determined by the dialectic of the individual and society, and Freud suggests that they are available to the unconscious even if not predicated on actual experience. I would say that the power of *The Homecoming* rests partly in its capacity to make such fantasies visible *as common, available structures*, that is, as phenomena that are not contingent on individual experiences or pathologies, but rather are symptomatic of basic social and psychological processes. Strong visceral responses to the play tend to confirm this psycho-structural reading.

In one final sense *The Homecoming* performs a kind of Freudian analysis on the unconscious of conventional family drama. In several ways, the play's basic scenario is reminiscent of Freud's account in *Totem and Taboo*. He begins by enquiring into what he considers the two key features of totemism, namely, the prohibitions against killing the totem animal and against sex with a woman of the same totem. Through a complex series of inferences he concludes that the totem animal is a substitute for the father, and then he wonders about totemic festivals in which the prohibition is ritually violated as the totem animal is slaughtered and eaten by the entire clan. Such a festival 'is a permitted, or rather an obligatory, excess, a solemn breach of a prohibition,' one that expresses the ambivalent mix of love and hate that marks the father-complex. Here, in a dizzyingly speculative move, Freud postulates the historical existence of a primal horde ruled by a single patriarch who monopolized all women and property and drove out his sons as they grew up. He continues:

> One day the brothers who had been driven out came together, killed and devoured their father and so made an end of the patriarchal horde. United, they had the courage to do and succeeded in doing what would have been impossible for them individually ... The violent primal father had doubtless been the feared and envied model of each one of the company of brothers: and in the act of devouring him they accomplished their identification with him, and each one of them acquired a portion of his strength. The totem meal, which is perhaps mankind's earliest festival, would thus be a repetition and a commemoration of this memorable and criminal deed, which was the beginning of so many things – of social organization, of moral restrictions and of religion.[46]

Yet any civilization that might emerge from this remarkable schema is bound to be haunted by guilt over the primal patricide. Civilization's guilt is partially assuaged by the social veneration of what we might call 'symbolic fathers' – gods of various kinds, certainly, but also rulers, authority figures, and the trappings and icons of wealth, power, and status in general. The brothers 'revoked their deed by forbidding the killing of the totem, the substitute for their father; and they renounced its fruits by resigning their claim to the women who had now been set free. They thus created out of their filial sense of guilt the two fundamental taboos of totemism, which for that very reason inevitably corresponded to the two repressed wishes of the Oedipus complex.'[47]

Though Freud does not put it in these terms, his account documents the inauguration of woman as sign and object of exchange, to return to a point raised by Jeanie Forte. It is the emergence of a sort of free-market economy of women – who are now 'shared' rather than monopolized – that allows the guilty anxieties of the patriarchal unconscious to be processed. I am reminded of Max's wildly incongruous admonition to Lenny as they consider Ruth's future living arrangements: 'I think you're concentrating too much on the economic considerations. There are other considerations. There are the human considerations' (87). But in this context the two amount to the same thing. The patriarchal 'human' is gendered and commercialized; flowing logically from Freud's account is the development of laws and institutions to regulate

private property and the distribution of resources among those in civilization's male fraternity. It is telling that *The Homecoming* begins with
seething masculine resentment and ends with a business deal. Patriarchal unrest is mollified by Ruth's arrival; the occupation of the
woman's 'place' would seem to accomplish an economic and social
restoration. Ruth's arrival also lends coherence and pseudo-harmony
to family rituals, with which the men struggle when left to themselves.
Lenny calls Max a 'dog cook,' Max complains that his cooking is unap-
preciated, and Teddy and Lenny squabble over a cheese roll. By contrast, Act 2 begins with the family luxuriating after Max has prepared
'a very good lunch' (61). Max pointedly praises the coffee that Ruth is
ritually serving, and the overall mood further leads him to a long
speech that begins, 'Well, it's a long time since the whole family was
together, eh? If only your mother was alive' (61). Later, Ruth demands
a drink, and Lenny is kind enough to ask, 'Drinks all round?' (77).
Freud provides a way of linking these rituals of food and drink with
gender and the underlying father-complex of bourgeois patriarchy.
Woman is the objectified guarantor of this system's uneasy coherence,
and the play throws the entire ideological structure into relief.

Indeed, *The Homecoming* centres on the overthrow of a primal patriarch and the emergence of a more fraternal – and bourgeois – mode of
patriarchy. We sense that the primal roots run deep when Max recol-
lects his own father: 'He used to come over to me and look down at me
... Then he'd dandle me. Give me the bottle. Wipe me clean. Give me a
smile. Pat me on the bum. Pass me around, pass me from hand to
hand. Toss me up in the air. Catch me coming down' (35). The combination of fear and envy in this self-infantilizing vignette becomes evident later, when the increasingly impotent Max tries to reacquire the
father's strength by describing how he bathed his own sons. The figures of Max's father, Max, and MacGregor collectively define a brutish,
authoritarian father whose demise is a source of both pleasure and
guilt for the next generation. When Freud links the origins of civilization with the Oedipus complex, he is suggesting that the history of civilization is predicated on sexual difference and repression. The father
and his symbolic surrogates continue to sanctify and perpetuate the
old psychic violence in updated rituals. This is the ideological foundation of much family drama, which *The Homecoming* negates by making
its architecture visible. Ironically, Ruth embraces her status as a commodity; she speaks back and negotiates. The woman refuses to disap-
pear quietly into her role as reward for the Oedipal journey. Moreover,

the play shows the trauma inflicted on the would-be fraternity of male descendants. Joey is emotionally stunted and narcissistic; Teddy ineffectual and dispossessed; and Lenny prey to severe psychosexual disorders. The father lingers as the cause of the play's neurosis.

The Homecoming's relation to family drama can be summarized by comparing it with two canonical examples of the form, namely, Eugene O'Neill's *Long Day's Journey into Night* (written in 1940) and Arthur Miller's *Death of a Salesman* (1949). For all their considerable virtues, it is clear that these plays privilege the Oedipal father/son relation and propagate the familiar misogynistic dialectic of madonna/whore. In O'Neill's play the mother, Mary, is stigmatized by her morphine addiction, which is attributed, in a punitive symbolism, to her sexuality (she became addicted after a difficult childbirth). When Mary is on morphine, she regressively drifts into an idealized, virginal past (she wanted to be a nun). The adult, sexual woman is rendered pathological, while the only other available role is that of a sentimentalized child. Tellingly, the other women who figure in the play are a maid and the prostitutes described by Jamie. In *Death of a Salesman*, the central woman is the mother, Linda, whom Miller punitively describes purely in relation to Willy: *'she more than loves, him, she admires him, as though his mercurial nature, his temper, his massive dreams and little cruelties, served her only as sharp reminders of the turbulent longings within him, longings which she shares but lacks the temperament to utter and follow to their end.'*[48] Linda is branded as a mere facilitator, a junior version of Willy. Otherwise, we are left with Happy's various conquests and the fittingly named 'The Woman' – Willy's stocking-obsessed guilty secret from years before.

These are Oedipal dramas par excellence. In its characteristically deconstructive mode, *The Homecoming* compresses into a single ideogram a gendered dialectic that is often sadistically elaborated. In the opening minutes of the play, Max says of his late wife: 'He was very fond of your mother, Mac was ... Mind you, she wasn't such a bad woman. Even though it made me sick just to look at her rotten stinking face, she wasn't such a bad bitch. I gave her the best bleeding years of my life, anyway' (25). Again, a submerged ideological pattern is wrested free and displayed. The madonna/whore double bind that *Death of a Salesman* tacitly installs over its duration is nakedly advertised on the third page of Pinter's play. From the standpoint of the ideology of family drama, *The Homecoming* might be read as the photographic negative of *Death of a Salesman*. In Miller's play, the wife is alive, the promiscuous woman is nameless and consigned to memory, and the play ends in tragedy. In Pinter's play, the wife is dead, a wife/mother/prostitute enters, and the play ends in farce. *The Homecoming* refuses to deploy the stereotypical roles of madonna and whore in their typical function as agents of a man's suffering or redemption. Instead, we are confronted with an ideologically overdetermined resolution that conjoins the economic and sexual logics of patriarchal society. This is a final sense in which *The Homecoming* might be said to negate conventional family drama. The negotiation of Ruth's prostitution gloriously resolves the unconscious conflicts of this drama while abjuring the prettifying structures by which these conflicts are often concealed.

CHAPTER TWO

The Modernist as Populist

Surely an admirer of Joyce and Beckett, adapter of Proust and Kafka, and collaborator of blacklisted film director Joseph Losey is likely to be inward, antisocial, and wary of the cultural mainstream. In some ways the early Pinter fulfils this expectation, but his increasingly noisy public persona from the 1980s onward signals a more complex attitude towards the public sphere. Indeed, with the benefit of hindsight it is possible to see that Pinter's formidable literary reputation has long coexisted with middlebrow celebrity, and to argue that the tension between these canonical and popular identities constitutes one of his most important legacies. In exemplary fashion, Pinter's career links the aesthetics of late modernism with those of an emergent popular culture. From the beginning his works have discouraged hierarchical distinctions between art and entertainment, precluding any rigid dichotomy between high- and lowbrow audiences. Visceral response to the plays has generally outpaced critical interpretation, and this pattern – the inverse of the obscure modern artist 'discovered' by intellectuals – raises significant questions about the decline of modernism and the blurring of traditional boundaries between high and low cultures.

The long, lucrative West End run of *The Caretaker* in 1960–1 suggests that Pinter almost immediately hit a cultural nerve, well in advance of his canonization as an important dramatist. The term *Pinteresque*, arising at roughly the same moment, underscores this lag between sensation and understanding: one knows it when one sees it but can't define what it means. Nonetheless, widespread use of the term signals quick incorporation of his plays' inchoate, still inarticulate ethos. The domesticated Pinteresque as an available, even fashionable signifier in British and (to a lesser degree) American popular culture dispels the refractory aura conventionally associated with difficult modern art. Moreover, Pinter's relatively successful work in film and television appears violently out of character for any direct descendant of Kafka or pure practitioner of hermetic modernism. These apparent contradictions should be embraced and explored. Collectively, Pinter's writings suggest an intermediate rather than a terminal figure, not a caretaker of modernism's legacy but a purveyor of its sensibility, less a throwback than a progressive popularizer.

In negative form, this populist tendency is reflected in the critical discourse. For professional commentators, the commercial aspect of Pinter's work has long been an elephant in the parlour. Before his ambiguity came to be celebrated in literary circles, crowds were unambiguously flocking to see his plays in the West End. This has been a vexing problem for critics, to whom Pinter often deals a losing hand. Writing about Pinter can have the unhappy feeling of explaining a joke or describing a dream: a morose and guilty activity that grows more elaborate in proportion to its basic inadequacy. Ingenious interpretations substitute for repressed emotions, guilty pleasures are relentlessly sublimated. Entertainment values are grudgingly acknowledged but are disavowed as by-products of skill rather than artistry. Pinter's work polarizes the critic and the fan, rendering commentary and enjoyment incompatible. This schism is fuelled by an underlying cultural tension, an anxiety connected to the popular. It is uncomfortable to write about a canonical dramatist with the suspicion that he may, in fact, be a craftsman or entertainer – a wordsmith, to use a favoured British epithet – or worse, a masquerading screenwriter. Thus, literary critics often describe Pinter's relationship to popular culture in purely ironic terms; it is argued that he parodies, subverts, or estranges the degraded pleasures of mass market entertainment. For a spectator, however, it may be precisely the visceral, 'low' cultural elements of Pinter's work that render it appealing and pleasurable.

Irony, I will argue, is not the primary mode of Pinter's relation to the popular. Rather, his plays inhabit and probe the limits of popular forms in what amounts to immanent critique. Pinter's populist aesthetic performs an insider's close reading of the structures and ideologies of popular culture; the tone of this reading is analytic rather than parodic. In so doing, he gives popular forms a distinctive inflection. As is the case with *The Homecoming* and family drama, Pinter's relation to these forms is typically one of determinate negation. Where conventional entertainments depend on narrative suspense, linearity, and progress, Pinter gives us distilled, ontological suspense, stasis, and even regression. Such formal negation is the focus of the following sections on *The Dumb Waiter* and *Betrayal*. The regressive quality of these plays fixates attention on concrete elements and episodes, frustrating semiotic and interpretive operations that might otherwise impose a sense of shape. To the extent that instrumentality and progress are watchwords of mainstream culture, regression embodies a negative value with its own array of perverse satisfactions. In this context, suspense is an exemplary cultural form that unites progress and stasis in a single figure. Typically, narrative suspense orients reception instrumentally towards a desired end but manufactures pleasure through deferral. In a variety of ways, Pinter severs such desire from its telos, exposing narrative as an ideological structure by encouraging audiences to feel a quasi-masochistic mixture of pleasure and displeasure.

The following sections are also concerned with Pinter's relation to points of cultural reference such as gangster films and melodrama, and with his relation to non-theatrical mediums such as radio and television. The question of medium is the principal focus of the section on *A Slight Ache*, a suggestive early play written for radio but also performed on stage. While one might expect something dilettantish in such an experiment, instead we find Pinter systematically exploiting the possibilities of the radio medium and finding sources of aesthetic energy that can be differently mobilized in theatrical works. I think it is only a slight exaggeration to say that radio aesthetics permeate Pinter's drama, accounting for some of the incongruous language, the distinctive and pleasurable suspense, that mark his work as a whole. Moreover, the question of radio also entails a regressive dimension, albeit historical rather than formal. The notion of radio drama carries some inherent cognitive and structural resistances when compared with the dominance of the visual in theatre, television, and film. The heyday of radio culture occupies an anomalous, transitional historical position, bridging the ascendancy of film and the coming of television. Radio culture flourished briefly in a supporting role, providing a kind of caesura in the relentlessly progressive narrative of visual culture. It is not surprising to find Pinter, as a card-carrying late modernist, drawn in the late 1950s and early 1960s to a vestigial form that runs against the prevailing cultural current.

Reading *The Dumb Waiter*

It may be noted, by the way, that there is no better start for thinking than laughter. And, in particular, convulsion of the diaphragm usually provides better opportunities for thought than convulsion of the soul.

Walter Benjamin[1]

Most of Pinter's admirers would concede that his work incorporates a motley assortment of cultural influences, a list that equally could include burlesque, vaudeville, Laurel and Hardy, gangster films, detective fiction, and *Waiting for Godot*. Disagreements might arise, however, about the tenor of this 'influence,' whether Pinter is seen to be innocently reproducing or ironically playing with existing sensibilities and conventions. Nowhere is this debate more pointed than in connection to *The Dumb Waiter* (1960), a funny, nearly flippant play that would likely be a mere footnote to the modern canon had it been written by someone else. At the same time, however, ambivalence about *The Dumb Waiter* is only an extreme – and therefore instructive – manifestation of conflicted critical attitudes towards pleasure, humour, and entertainment. The play usefully amplifies neglected questions raised by Pinter's use of comedy generally. The goal in this section is to read *The Dumb Waiter* as a thorny case study in the poetics and politics of comedy.

Broadly speaking, discussions of comedy in Pinter are welcome insofar as they tend to oppose the metaphysical tendencies that run through some criticism of his 'serious' work. In this respect such discussions share the anti–interpretive legacy of Austin Quigley, who in 1975 usefully pointed out that all symbolic readings of Pinter were equally conjectural unless grounded upon 'an accurate understanding of the functions of the language in the plays.'[2] Likewise, attention to comedy is initially more concerned with concrete language and action than with abstract significance. For those who read Pinter's comedy as parody, however, the concrete soon becomes abstract and ironic. The rhetoric of his plays is taken as satire, as mocking speech in a dead language of cultural codes, conventions, and cliches. While Quigley treats Pinter's stage as a textual laboratory of specific speech-acts and interactions, interpretations based on parody stress the intertextuality of the plays as they mimic and subvert outside points of cultural reference.

Here, ironically, the argument for parody resembles the modernist hermeneutics directed at Pinter's full-length masterworks. Like the canonical author of these 'major' plays, the parodic Pinter becomes a solitary, revolutionary figure breaking with a stale and oppressive cultural inheritance. This narrative depends on a perceived tension between 'the public domain of literary and theatrical styles and the playwright inevitably in conflict with them,' in Elin Diamond's words. The *mise en scène* of parody is similar to that of Harold Bloom's well-known *The Anxiety of Influence*, which suggests that artists creatively misread the work of their predecessors 'so as to clear imaginative space for themselves.'[3]

Parodic interpretation needs to be considered as a rhetorical strategy that makes particular historical and aesthetic assumptions and confers particular intellectual advantages. One consequence of its model of authorship, for example, is the suppression of social reality as a determinant of aesthetic production, to the point that a monolith of 'culture' is very nearly substituted for history. The image is of history and art running in parallel horizontal lines with few, if any, axes of vertical connection. A related problem is that once cultural history is seen as a 'dead language,' parody is taken to be a relatively simple enterprise, as if prior forms and conventions themselves were not determined by complex and contradictory social forces. At the same time, such reductions are a kind of necessary price in the profitable mining of ironic values. Like the Borges story in which a modern author painstakingly rewrites *Don Quixote* word for word, believing he has improved a frayed original,[4] the notion of parody implies a text that is not quite self-identical. To explicate a purported parody is to write a new, subtly different text that you, the critic, have now co-authored. As a practical matter, such readings reward the author and the critic simultaneously. If the work is found to be playfully subverting rather than innocently mimicking codes or conventions, part of the credit for this sophistication naturally accrues to its discoverer.

In what follows I want to outline an anti-parodic reading of *The Dumb Waiter* – certainly one of Pinter's least 'serious' and most popular plays – and there is a strong parodic reading, by Elin Diamond, that I want to engage. Here, it would seem that the argument for parody is at its most urgent, if this light or 'minor' play is to be assigned a stature befitting the reputation of its author. This critical rescue has consequences, however, since it presupposes a particular understanding of humour, entertainment, and pleasure and implicitly defines an appropriate range of response. Academic and professional critics may have a vested interest in positing less visceral, more cerebral kinds of pleasure – with this play in particular – in order to sustain Pinter's status as an important dramatist. Intentionally or not, this perspective may adopt an elitist position in relation to audiences by installing an idealized, authorized source of humour and thereby devaluing other kinds of laughter. As an alternative, I want to emphasize the play's complex, specific materiality – centred on the characters' relationship to their object-world – as a source of affective energy that I feel has been elided. The counter-reading lastly turns to the problem of *suspense* (which I take as an unironic, or at least anti-ironic, register in the play) as a way of exploring the question of entertainment and its links to narrative.

At the level of raw material, I think Pinter's works appeal to a phenomenological rather than an ironic eye. Irony presupposes critical distance; by contrast, watching a Pinter play, one may feel aligned with the characters in their heightened receptivity to the sheer strangeness and recalcitrance of *things*. For characters and audiences alike, interpretive circuits are often shorted by the stubborn density of perception. This elemental resistance has significant consequences for hermeneutic approaches. The phenomenological heaviness of the plays clouds the semiotic transparency that abstract interpretations require. Umberto Eco has suggested that 'phenomenology undertakes to rebuild from the beginning the conditions necessary for the formation of cultural units which semiotics instead accepts as data because communication functions on the basis of them.'[5] In these terms, it seems to me that the lack of reliable cognitive data in Pinter – for characters and audiences – suggests phenomenological rebuilding of the 'cultural units' that might sustain a semiotic economy of meanings and interpretations. It is useful here to briefly turn to Bert O. States, who has written suggestively about the theatre's phenomenological building blocks. States describes what he calls the 'frontality' of experience, the necessarily partial perception of only that which presents itself directly to the eye. The principle of frontality requires an apperceptive network of 'co-presences' and signifying absences before anything like an object or an experience can surrender itself to intuition as a singular thing.[6] It is the task of phenomenology, he argues, to reflect on these perceptual mediations in order to redeem and reawaken dimensions of the 'obvious' hidden by familiarity and repetition.

The theatre is a privileged space from States's perspective, depend-

ing as it does on the suspension of reality and the acceptance of illusion, the dialectic of presence and absence between stage and offstage,
and the problematic ontological status of bodies and scenery that are
demonstrably pretending and posturing while claiming a certain
brand of authenticity. Theatre is like a phenomenological gallery,
affording a thick multiplicity of realities, illusions, and perceptual
compromises as preconditions of understanding. I would argue that
Pinter's plays alter the standard phenomenological contract with spectators, obsessively estranging objects, language, and identities until a
second performative dimension begins to open in the onstage space.
Pinter's characters seem to regard phenomenologically the 'otherness'
of their environments, encountering objects and others in a kind of pre-
theatre, where the obvious is haunted by the principle of frontality.
'Behind' concepts, objects, and utterances are new facades, and one
never arrives at a fully rounded sense of the thing-in-itself. On Pinter's
stage, the normal phenomenological collusion between the real and the
illusory verges on betrayal; everything is on the brink of being something other, not-itself.

As a small counter to interpretive trends, my reading of *The Dumb
Waiter* seeks a naïve, fixated encounter with Pinter's iconography – as
Bert States puts it, a 'phenomenological attitude that uninhibitedly
accepts everything it sees.'[7] Interpretation, after all, depends on perception; in what follows I hope to take *The Dumb Waiter* rigorously at
face value. It could be plausibly objected that this is but a new, politically dubious hermeneutic, yet a phenomenological attitude at least
has the virtue of restoring what much well-intentioned criticism has
obscured. Such an approach might be a partial antidote to the critical
malaise that has lingered since Quigley's 1975 description of the Pinter
problem. Interpretive scenarios tend to critique the totalizing pretensions of their predecessors while smuggling in a more appealing image
of totality. Phenomenology begins with a gaze at things-in-themselves.
To take an example central to *The Dumb Waiter*: under close examination, the debris of social realism that clutters Pinter's drama is perhaps
not only a matter of theatrical style but instead a preoccupation with
the verbal and material bric-a-brac of modernity. Materiality in Pinter
is not a casual business but an obsessive concern. Doubled-edged
clichés, idiomatic quibbles, and malevolent paraphernalia occasion
cognitive alarm in the characters. Their discomfort disturbs the raw
material of our own habitual perceptions, underscoring a deeply
uncertain relationship to the world.

Reading backward, as it were, may disclose something fundamental about the affective energy of Pinter's work, about the visceral disquiet linked to even the apparent playfulness of *The Dumb Waiter*. From its opening, the play manipulates conventional expectations in a manner that constantly verges on phenomenological alarm. In a claustrophobic room we meet Gus and Ben, two hit men waiting for instructions in what turns out to be the basement of a former restaurant. After periods of tense and unproductive chitchat, an old dumb waiter in the back wall starts to operate, bringing slips of paper with requests for gourmet meals. Gus and Ben cope as best they can, desperately sending up their remaining provisions of chocolate and chips, which are not greeted with much enthusiasm by the unseen diners. Finally, after the two have discussed the procedure for gunning down the target if and when he enters the room, Gus exits to get a drink. The dumb waiter's previously silent speaking tube tells Ben the target is on the way; Ben draws his gun, and when Gus re-enters in disarray, we are meant to wonder if he is the intended target. Nothing happens; the two men confront each other in a frozen tableau, a kind of skeletal visual cliché symbolizing the film noir double-cross.

This scenario is ripe for the kind of parodic reading performed in Elin Diamond's study *Pinter's Comic Play*, perhaps the most thorough discussion of Pinter's comedy. The chapter in question begins with a remark of Eric Bentley, 'Parody is more important to the modern than to any previous school of comedy.' In Diamond's view, Pinter is the kind of parodist 'who ironically plays with and criticizes a tradition even as he establishes himself within it.' Parody is characterized by the rejection of realism and a tendency towards intertextuality and a presumably subversive reworking of existing styles: 'since parody is not a "mirror of nature" but a deliberately skewed imitation of another representation, it lays bare the convention of mimesis, exposing it as a device.'[8]

With respect to *The Dumb Waiter*, Diamond argues that the play is distinctively modern in its self-reflexive, parodic use of pre-existing cultural forms – the detective story, the revue sketch, the gangster film – in a grand theatrical transformation of the structures and rhythms of classical comedy, which now are lent a second level of irony. She contends that 'parodists frequently target the conventions of naively mimetic art (well-made realism, television soap opera),' and '*The Dumb Waiter* parodies the gangster movie and the detective plot.' For Diamond, gangster and detective narratives seem readily analysable as a series of isolable stereotypes and 'conventions of standard gangster behavior,' which are then available for parody. This interpretive model necessitates an abstracted view of the play's concrete dialogue, situation, and *mise en scène*. From Diamond's perspective, these materials compose a 'skewed imitation' of pre-existing clichés whose ultimate significance resides in the debunking of conventions. In relation to the play's final image, she concludes, 'Pinter's guns are props and his characters richly parodic pawns, tough and desperate but mostly funny. Placing them in tableau, Pinter imitates and, of course, parodies the well-made play ... We can almost sense the playwright in the wings, bringing down the curtain.'[9]

Though Diamond's account is free of metaphysics, it does repeat two familiar interpretive gestures that are problematic from the standpoint of this chapter's methodology. First, her argument generally precludes social or ideological analysis by making such 'realist' considerations a function of intertextuality and aesthetic play. Second, this view privileges the position of the parodist, and it is therefore consistent with other readings that celebrate Pinter by placing him in a superior ironical relationship to his social, mythic, linguistic, or cultural raw materials. This move disarms the problems of realism, mimesis, and ideology in favour of a modernist conception of authorial originality. As a result, there is little to be said about the cultural and historical contexts of *The Dumb Waiter*, or about the subtle determinations and interpenetrations that inevitably complicate the responses of a particular audience.

A key difficulty is the idea that conventional cultural forms designate stable, definable collective experiences that can then be parodied or subverted. Yet even a preliminary look at the topic suggests that gangster films, for example, are intricate symbolic mediations of a variety of historical tensions rather than reflections of some timeless fascination with cops and robbers. A spectrum of conflicts and determinants connected to modernity – the ideological contests of communism, fascism, and capitalism, shifts in the ideologies of gender, the changing dynamics of the city – was combined with the mode and style of classical Hollywood production to shape the iconography of film noir. A range of cultural influences, from hard-boiled fiction to German expressionism, also contributed to the visual and ethical contrasts characteristic of the style.[10]

The cynical private detective of 1920s and 1930s popular fiction – the iconic precursor of subsequent anti-heroes – is a lonely, threadbare, compromised moral figure on the fringes of social institutions and mass movements stained with collective guilt.[11] A compressed moral continuum linking private eyes, the wealthy and powerful, and gentlemen gangsters is established in seminal films such as *The Big Sleep* (1946) and *Out of the Past* (1947), often through the competitive circulation of women. Corruption is ubiquitous, a matter only of degree. From the moral equivalence of detective and gangster it is no great distance to the romance of pathological deviancy in Cagney films or the later gangster chic of *Pulp Fiction* and its imitators. Marc Vernet has argued that early noir detectives and gangsters express nostalgia for a mythic frontier individualist, for an older populism lost to capitalist industry, and he identifies classic noir with the narrative form of the jeremiad.[12] As we move towards Mafia films of the 1970s, the nascent anti-capitalism embodied in much early noir is ideologically transformed. In relation to *The Godfather*, Fredric Jameson suggests that the libidinal appeal of the Mafia rests on a reconfigured old-world entrepreneurial and familial ethic now ironically embedded in the charismatic mob community. Fascination with the mob displaces anxiety over shifts in family and community structure, as well as the fears and desires aroused by legitimate corporate big business.[13]

The gangster ethos in *The Dumb Waiter* is further complicated by tonal ambivalence. Michael Billington suggests that echoes of English music-hall comedy infiltrate the noir sensibility: 'Hackney Empire cross-fertilises with Hemingway's *The Killers*.'[14] Tellingly, Billington concludes that the result of such cultural over-coding is not light satire but a serious evocation of 'political terror.' As this dense network of associations indicates, complex histories and energies may be elided when a cultural motif is approached as a cliché. Gus and Ben won't submit to easy digestion or processing; *The Dumb Waiter* does not so much allude to other representations of gangsters as refigure some of the cultural tensions of the gangster in different form. The gangster is an overdetermined concept and, in a further sense, Gus and Ben are overdetermined characters; indeed, Diamond goes on to note their links to Vladimir and Estragon, Laurel and Hardy, vaudeville, and the like. In the familiar rhetoric of literary criticism, such fragments of cultural raw material are commonly rendered in generic ironical formulations, such as 'Pinter cites _____ in order to subvert it,' 'Pinter capitalizes on the tradition of _____ in order to complicate it,' or 'Pinter draws on the conventions of _____ only to expose them as illusion.' Such assertions impute a rhetorical posture to Pinter in theory, a posture that the critic assumes in practice. The critic is predisposed to find those latent political tendencies, masquerading as literary devices, which in some abstract way can be politically fulfilled simply by bringing them to light. If aesthetic operations such as demystification and parody are considered politically progressive a priori, then the detection of aesthetic ironies at the level of the text becomes a political act in the world of the critic. The revelation of subversion is subversive, QED.

Leaving aside the Gordian knot of criticism and politics, the difficulty here is that *The Dumb Waiter* only occasionally manages to find a stable ironic distance and therefore lacks the fixed positions essential to the subversion argument. Indeed, the play adopts a curious stance towards its raw materials from the outset, a faintly pathological disposition towards condensation in relation to the cultural imaginary rather than the more efficiently sublimated forms of displacement associated with parody. The play grasps for a cultural handhold from within rather than confidently playing with conventions from without. The argument for parody invokes an iron rule of textual displacement, which becomes the method behind the 'dream' of the text, at the expense of elements that insist on a separate relationship to the real and require further interpretation. In almost Freudian fashion, Pinter seems more concerned with the many avenues of significance emanating from concrete details – the messy plurality of dream thoughts linked to manifest dream content – than with empty combinations of parodic signifiers.

This view resembles my earlier discussion of the concrete and the abstract, of phenomenology and semiotics, in relation to Pinter's work. In this vein, the final problem with Diamond's analysis is the impoverishment of the play's materiality. When she writes that 'Pinter's guns are props,' the point is uncontestable, yet it casts little light on the gun as a central artefact of modernity. Onstage guns must surely arouse feelings of desire, guilt, and anxiety, mediated by an entire cultural and historical iconography, before they function simply as jokes. Indeed, we see in *The Dumb Waiter* an elaborate struggle between the forces of concretion and abstraction in the characters' fitful attempts at 'cognitive mapping' (to borrow Fredric Jameson's phrase[15]), within a troubled social, political, and cultural space. The play's opening – after Gus silently ties his shoes, looks for matches, and goes to the lavatory, while Ben struggles to read a newspaper – anchors this tension in the *mise en scène*:

BEN: Kaw!
He picks up the paper.

What about this? Listen to this!

He refers to the paper.

A man of eighty-seven wanted to cross the road. But there was a lot of traffic, see? He couldn't see how he was going to squeeze through. So he crawled under a lorry.

GUS: He what?

BEN: He crawled under a lorry. A stationary lorry.

GUS: No?

BEN: The lorry started and ran over him.

GUS: Go on!

BEN: That's what it says here.

GUS: Get away.

BEN: It's enough to make you want to puke, isn't it?

GUS: Who advised him to do a thing like that?

BEN: A man of eighty-seven crawling under a lorry!

GUS: It's unbelievable.

BEN: It's down here in black and white.

And a few moments later ...

BEN (*slamming his paper down*): Kaw!

GUS: What's that?

BEN: A child of eight killed a cat!

GUS: Get away.

BEN: It's a fact. What about that, eh? A child of eight killing a cat!

GUS: How did he do it?

BEN: It was a girl.

GUS: How did she do it?

BEN: She –

He picks up the paper and studies it.

It doesn't say.

GUS: Why not?

BEN: Wait a minute. It just says – Her brother, aged eleven, viewed the incident from the toolshed.

GUS: Go on!

BEN: That's bloody ridiculous.[16]

The first way to read this exchange is to register the economy of its response to conventional theatrical requirements: the opening of narrative expectation (what are these men doing here?), the ingratiating use of comedy, and the rudimentary introduction of character. Reaction to the scene depends in part on recognition of these familiar mechanics, perhaps filtered by a sense of Pinter's distinctive tone, coupled with a progressive desire to see what happens next. I want to argue, however, that there is a regressive manoeuvre at the heart of these recognitions, which directs attention to a foundational unease. The two characters, for example, initially seem to have isolable and complementary voices. Ben is senior, aggressor, narrator, while Gus is junior, victim, audience. At moments, however, their relationship is so reciprocal that the two appear halves of a whole rather than separate, psychologically coherent entities. Ben is not an especially funny or compelling storyteller, and Gus is not a particularly helpful or compliant straight man. The roles begin to merge and reverse. Gus's sporadic contributions acquire the ring of a genuine crisis ('It's unbelievable'), while Ben is unable to find a perspective from which to make a cutting, ironic remark. 'It's bloody ridiculous' is not a quip but what one says when no good line presents itself. Gus and Ben are co-conspirators in a comic aura that springs from the mutual ambiguity of their relationship to the referential world (signalled by the would-be factuality of the newspaper) rather than from witty dialogue between two self-assured and separate beings.

Moreover, the comedy of the exchange is interwoven with increasingly disturbing and traumatic imagery, finally circling a primal scene embedded in the once benign newspaper. The old man killed by a lorry, while not conventionally hilarious, might at least be construed as a bizarre accident and grimly laughed at in defiance of a capricious world. The murder of the cat, by contrast, is in human terms minor, yet as an anecdote much more alarming and perverse. For example, the idea of the boy who 'viewed the incident from the toolshed' compels the question of why he was in the toolshed in the first place. Surely the toolshed is no place for a young boy. To a parental eye, axes, saws, and lawnmowers are literally hazardous, and the taboo imposed on the space further extends to all the dark associations of private childhood naughtiness. In every sense, a child in the toolshed alone is out of place. Thus, the toolshed carries the unexpected connotations of parental discipline and punishment, while at the same time injecting the remembered libidinal charge of playing doctor and other forms of childish experimentation. In the context of the scene, these conflicted feelings are uncomfortably coupled with the manifest sadistic and voyeuristic overtones of the cat-killing and its perverted 'viewing.' The ostensibly innocent news item resurrects the secret shame of childish

The Modernist as Populist 89

desire, overlaid by adult awareness of the vaguely barbaric metal implements in the toolshed, its literal and figurative distance from the house, and the nefarious potential of abduction and abuse that haunts this banal but now guilt-laden imaginary space.

The threat of unpleasure is deepened by the many displacements and dislocations suggested by the *mise en scène*. The play's reassuring realism, the apparent familiarity of its spatial and cultural coordinates, is offset by existential queasiness – hence the desperate, petulant tone of Ben's declaration: 'It's down here in black and white.' The black-and-whiteness of the newspaper and the civilization it purports to represent are called into question. We are initially presented with two men and a newspaper, with all the orderly bourgeois-patriarchal associations of this ideological scenario, but are quickly ensnared by the dehumanizing and fragmentary logic of the modern human interest story. Contrary to their ostensible purpose, these stories alienate rather than expand the sphere of the normal until everyday life is 'enough to make you want to puke.' An iconography – a newspaper, professional men, the overall scenario – that typically centres and naturalizes an ideological worldview here is used to estrange it.

Elin Diamond writes that the newspaper items in *The Dumb Waiter* are 'parodies of our own lurid headlines.'[17] One might ask, however, why Pinter's newspaper must conform to present-tense cynicism about the media before being simply a newspaper in the world of the play, one touched by the newspaper's history as an emblem of early mass culture and of the cognitive tensions of modern social life. The newspaper is not a facile or neutral object that quietly takes its place in a grander signifying scheme; the materiality of the newspaper remains ambivalent. On the one hand, a newspaper may tap into nostalgia for literary modes of historical knowledge, a nostalgia organized around the anachronistic pleasures of ink stains, rustling, folding, turning, and spreading its pages, tactile sensations opposed to the passive receptivity required by television. At the same time, the newspaper signals the abstraction and instrumental reorganization of the represented world, the scientistic reduction of life to facts. Socially, the newspaper is likewise contradictory. It trumpets diversity and individual taste while binding this diversity to a totalizing narrative; it yields a spectacle of sociality while fostering a spell of alienated private consumption. As Walter Benjamin wrote in the 1930s, the content of the newspaper is

'subject-matter,' which denies itself any other form of organization than that imposed on it by the readers' impatience. And this impatience is not just that of the politician expecting information, or of the speculator on the lookout for a tip; behind it smolders that of the man on the sidelines who believes he has the right to see his own interests expressed. The fact that nothing binds the reader more tightly to his paper than this impatient longing for daily nourishment has long been exploited by the publishers, who are constantly opening new columns to his questions, opinions, protests. Hand in hand, therefore, with the indiscriminate assimilation of facts, goes the equally indiscriminate assimilation of readers who are instantly elevated to collaborators.[18]

Aggression 'smolders' in the newspaper's supposed neutrality. Gus and Ben's impatience begins to mirror the mystifying and inaccessible barbarity of the recounted events. The commodity-world, as epitomized and marketed by the paper, fuels and organizes the symbolic violence of a consumer life that impatiently demands the right to make the world conform to its preconceptions ('It's bloody ridiculous'). Cultural producers and consumers collaborate in transforming reality into 'facts' that can be systematized and exchanged.

Pinter's newspaper embodies a tension between the concrete and the abstract, between reality and interpretation, and it also acts in the play as linchpin for the various objects, phenomena, and cryptic messages that alternately unite Gus and Ben in detective endeavour and set them violently at odds with one another. The interpretation of reality provides the engine for development of individual scenes and the broader narrative. The motif of investigation, which Elin Diamond treats as part of a 'parodic detective plot,' may, in fact, express a more complex and genuine hermeneutical impulse. As the play proceeds, we sense that the phenomenal world exerts a palpable pull on the characters. *The Dumb Waiter* then invites the spectator to reflect on the contradictions emanating from its object-world, to cut through the dense ideological histories of material things whose electricity the play amplifies. Earlier in the play, for example, Gus expounds at length on the attributes of the crockery and appears desperately to feel that if he could only fully speak its name, he could enter some more complete relationship with the thing itself: 'There's a white stripe ... You know, sort of round the cup. Round the rim. All the rest of it's black, you see. Then the saucer's black, except for right in the middle, where the cup goes, where it's white' (131). There is a doomed utopian strain in the evocation of a black-and-white world where saucers are saucers and cups are cups, and a consequent pathos mixed with the humour of Gus's conclusion, 'Yes, I'm quite taken with the crockery' (131).

This last line is funny because of its insufficiency, but it also hints at a deeper crisis in understanding. Gus's cognitive struggle is engendered by the crockery's phenomenological aggression, the provocative black-and-whiteness of its design, but his attempts at rational mastery finally short-circuit, returning the plates and saucers to their ontologically separate realm. Ben, presumably more cultured and adult, is disgusted with Gus's embryonic philosophizing, accusing him of having no 'interests.' Ben boasts, 'I've got my woodwork. I've got my model boats. Have you ever seen me idle?' (134). Ben provides an ideological reading of the crockery episode. His impatience with Gus disguises his own retreat from the world. He desperately evades the sense of phenomenological alarm continually created by circumstances. Like newspaper items, the idea of 'model boats' suggests a schematic and microscopic subjugation of life to the logic of facts and systems – as an advertised antidote to 'idleness,' which in other respects is its mirror image. 'Interests' are not experience but a symptom of its degradation; Ben's critique of Gus takes consolation in leisure activities that closely resemble labour.

One could extend this kind of analysis to many other objects and phenomena that exert an uneasy influence on both characters and audience. To develop the anti-parodic reading I want to briefly consider two items that refuse to submit to generalizing interpretations, items that harness particular historical anxieties created by the past brushing against the present. The first is the long-running offstage toilet with the possibly 'deficient ballcock' (133), which continually bewilders Gus and occasions several exits and entrances; the second is the vaguely monstrous bourgeois apparatus of the dumb waiter itself. Both are the offspring of pre-electrical mechanical ingenuity: the first a triumph of ergonomics and efficiency, with a hidden hydraulic system of floats, valves, and stoppers; the second a curious box and shaft concealed in a wall, using pulleys and counterweights to render labour invisible and to add an illusory, magical dimension to the performance of domestic ritual.

The two items are incorporated in different ways. On the one hand, the familiarity of the toilet is estranged by its absence from the stage. Gus's puzzled assessments of its operation have a disembodied quality that focuses the imagination on one's own intimate experiences of the mysterious object. Indeed, the toilet acts as a controlling motif, defining and colouring the imaginary offstage where Gus intermittently ventures, flushing and tinkering. To this extent, the toilet creates tensions connected to offstage space in a manner similar to other Pinter plays. The anxieties of the visible room are heightened by the intimation of barbarity beyond the door. Thus, a standard case might be made for the toilet as a structural device in the play, serving as locus of motivation and desire, generating suspense, and furnishing peripheral humour of an absurdist variety.

The raw material of the toilet, however, does not seem wholly gratuitous or ephemeral in this context. It functions here as an ideogram of modernity, imbuing the offstage with signs of specific and troubling material, concretizing the imaginary space in a pointedly affective way. The toilet resonates beyond its status as a narrative diversion or a source of theatrical business. Surely, there are few people, however prosperous or erudite, who have not at some time felt an existential shudder or moment of affective disorder when confronted with the mysteries of a toilet, the baffling, unaesthetic, seemingly arbitrary mechanics concealed in the tank, the sheer and enormous dependence on this strange object to exercise a civilizing hygiene on the most rudimentary organic processes. The experience of a toilet in some way carries the echoes of a more primitive encounter with nature: early aqueducts or irrigation canals; the historical, biological, and sexual implications of hydraulics and fluids; nearly unconscious fears and desires signified briefly by the liquid, material reservoir of the toilet bowl.

The anxiety of Pinter's toilet is not easily soothed by the abstract categories of absurdism or general assertions about the alienation of the object-world. The toilet is a fetish of modernity, hiding trauma, enacting on a daily basis the foundational modern encounter of technology and organic life. At the most literal level, the toilet situates and privatizes the body, converting the common human experience of excretory processes into a ritualized, hygienic erasure performed alone. Some of the psychosocial energies diverted and contained by this process, including feelings of shame, curiosity, and aggression, are resurrected in the desperate, understated tone of Gus's phenomenological questions: 'Have you noticed the time that tank takes to fill?'; 'What do you think's the matter with it?' (133).

By contrast, the dumb waiter unsettles the room by its sheer, insensible presence on stage. It stands as a relic of bygone invention, an artefact that by the force of its incongruity asserts the barbarity of bourgeois civilization. The dumb waiter obliges us to accept an unsavory cultural inheritance predicated on class struggle, artifice, and the suppression of labour. The unreason of this rational contraption is sewn into the mythos of social progress. The dumb waiter functions as an instrument of regression. It is a guilty reminder of the irrational perversity of a supposedly rational society and is a manifest anachronism in the play's 1960 milieu. Ironically, the regressive character of the dumb waiter, its refusal to signify referentially in the present tense, has invited elaborate hermeneutical approaches. In Pinter studies, the dumb waiter has been subjected to a number of symbolic and allegorical readings, interpreted as a voice-box of the supernatural, an oppressive mechanism inflicted by capitalists on alienated labour, and other options in between.[19]

Again, however, Gus and Ben invite more pragmatic interpretations. They resolutely investigate the mysteries of the dumb waiter's pulley system and speaking tube, developing questions and theories about the ontological status of the unoccupied floors above and gradually concluding that the basement was once a restaurant kitchen. This impulse towards the concrete is reinforced by the brutal and opaque specificity of the dumb waiter's demands, which begin with two braised steak and chips and escalate to Macaroni Pastitsio, Ormitha Macarounda, Char Siu and Beansprouts, and finally Scampi, which leads Gus to scream in frustration at the speaking tube, 'WE'VE GOT NOTHING LEFT! NOTHING! DO YOU UNDERSTAND?' (162). To this point, the two bewildered assassins, ever sensitive to authority, had obligingly attempted to meet the mystifying requests with whatever was at hand, including one Eccles cake, one Lyon's Red Label, a Cadbury's Fruit and Nut bar, and a packet of Smith's crisps.

The dumb waiter, by virtue of its resistance to realist interpretation, clears a broad imaginary space. It suggests mediation and disjunction; here, it entails consumer demands and transactions anchored to commodities; it symbolizes cultural and class conflicts through the culinary opposition between gourmet dishes and proletarian snacks such as chocolate bars and Eccles cakes. One might then begin to consider the object as an ideological cipher for modern apparatuses of mass communication that create similar tensions between sender, message, and recipient. After all, modern culture works to create, maintain, and satisfy a spectrum of consumer desire that ranges from haute cuisine to pre-packaged food. The incongruity of the dumb waiter motif allows us, with a bit of imagination, to posit the modern object that would most neatly fill the literal and symbolic void: a television set. Television had begun to change the world in 1960, its perpetual illusion of presence transforming older cultural objects and forms into ghostly relics or phantasms of dead history. On closer examination, the innocent dumb waiter – funny theatrical device, instrument of gangster parody, token of absurdism, signifier of existential alienation – unexpectedly summons a crisis in historicity.

Finally, I want to consider *The Dumb Waiter* more integrally, as an entire performative compendium that structures momentary experiences of pleasure and unpleasure in particular ways. At the level of narrative, the organizing principle is *suspense*, although, like the play's humour, its suspenseful pleasure is not unequivocal. Suspense is a dialectical concept. In his discussion of fore-pleasure and end-pleasure near the conclusion of the *Three Essays on the Theory of Sexuality*, Freud acknowledges that while pleasure usually derives from a lessening of tension, sexual excitement often craves a prolongation and increase of stimulation. End-pleasure is thus paradoxical, since orgasm extinguishes a tension that had become pleasurable. Similarly, narrative suspense implies the anticipation of closure, which is pleasurable; at the same time, closure threatens the end of anticipation (and thus pleasure), which occasions anxiety or fear. Reaching the end is desirable, yet the condition of desiring allows deep experiences of playfulness and arousal possible only in a state of suspension or deferral: the end of desire is the end of desiring, which is an ominous prospect to the extent that 'desiring' becomes an end in itself. Conversely, the infinite suspension of closure severs desire from its object; hence, experience is no longer 'desiring' but rather a condition of stasis or habitual estrangement.

I would argue that Pinter crystallizes suspense, boiling its two phases down to an elemental state of tension. Pinter's suspense is not readily perceptible at the macro level of narrative or plot, but rather is evident in microscopic gestures that attempt to close circuits of communication through dialogue, to bridge silence with language, to reconcile self and other, to ease the phenomenological trauma of self and world. The movement to complete these gestures, to resolve existential tension moment by moment, word by word, drives this and other Pinter plays. Moreover, it is often the individual moments and scenes that refuse completion – even as we seek it – that engender the deepest affect. Consider this apparently semantic debate between Gus and Ben on the subject of making tea:

BEN: Go and light it.

GUS: Light what?

BEN: The kettle.

GUS: You mean the gas.

BEN: Who does?

GUS: You do.

BEN (*his eyes narrowing*): What do you mean, I mean the gas?

GUS: Well, that's what you mean, don't you? The gas?

BEN (*powerfully*): If I say go and light the kettle I mean go and light the kettle.

GUS: How can you light a kettle?

BEN: It's a figure of speech! Light the kettle. It's a figure of speech!

GUS: I've never heard it.

BEN: Light the kettle! It's common usage!

GUS: I think you've got it wrong.

BEN (*menacing*): What do you mean?

GUS: They say put on the kettle.

BEN (*taut*): Who says?

They stare at each other, breathing hard.

(*Deliberately*). I never in my life heard anyone say put on the kettle.

GUS: I bet my mother used to say it.

BEN: Your mother? When did you last see your mother? (141–2)

At its most banal this scene is an exercise in confusion. Gus and Ben cannot quite reach consensus on the precise terminology for boiling water. It is possible to regard the exchange from an abstract perspective, as a demonstration of miscommunication or of the instrumentality of language. Austin Quigley, for example, argues that the 'trivial topic' of the kettle masks the deeper issue of 'the mutual status of the characters in the relationship.' He goes on, 'There is, however, another dimension to this situation – the danger for both Gus and Ben if no satisfactory solution is arrived at. Mutual certainty about language is also certainty about a shared reality. As we have stressed that language has no given core or given boundary, words have no final fixed function.'[20]

At the same time, granting the notion of struggle, the possible lack of a 'solution,' and the variability of language is not the same as agreeing that the substance of the exchange has no referential or ideological meaning or that its content is inherently 'trivial.' The concrete elements of dialogue may answer in their own way to 'shared reality' rather than acting purely as markers of abstract interpersonal struggle. I would argue that it is the apparent triviality of the scene, the regressive movement from 'Go and light it' (the first words) to 'your mother' (the last), which suspends the progressive mandates of narrative and rational discourse and creates a space in which details speak differently. In this exchange one might perceive, for example, the contradictions of the empire, from the conquest of India and its tea leaves to the reproduction of colonial ideology in afternoon tea rituals of the nineteenth-century drawing room. 'When did you last see your mother?' expresses a painful loss of primary plenitude, the golden age of bourgeois childhood, perhaps, here linked historically to the lost golden ages of Elizabeth and Victoria. This chain of associations occasions both sentimentality and guilt over the disconnection from origin – when did any of us last see our mothers? The arc from the kettle to maternity defines an absence, an ineradicable modern fact that manages to be social and personal at the same time. The prehistory of modernity cannot be imagined or conceived in a divided and uncertain vernacular, where 'tea' can no longer be discussed, much less made.

Beyond the parodic humour of two grown gangsters debating colloquialisms, I want to emphasize the importance of regression in the exchange. Literally speaking, the disagreement functions as a digression, an interruption to the course of the action. It inverts the ideological tendencies of progressive narrative by symbolically reverting to stasis, memory, childhood, and history. By foregrounding these antinomies, *The Dumb Waiter* turns a critical eye on progress, adulthood, and the present tense as watchwords of conventional narrative. Pinter adopts suspense as a formal principle in its smallest, barest shell, to the point that the exchange 'Light it.'/'Light what?' carries a narrative impulse on which entire Hollywood films are built. The image here, like the play's final tableau, is stillness rather than action. In deadly earnest, *The Dumb Waiter* receives the mechanized progress of Hollywood film, where even the slightest raised eyebrow brings the promise of another adventure.

Pinter magnifies a quality implicit in commercial narrative: compulsory deferral designed to stimulate further consumption. Popular culture has no end; closure is always temporary. In this sense, *The Dumb Waiter* works as a distorted mirror image, reflecting in its final tableau a basic premise of Hollywood entertainment. As technique and tendency, regression can operate only as negation. *The Dumb Waiter* does not disclose some hidden truth or create a new aesthetic value. Ironically, the power of the play lies in forcing the audience to grapple with the sheer power of convention; its perverse pleasure derives from the persistence of desire even in the absence of gratification. In an odd way, the assault on progressive narrative expectations underscores their potency. Like the characters, the audience may hopelessly await the lighting of the kettle, the return of the lost mother, or a shot that breaks the deafening silence of Ben's unfired gun.

A Slight Ache and the question of radio

'No more masterpieces!' Antonin Artaud famously declared, and something of the spirit of this 1930s rallying cry persists across Pinter's eclectic résumé. Short plays, sketches, teleplays, film scripts, and radio dramas balance and gradually displace full-length masterworks, which appear more infrequently after the frenetic output of 1958–65. From the beginning Pinter wrote in a variety of forms and for a variety of non-theatrical mediums, which means that no single set of aesthetic standards fits the oeuvre as a whole. In this context, *A Slight Ache* (1959) – a short piece sandwiched between the comparatively massive plays *The Birthday Party* (1958) and *The Caretaker* (1960) – emerges as a key problem text. Originally a radio play, later staged and televised, *A Slight Ache* announces aesthetic promiscuity at the outset of Pinter's career. In this section *A Slight Ache* is examined as it bears on larger questions of medium, with particular attention to Pinter's language. I argue that the play creates auditory pleasure through sonority, and that this sonorous materiality works to alienate familiar meanings and to create suspense. It is suggested that Pinter's experiments in non-theatrical forms are central rather than incidental, and that radio aesthetics sheds particular light on his use of language. Historically, Pinter's complexity as a cultural figure stems from his liminal status, his links to both modernism and mass culture. In this sense, *A Slight Ache* anchors his career at a transition. In the play the aesthetic possibilities of radio and its cultural moment are explored, and this formative encounter is echoed in other works.

The fact that *A Slight Ache* was originally written for and performed on radio is initially vexing; for several reasons the question is a thorny one. Difficulty finding *A Slight Ache* in recorded form[21] only underscores the fact that there can be no simple recourse to the text, since the differing performance texts of radio and stage are precisely at issue. For anyone writing about Pinter, it is easier to emphasize the play's typical rather than anomalous features – to treat it as a play with an asterisk – and thus to acknowledge medium difference without really engaging the topic. Martin Esslin, for example, analyses the play as a piece of theatre but grants that 'in its radio form the play is bound to be more effective, because then it can remain open whether the central character, the match-seller, who never speaks, actually exists or is no more than a projection of the two other characters' fears.'[22] An alternative aesthetic stance is advanced by Elissa Guralnick, who argues that radio plays achieve 'at their best, a profound expressivity, not *despite* limitations in scale, but *because* of them.' Guralnick contends that the epistemological constraints of radio create a basic cognitive uncertainty that opens the imagination and allows consciousness to reflect on itself. In relation to *A Slight Ache*, she writes that 'the play emerges as a baffling mind game, which implicates the audience before the play's end' and that it exploits 'radio's aptitude for creating indeterminacy, a condition conducive to contemplating consciousness.'[23]

In different ways, both of these positions mobilize an aesthetic purism. From a theatrical perspective, Esslin nods at the question of medium difference while focusing on the stage play. The problem of radio becomes a footnote, a quirk. In contrast, Guralnick's study is a manifesto for the specific values of radio drama, and she systematically enumerates the pleasures and possibilities of radio and evaluates *A Slight Ache* accordingly. Esslin's account implies an important dramatist who dabbles in other mediums, while Guralnick annexes this single work to support a theoretical discussion of the separateness of the radio form. The two positions recruit *A Slight Ache* to their respective camps, thus resolving an aesthetic tension at the heart of the play. Ironically, the play's appeal to the two critics stems from a problematic medium-flirtation that is partially suppressed in each account; for the purposes of this section, the interest of *A Slight Ache* is not exhausted in either, but rather is implicit in the existence of both. The play's duplicity and aesthetic promiscuity – its slight ache, as it were – should be placed in the foreground.

To put the question of radio first is to leave aside spatial preconceptions and embrace a dislocating and increasingly unfamiliar epistemology. As every introduction or primer attests, the first structural principle of the radio medium is its blindness. This fact is the source of both its appeal and its marginality. On the one hand, radio is limited to audible words and sounds and can never in any material way engage the other senses. In this respect, listening to radio is similar to the process of reading, which is confined to the mere visual perception of words on a page. On the other hand, both reading and radio forcibly empower the imagination – with its enormous visualizing potential – by virtue of their inability to furnish the objects of sight. Like reading, radio seems intimate and personalized in contrast to visual forms of mass culture, fostering private introspection apart from the sensory overdetermination that marks the noisy spectacle of film and television. Unlike reading, however, radio is materially anchored to specific voices and their presumptive embodiment in particular speakers; words are not completely free to combine, resonate, and signify, but instead emanate in a manner partly bounded as a material enactment and partly open to sensory imaginings and speculation.

In a variety of ways, *A Slight Ache* invites us to think about the implications of these differences. The play's characters, content, and structure have a quality somehow expressive of the radio medium; its combination of uneasy suspense and overwrought speech seems a signature of radio drama. More fundamentally, the play's governing motif and dramatic engine is the silent match-seller, whose unverifiable status on radio and hulking presence on stage position the play on a fault line of medium difference. On stage, *A Slight Ache* is bound to be a much different work. Directors are forced to cast a live actor who then stands in uncomfortable silence as he is addressed by an hour's worth of monologues. On radio, the ontological status of the match-seller is the constitutive source of dramatic tension. Is he genuinely plying his trade (on a deserted country lane in the late 1950s), or is he a figment of Edward's and Flora's overheated imaginations? But this tension is short-circuited by the presence of an actor, which changes the dynamics considerably. On stage, the dramatic premise is estranged by virtue of its origin in a different aesthetic.

Moreover, *A Slight Ache* provides a virtual meta-commentary on distinctions between hearing and sight. The play constantly, almost neurotically, returns to problems of vision and verification, offering in its language, structure, and basic scenario a kind of meditation on the limitations of the radio medium just described (even the 'slight ache' of the title refers to an ailment detected in the eyes). The play begins at the breakfast table with Edward and Flora, a middle-aged couple, in an isolated country house. Edward comes across as an ineffectual, irascible prig – quibbling childishly, boasting of arid scholarly treatises, whining about headaches. Flora is more desultory and enigmatic, though both she and Edward spring to action when menaced by a wasp, which is eventually drowned in the marmalade. The action then abruptly shifts with the sighting of a sodden, disreputable-looking match-seller loitering near the house's back gate. To Edward, this is not an advantageous spot for selling matches, particularly since no one ever uses the deserted lane. Finally, the match-seller is invited in and remains absolutely silent during extended separate 'conversations' with Edward and Flora. Conversation becomes monologue, and the match-seller's silence functions like the silence of an analyst, activating processes of transference and projection. Edward and Flora take turns re-experiencing anxieties, traumas, memories, and sexual fantasies. Edward reaches a state of exhausted desperation, while Flora treats the match-seller as an object of desire. She offers to give him a bath, put him to bed, show him the garden, and serve lunch by the pool. At the end of the play Flora hands the match tray to Edward, who, now mute, assumes the match-seller's place.

This semiotic cornucopia invites exegetic commentary. Readings have explored the construction of gender, the question of whether the play takes the perspective of Edward or Flora, the role of memory, the attitude towards nature embedded in the many references to the garden (and Flora's suggestive name), and the ontology of the match-seller as pure silence, nothingness, impotence, or death. While Pinter's work typically invites a variety of interpretations, I would argue that *A Slight Ache* exhibits an overabundance of signification in relation to the meticulous, fixed understatement of Pinter's theatrical work, and that this plenitude is in inverse proportion to the signifying limitations of radio. Collectively, the play's verbal efflorescence and its many evocations of vision and the visible compensate for the blindness of the radio medium. The dialogue is saturated by lush, improbable descriptions and vivid renderings of the characters' fantasies and experiences. Complicating matters is the fact that Edward and Flora are of the educated middle class (Edward is apparently a former businessman, who has secluded himself in order to write essays), and here Pinter weds their class affiliation to a flowery, pedantic idiom. In any case, the foliage of figural language in *A Slight Ache* multiplies in inverse proportion to the limits of radio, which forecloses visible figuration.

Moreover, the play works hard to convert this blind figuration into a source of aesthetic pleasure in its own right. In *A Slight Ache* we find two axes of tension with the visible, both potentially pleasurable. Textually, the play's language feels emancipated from the strictures of narrative and conventional signification, even as it seeks hallucinatory vividness and ecstatic reconnection with the visible; contextually, the play systematically exploits the medium's cognitive uncertainties, fuelling (and frustrating) the distinctive narrative pleasures of radio suspense. Both dimensions are engaged in the play's opening:

FLORA: Have you noticed the honeysuckle this morning?

EDWARD: The what?

FLORA: The honeysuckle.

EDWARD: Honeysuckle? Where?

FLORA: By the back gate, Edward.

EDWARD: Is that honeysuckle? I thought it was ... convolvulus, or something.

FLORA: But you know it's honeysuckle.

EDWARD: I tell you I thought it was convolvulus.

Pause.

FLORA: It's in wonderful flower.

EDWARD: I must look.

FLORA: The whole garden's in flower this morning. The clematis. The convolvulus. Everything. I was out at seven. I stood by the pool.

EDWARD: Did you say – that the convolvulus was in flower?

FLORA: Yes.

EDWARD: But good God, you just denied there was any.

FLORA: I was talking about the honeysuckle.

EDWARD: About the what?

FLORA (*calmly*): Edward – you know that shrub outside the toolshed ...

EDWARD: Yes, yes.

FLORA: That's convolvolous.

EDWARD: That?

FLORA: Yes.

EDWARD: Oh.

Pause.

I thought it was japonica.

FLORA: Oh, good Lord no.

EDWARD: Pass the teapot, please.

Pause. She pours tea for him.

I don't see why I should be expected to distinguish between these plants. It's not my job.

FLORA: You know perfectly well what grows in your garden.

EDWARD: Quite the contrary. It is clear that I don't.[24]

Shortly after, Flora asks if Edward has something in his eyes, and he responds 'I have a slight ache in them' (172). This could serve as a caption to the preceding exchange. Edward and Flora here seem bounded by the phenomenological malaise of radio, unable to visually verify from within what the listener can likewise only imagine from without. Dysfunctions of the visible are endemic, from the 'slight ache' in Edward's eyes to the vivid, almost hallucinatory evocations of convolvulus and clematis, honeysuckle and japonica, the toolshed, the pool, and the garden. These images compose a sensory realm that, as Edward later moans, is 'now denied' (176). Many of Pinter's early stage plays centre on clipped, malevolent banter amid the isolation and estrangement of barren rooms, while this radio play provides a lush, hallucinatory travelogue of Eden. The first world is inarticulate, the second blind; collectively, these tendencies suggest two halves of a single, broken life.

As Edward's character develops, we begin to sense a full-scale cognitive retreat from the world. He obsessively tries to make good the lack or loss of the world through verbal excess. His persona is a kind of pastiche of insufferable pedantry; he is responsible for a memoir on the Belgian Congo, naturalistic descriptions of African fauna, and 'theological and philosophical essays' on 'the dimensionality and continuity of space ... and time' (177). These gratuitous writings signify a scientistic attempt to domesticate and classify the material world through a network of reassuring abstractions. The mastery afforded by Edward's pedantry is more apparent than real; his loquaciousness compensates for blindness. From the outset, Edward's disorders are mirrored by the listener's sightless cognitive dislocation in the grip of radio suspense. The play poses a number of ontological questions that would be less alarming in the light of the visible. For example, given two recognizably effete and plutocratic characters, uncommon in early Pinter, one begins to wonder with some justification why the drama is taking place not in a Mayfair flat or a stuffy Hampstead cottage but instead in a country house, on an abandoned lane, near a monastery, of all places. But such cognitive dissonance is characteristic of radio, where the necessary evisceration of space can render location and enunciation deeply problematic. *Where* is constructed rather than factual, and the gap between signifier and signified takes on existential as well as linguistic implications. Moreover, from the standpoint of narrative, the question of what will happen next is accompanied by the question of what has *already happened* to make the (re-)narration necessary or desirable. Is the litany of radio drama simultaneous or prior, and do the disembodied voices reflect a recitation or an event? Radio alters the experiential rhythm of speech and response, withholding the ontological and epistemological reassurances of presence and visibility.

Here, *A Slight Ache* capitalizes on radio's dialectic of freedom versus compulsion, one that has a complex cultural and ideological history. One the one hand, unlike other mediums, radio has an essential structural freedom, liberating the listener from the burden of complete immersion and opening the possibility of other kinds of simultaneous activity. At the same time, the ostensible utopianism of this structural fact may work to conceal radio's power as an instrument of social organization. In hindsight, the heyday of radio drama has certainly acquired an ideological tint. Perhaps because of the brevity of its cultural pre-eminence, the image of a polished walnut radio cabinet in a 1920s or 1930s living room is endowed with an almost unbearable quaintness, linked in the American cultural imagination to a pipe-smoking, newspaper-reading father, a knitting mother, young girls playing with dolls and boys with toy soldiers. Nostalgic fantasizing about radio resurrects a once potent and still disturbing domestic ideology, and the political force of this apparently innocent commodity to organize and marshal collectivities is further underlined when we recall the centrality of radio as an instrument of the cultural policies of fascism. The Nazis' use of radio to shape attitudes and pervert discourse on a daily basis casts a menacing shadow on the apparent freedom of radio listening. Distraction may disable rather than encourage critical thought, providing 'relief from both boredom and effort simultaneously,' as T.W. Adorno said of popular music.[25] Further, the social function of radio is now centred on car radio and workplace radio, cultural epiphenomena whose main purpose is to provide a pseudo-contentment or quasi-narcotic compensation for the daily commute and the travails of the workday.

At the same time, radio once did presumably encourage a kind of pluralized unity in domestic space, allowing for distinct and individuated kinds of activity under the cognitive spell of shared listening – a possibility decisively foreclosed by television. There is a certainly a utopian strain that runs through various discourses on early radio, an optimistic sense of the progressive potential of the new medium. In the life-world of the 1920s and 1930s the radio was a transitional object not yet fully assimilated to an established regime of social purposes and lifestyles. In Britain, the cheap availability of radios in this period, the growing diversity of programming under the BBC monopoly, and, subsequently, the cultural centrality of wartime radio, which mixed high-grade factual reporting with propaganda – all undeniably contributed to British nationalism and wartime unity, establishing radio's populist credentials and conferring on it a favourable aura. Radio thus carried a large sum of goodwill to its British renaissance in the 1940s, when a formidable array of educational, comic, news, entertainment, and more highbrow programs – including an abundance of radio drama by aspiring and established literary stars – reached an apex of efficient cultural dissemination. The decline of radio coincided with the ascendancy of television in the 1950s and led to a qualitative change in the nature and content of radio broadcasts. The shift towards popular music, talk radio, and short newscasts was designed to accommodate occasions that precluded the rapt encounter with television. The radio was now tailored to the divided attention spans of the kitchen, the workplace, and the daily commute and likewise entailed a regression from 'listening' to 'hearing,' as one author writes.[26]

Among writers and theorists of the European Left, there had been some feeling that radio technology might contribute to the annihilation of the ideological aura of bourgeois culture and provide a new basis for mobilization of the masses. This view depended on a move towards interactivity and communication in radio culture, with listeners as collaborators rather than recipients. Radio participants would be simultaneously producers and consumers. As Bertolt Brecht remarked in 1932, 'there was a moment when technology was advanced enough to produce the radio and society was not yet advanced enough to accept it.'[27] For Brecht, radio tended (as did all mechanisms of official culture) to encourage unthinking ('culinary') responses and to revert to propagation of bourgeois ideology, yet he characteristically retained a measure of faith in the potential of this new technology to produce more genuinely collective and progressive modes of social life. It is outside the scope of this section to assess the commensurability of cyberspace with this goal, but in the case of radio the desired transformation never fully took place.

From this overview one may argue that radio exists, historically and ideologically, in relation to the visual. Radio culture is in some sense a negative phenomenon, a temporary impediment to the cultural apotheosis of the eye. The heyday of radio constituted a backward crease in the advancement of the technologies of vision begun under the ecstatically visual banner of Enlightenment, extending from perspective painting through photography to the mimetic ideology of naturalism and, shortly thereafter, to the beginnings of motion pictures. To historicize what is by now an internalized and largely unconscious sensual arrangement is to imagine a process by which sight is constituted as the privileged organ of sense, with an evolving economy of fetishes and taboos, desires and gratifications. The period between the development of both the phonograph and the motion picture in the 1880s and the perfection of synchronous film sound in the late 1920s was one of continual, frantic efforts to unite the two technologies in what promised to be an ontologically distinct form of pleasurable entertainment. Indeed, this union had been envisaged by Edison from the first.[28] In this sense, the collective ebullience that by all accounts attended the premieres of early 'talkies' is best understood not as the unveiling of simply one more dish for the visual appetite, but as a consummation of the ideology of vision, with the visible now projected in a despotic relation to the auditory, on screen as in life.

This is the visual corollary to Brecht's description of radio, above. The early twentieth century, with a preceding hundred-year obsession with rudimentary optical tricks and games and then with photography, was eminently well prepared for a pleasure that technology could not yet afford. The gap between the 'talkie' and television was the heyday of radio, which then played an odd and short-lived supporting role. While filmic entertainment is a spectacular and erotic, dynamic and multi-vocal *experience*, suspenseful radio drama – one of the period's most prominent genres – now seems grim and monotonous, arousing by its disembodied, prehistoric aesthetic a kind of cultural castration anxiety. Indeed, the pleasures of radio suspense depend on precisely this kind of threat, one that embraces rather than disavows the limitations of the medium. The medium's regressive tendencies are seized as a source of difference and advantage. Radio pleasure is not visual pleasure, and it can therefore direct a listener's libido towards different kinds of fantasy and perversion.

The illusion of diachronic experience harnessed by visual entertainment is well suited to the omnivorous, insatiable eye. By contrast, the radio may create a feeling of 'synchronous recognition,' in Fredric Jameson's phrase.[29] We hear, as it were, in reverse: making meaning retroactively, anchoring ourselves in small bursts of backward clarity that posthumously structure and resolve the potential incoherence of an unfolding semantic chain. Suspenseful radio drama extends this tension to the form as a whole by directing attention towards the end of the enunciation, the final syntactic unit that promises to organize the preceding discourse. In the meantime, the listener is left to speculate whether the entire sequence is being retold from an ill-fated and unsavory present tense to which it has already arrived and we are fast approaching. Like noir films that begin and end in a police interrogation room, narrated as one long confession to a tape machine or stenographer, the feeling is one of inevitability rather than progress, doom rather than catharsis, stasis rather than evolution. In radio suspense, the case is long since closed; in perverse and regressive fashion, 'what you are about to hear' has already taken place.

Visual narration fixes characters, locations, and events in the psychic economy of the perceiver, while radio concentrates its energies on the instance of retelling and the complicity of the listener. Listening to the radio always potentially resembles eavesdropping; the apparatus is a source of inappropriate knowledge. The primal scene of radio aesthetics is the violent technological transformation that severs voices and bodies while making the captured voices audible for the pleasure of a privileged listener. The line between the human and the mechanical blurs. The apparent plurality of voices becomes monotonous when anchored to a single apparatus of intonation. Are real human beings speaking, one may wonder, or is this somehow the voice of the apparatus? When properly exploited, suspenseful radio drama capitalizes on these cognitive and epistemological qualities of the medium. Managed skilfully, the listening process can be rendered pleasurably illicit. The visual is driven by desire and acquisition, while the auditory seems more intimately concerned with absence, guilt, and fear. To put this proposition in negative form: the radio, by negating space, can recharge it. In making an unobtainable fetish of the visible, radio reawakens the latent power of an object-world that refuses to coalesce into reassuring imagery. Listen hard to a recording of *The Shadow* and stare closely at the bric-a-brac of the living room. It looks back at you.

It is now difficult to distinguish the pleasures of an individual radio play from the anachronistic cultural associations of radio drama in general. When *A Slight Ache* was first broadcast – and increasingly thereafter – the liminality of the medium became part of the message. The idea of radio drama mobilizes fantasies about earlier forms of mass culture and anxieties about the mercilessly visual nature of contemporary life. The medium's historical determinations are accompanied by its epistemological peculiarities, which, as we have seen, can be deployed for both compulsion and pleasure. In the context of Pinter's career, *A Slight Ache* appears as a local instance of negation, which harks back over radio's historicity in a regressive, late modernist gesture. Formally, the play uses the possibilities of the medium to forge a peculiarly energized and resistant linguistic structure, one with both aesthetic and political implications. What organizes the linguistic field of *A Slight Ache* is its negative pole – namely, the semiotic black hole of the match-seller, which exercises an almost magnetic pull on speech. Again, the meaning of this absence, its radical invisibility, only emerges in relation to a desire for visible presence. This determinate negation refers us back to the question of medium.

In the theatre, the visibility of the performing body can be a source of both ambiguity and consolation. As both a real and a pretending body – a body standing for another body (and our bodies) – the actor enables the pleasurable recognition of both reality and illusion, providing a sense of mastery over the anxieties that such existential flickering might otherwise cause. In the theatre, such engagements are relatively *consensual*: the sociality of theatre-going, the framing proscenium arch, the darkness of the house and brightness of the stage all foster a sense of *willing* suspension and cognitive play. Radio, by contrast, presents problems of verification. The utopian potential imagined by Brecht and other early champions of radio as an instrument of populist interaction does not mesh comfortably with the broadcast of fiction. The disembodied apparatus creates a suspension that is compulsory rather than consensual. The impersonal technology and its unverifiable authority can foster anxiety in the sequestered listener. The radio audience is privatized and fragmented, denied the communal comfort of shared theatrical participation. The public panic occasioned by the broadcast in 1938 of Orson Welles's *War of the Worlds* is evidence of the social force of the medium and its epistemological peculiarities.

By pursuing the potentially coercive implications of this indeterminacy, the match-seller functions as a critique of the epistemology of radio. The critique gains power and complexity as it becomes clear that the match-seller is less a character than a cipher designating a complex, overdetermined imaginary space. First, the listener must partly identify with the match-seller even while speculating about his ontology. Like the listener, the match-seller is a distant object, an addressee, and later a mute witness. The aggressive energies directed at him begin to function as an unrelenting confession or harangue directed at the audience. At the same time, the fact that the match-seller is evidently an enigma to Edward and Flora implicates the characters and listener in a common suspense. At an abstract level, for critics, audiences, and characters alike, the match-seller acts as a kind of signifier without a signified; he symbolizes the extra-symbolic or a final, inaccessible referent. He serves as the desired end of much figurative language in the play, perpetually at its fingertips but just beyond its grasp. He is repeatedly enjoined and incited to speak, and his silence thus functions as an interruption or failure in language, a marker of lack or absence.

Within the play, the match-seller is variously described as old, a bullock, disgusting, youthful, smelly, vile, a solid old boy 'not at all like a jelly' and is even given the pet name Barnabas by Flora, in one of her amorous moods. Critics have reciprocated with a similarly long and varied list. The match-seller has been taken as death, silence, materiality, immateriality, the ineffable, and the transitory. Because the impenetrable figure tends implacably to reflect back one's interpretive desire – neither confirming nor denying – many abstract readings sound equally plausible. At the same time, however, I would suggest that there is at least a particle of concreteness in the match-seller that still needs attention. All we have is the name, the opaque image, the appellation; we cling more fiercely to the bare sign of the match-seller because of the ambiguity of its referent. From his window early in the play, Edward invites our identification through his doggedly rational (albeit paranoid) efforts to explain the match-seller according to an imagined practical logic of match-selling as form of commercial enterprise: 'And do you know I've never seen him sell one box? Not a box. It's hardly surprising. He's on the wrong road. It's not a road at all. What is it? It's a lane, leading to the monastery. Off everybody's route. Even the monks take a short cut to the village. No one goes up it. Why doesn't he stand on the main road if he wants to sell matches, by the *front* gate? The whole thing's preposterous' (176).

The regressive chill here is of ill-fated reasonableness, of logic forever betrayed by illicit back gates off everyone's route. Lucrative and efficient match-selling appears to be a losing proposition in the 1950s English countryside; Edward's pedantic speech is 'preposterous' from the outset. In one broad and unexpected stroke, this suspension of reality evokes a historical life-world in which match-selling occupied an assured and integrated place in the social system, or perhaps even constituted an economically viable working-class activity. One might begin to nostalgically imagine the match-seller as a cog in a benign commercial system of distribution as partial antidote to some of the more uneasy associations surrounding this signifier. As Edward's paranoia turns inward, the cipher begins to generate more primal

forms of anxiety, going finally perhaps to a fear of matches as regressive emblems of some more archaic and threatening relationship to
fire:

> He's sold nothing all morning. No one passed. Yes. A monk passed. A
> non-smoker. In a loose garment. It's quite obvious he was a non-smoker
> but still, the man made no effort. He made no effort to clinch a sale, to rid
> himself of one of his cursed boxes. His one chance, all morning, and he
> made no effort. I haven't wasted my time. I've hit, in fact, upon the truth.
> He's not a match-seller at all. Curious I never realized that before. He's an
> impostor. I watched him very closely. He made no move towards the
> monk. As for the monk, the monk made no move towards him. The monk
> was moving along the lane. He didn't pause, or halt, or in any way alter
> his step. As for the match-seller – how ridiculous to go on calling him by
> that title. What a farce. No, there is something very false about that man. I
> intend to get to the bottom of it. (179)

Matches become 'cursed boxes,' and Edward defensively uncouples
the title of the match-seller from the maddening and insensible resistance that the concept has begun to signify. The idea of an impostor is
somehow more consoling than the inscrutable barbarism of selling
matches. The movement of these two passages re-enacts the structural
logic of the entire play, which begins with innocuous, though intermittently electric repartee ('FLORA: You know perfectly well what grows in
your garden'; 'EDWARD: Quite the contrary. It is clear that I don't'),
broadens to vividly sensual imagery ('EDWARD: It will not bite you.
Wasps don't bite. Anyway, it won't fly out. It's stuck. It'll drown where
it is, in the marmalade'), and proceeds by regression towards an
increasingly monologic and ecstatic conversation with the imaginary.
In response to Flora's question about the honeysuckle, Edward's first
line in the play is 'The what?'; his last is the desperate question to the
match-seller, 'Who are you?' Between is an eruption of verbal excess
oriented finally towards the conflicted symbolic space of the match-
seller cipher.
   At the same time, regression allows a kind of radio freedom, an
emancipation of language from the strictures of referent and significance. For example, it is clear from Edward's speech, above, that the
eminently reasonable question of whether a given stretch of ground
should be described as a road or a lane is, in this play, a dubious undertaking. The words, once spoken, begin to concretize and organize

themselves as separate and ultimately indecipherable formal entities. As the play proceeds, language is increasingly open to complex combinations that refuse to be digested or exhausted as mere figures of speech. The non-smoking monk 'in a loose garment' or the wasp drowning in the marmalade are relatively unyielding from a semiotic perspective, yet both hold themselves out with all the brittle and irreducible force of a fully determinate Raymond Chandler simile (e.g., 'About as inconspicuous as a tarantula on a slice of angel food').[30] I would argue that these small, retrograde linguistic entities are tokens of Pinter's connection to radio. The constitutive blindness of radio animates the language of *A Slight Ache*, and this may be taken in analogy to the troubling materiality of language in Pinter's stage plays. In one way or another, nearly all of Pinter's work strives to make us hear differently. Even with eyes open in the theatre, Pinter's harsh and often minimalist language reverberates as if from a disconnected loudspeaker, which encourages us to cognitively respond as if our eyes were closed. The suspense and anxiety engendered by disembodied, reproduced language begins to infect the visible stage. Something in Pinter continues to reside at the intersection of technology and language and its brief embodiment in the culture and drama of radio.

Unease, malaise, menace, malevolent quibbles, threatening small talk – these motifs of the Pinteresque can be re-examined in relation to radio suspense. The exemplary linguistic episodes of *A Slight Ache* are only extreme cases of familiar tendencies in Pinter's language. Words slide towards inaccessible reality, acquire the elemental resistance of objects, become opaque and unfamiliar. The booming resonance of Pinter's stage language, its aura of dominance and invisible authority, also has something in common with the cognitive spell associated with suspenseful radio drama. Reading Pinter's stage plays *in relation* to radio, rather than regarding the two mediums as ontologically opposed, acknowledges the idea of cultural connectedness. Individuals presumably do not encounter theatre, radio, film, and television in schizophrenic fashion, but they are likely to respond to cultural experiences within familiar existential parameters of leisure, logistics, time, expense, pleasure, and boredom, and these responses are almost certainly tinged by memories of things heard and seen before. Again, the problem of *pleasure* can be a useful corrective to the hegemony of abstraction. Relationships between Pinter's works in various mediums become tangible at the level of lived experience in a manner often precluded by specialized criticism.

At moments, *A Slight Ache* suggests a cognitively distinct kind of auditory pleasure, one that is intensified by the aesthetics of radio. Language is intermittently relieved of its narrative obligations, and the listener is freed from the overwhelming sensory plenitude of the stage and movie-screen. Late in the play, Edward innocently offers the match-seller a cocktail, and the litany that follows plays on the negative potentialities of both the radio and the ear: 'Now look, what will you have to drink? A glass of ale? Curacao Fockink Orange? Ginger Beer? Tia Maria? A Wachenheimer Fuchsmantel Reisling Beeren Auslce? Gin and it? Chateauneuf-du-Pape? A little Asti Spumante? Or what do you say to a straightforward Piesporter Goldtropfschen Feine Auslese (Reichsgraf von Kesselstaff)? Any preference?' (185). On the one hand, there is no way to reconcile the Caribbean, British, German, Italian, and French polyglot suggested by these beverages. After the endless description of the Reisling, Edward's abrupt 'Gin and it?' directs attention back to the brute materiality of the previous nonsensical utterance (while making most gin-drinkers slightly nauseous). The listener is free to indulge whatever exotic, banal, or purely auditory reverberations the cocktails may provide.

Beyond its force as an instance of verbal play, Edward's speech has a latent political (or at least psychosocial) content at the same time. Given the context of the speech, delivered to the void of the match-seller, the incongruousness of Edward's language takes on social specificity. It is difficult to harmonize the bourgeois feeling-tone of a glass of Tia Maria or Châteauneuf-du-Pape with wet matchboxes that 'smell suspiciously like fungus' (186), as Edward later remarks. Throughout the play Edward uses language as a defence; he restlessly tries to define and control others while clothing himself in a protective cultural uniform. In this sense, there is a psychotic quality to the litany, a sense in which the exaggerated sonority of the drinks and the bizarre civility they symbolize can no longer effectively sublimate the dark truth of this damaged life. The overflow of names once again places Edward in the position of a pedantic consumer, losing sight of the world through remorseless classification. One is reminded of the spectacle of the modern supermarket with all its glorious and unabashedly totalizing overtones. Here the modern utopian synthesis of wide aisles and 'product visibility' – to borrow an unpleasant-sounding phrase from advertising – is presumably intended to echo and update the spatial and social pleasures of a nineteenth-century boulevard. Yet, like Edward's speech, the supermarket's signifiers begin to grate. The irrational strain of a reduced-fat, all-natural, economy-sized shopping polyglot can still produce local and primitive resistance in the inner ear. *A Slight Ache* and the radio society it evokes symbolize a kind of redness in the eye of visual culture; dominant ideologies of vision may be subtly compromised by the pleasures and limits of the second sense.

In the context of Pinter's career, *A Slight Ache* underscores in salutary fashion the plurality of his authorship – both its populism and its dispersion across a variety of mediums. In various ways, authors like Pinter encourage a healthy revision of conventional wisdom. Such revision is especially welcome in the field of modern drama, where the problem of medium specificity has been compounded by historical factors. The separation of artistic media according to particularities and potentialities is as old as aesthetics, but during the modern period the process of separation becomes more adversarial. Modernist painting recoils from the representational hegemony of photography towards more abstract realizations of paint and canvas. Modernist filmmakers, broadly speaking, react in similar fashion against the parasitical dependence of commercial film on the play and the novel, towards theories and practices emphasizing the potential of film as film.

In the case of modern drama, these tensions are exacerbated by the increasingly marginal status of the theatre in relation to film, television, and newer mass cultural technologies. This marginality can be viewed as both an asset and a liability, but in either case it may foster a kind of disciplinary separatism. Practitioners, critics, and scholars of modern drama have understandably been concerned with preserving the *difference* of theatre – its historicity, its essential collectivity and presence – while arguing for its contemporary relevance as a progressive source of intellectual development and resistance to the prevailing winds of commercial culture. At the same time, the comparative isolation of modern drama as both practice and object of study – particularly in relation to the trendier objects of recent cultural studies analysis – underscores the need for a more holistic approach.

Radio, theatre, television, and film are not ontologically discontinuous realms. At the same time, an undifferentiated mishmash of culture is not a desirable proposition, even where commercialization encourages us to think in this way. The work of plural writers like Pinter demands that we balance the two extremes, that we conceptualize culture as a totality while remaining alert to distinct subcultures, to varying modes of production and reception and their aesthetic and political differences. In this sense, the radio-problem of *A Slight Ache* broadens

into larger questions about mass culture and the popular. As an apparatus of mass cultural dissemination, radio serves as a reminder of the
millions who have heard or seen Pinter's work in forums other than
the theatre. The blunt, factual, silent nature of this popular consumption opens a cultural divide when it is compared with the noisy, articulate responses that are the currency of professional commentators.
Radio is a reminder of Pinter's direct and powerful bond with audiences, a bond that urges attention to matters of pleasure, popularity,
and reception.

Cultural studies discourse has shown that complex ideological,
structural, epistemological, and institutional determinants can be disentangled from a particular aesthetic experience, and that the analysis
of cultural texts benefits from this kind of attention. Pinter's career has
taken frequent iconoclastic turns towards radio, television, and film,
thereby damaging any sweeping interpretation that rests on the singularities of one medium. His work demands attention to particularity
and specificity by refusing to succumb to the dominion of a single
medium, mode, or style. We are led to ask whether 'modern drama'
itself is a stable, isolable phenomenon, or whether this disciplinary history likewise needs rewriting in relation to radio, television, film, and
other forms of cultural production.

Betrayal and mass culture

The word regression is a way of referring to those states of mind (or mindless-
ness), either inarticulate or on the verges of representation, that defy or confound the already known.

Adam Phillips[31]

Much work in cultural studies has been devoted to the dialectic of
modernism and mass culture, and I hope the foregoing discussions
have shown that Pinter traverses the two extremes. The tension
between high and low cultures is directly and provocatively incar-
nated by Betrayal (1978), a mid-career play whose style and subject
matter seem better suited to the screen than to the stage (a film version
was made in 1982). To be sure, Pinter had worked extensively in the
mass media before 1978 and would continue to do so after. Yet Betrayal
juxtaposes the aesthetics and pleasures of art and entertainment in a
singular, hybrid form. Betrayal serves as a culmination and turning

point in Pinter's relationship to popular culture. This relationship, as the play underscores, is complex and intimate rather than one-sided. In this section I analyse *Betrayal* as a puzzling hybrid, a play that is neither a commentary on nor an example of popular culture yet is somehow both.

The play does not comment on the popular from a safe, ironic distance, but instead inhabits and implodes the architecture of conventional narrative. As anyone familiar with *Betrayal* knows, the drama performs radical surgery on what I will call instrumental narrative: linear, teleological narrative that subordinates its substance (means) to its goal (closure, resolution, ends). Despite its formal radicalism, however, the play leaves the apparatus of instrumental narrative strangely intact, suggesting an author who is aware that there are no easy alternatives to the conventions and consumer expectations of contemporary mass culture. Moreover, *Betrayal* reflexively erodes Pinter's monolithic literary status by introducing a slightly disreputable, lowbrow version of his authorial persona. Here, the univocal modernist Harold Pinter, an authoritative, high cultural voice in opposition to the marketplace, begins to yield to a postmodern Pinter, an elusive, unpredictable figure fighting guerrilla battles on the terrain of commercial culture. I first briefly discuss instrumental narrative in the context of reification, pleasure, and mass culture and then read *Betrayal* in its formal and thematic relations to popular culture, particularly melodrama and soap opera. Finally, I argue that the play represents a bitter, nearly nihilistic critique of conventional aesthetic pleasure.

The problem of narrative pleasure requires some brief background. Particular forms of entertainment are not exempt from larger social processes, and aesthetic pleasures need to be grasped in the context of other kinds of cultural experience. Theatre is a pre-eminently social activity that exists in relation to other social activities, such as working in an office or going to a ball game, and also, more sequentially, to the cocktail hour before the performance or the cab ride home. 'Culture is ordinary,' to borrow the title of an essay by Raymond Williams, and, like supermarket etiquette or a subway ride, theatrical experience imposes a particular shape on collective life. One task of cultural studies is to yoke such varied phenomena, to discern ideological patterns across a range of social and consumer activities, to resituate local acts of reading and reception in a larger social frame. Here, I want to suggest that in the modern period encounters between individuals and representations are increasingly defined by the broader logic of markets and commodities.

Reception closely approximates the instrumental character of cultural production; significantly, the term 'consumption' begins to displace 'reception' with respect to cultural as well as material goods. The instrumentality of acquisitive consumer consciousness is mirrored and reinforced by products and texts that trumpet easy, pleasurable utility. In contrast to traditional aesthetic notions of art as a realm of freedom in which 'purposefulness without purpose' may be pursued or as a genuine and organic expression of collective spirit, the birth of mass media culture compels aesthetic work to define itself in relation to its values or ends in the sphere of consumption.[32]

Culture thus begins to conform to the processes of rationalization and instrumentalization in modern society – to borrow unwieldy terms from both Max Weber and the Frankfurt School. These twin concepts document the ways in which the values and pleasures of older forms of human activity are fragmented and restructured according to rational paradigms of usefulness and efficiency. The ends or intrinsic values of these various activities are suspended, and what remains is a society of goal-directed, procedural behaviours organized by the universal 'end' of exchange-value or money.[33] In the sphere of culture, this instrumental, commodity-driven logic is visible in a variety of modern forms, such as the emergence of the director-centred theatre, where a unified and coherent production becomes an ultimate value towards which all creative and technical labour is directed. More notorious are the Hollywood studios of the 1930s and 1940s, where film production is literally reorganized around the assembly-line model of Henry Ford, and films are increasingly composed of repetitive structures and interchangeable parts. To cultural consumers instrumentality is familiar as the principle of delayed gratification at work in the serial fiction and cliffhanger movie 'shorts' of the 1920s and 1930s, espionage fiction, the detective novel, the compulsory Hollywood happy ending, and the ultra-modern form of the contemporary soap opera. As described in Veblen's 1902 critique of 'conspicuous consumption,' we habitually read individual chapters or watch individual episodes under the promise of an endlessly delayed gratification, until whatever minimal pleasure remains now resides in the experience of ourselves as consumers, and consumption becomes the unifying goal of social life.[34]

At the level of common sense, it is initially not clear if one 'consumes' art as one would gasoline or a sandwich, or even a Nike ad or *Days of Our Lives*. On the one hand, the notion of consumption seems to provide a metaphor for cultural experience with its own integrity, duration, and intensity while, on the other hand, orienting experience towards a final and non-durational form of transaction or value – as if watching a Pinter play were roughly the equivalent of drinking a can of Coca-Cola. Consumption is another way of speaking about instrumentality; the nature of the concept requires that the means of a particular work be balanced against its ends. The structures and contents of a cultural experience are measured against its ultimate commodity status, and, conversely, assessments of its use value are dictated by the specificities and differences that make it ideologically comprehensible.

Clearly, conventional wisdom disposes us to approach entertainment as Coca-Cola and art as a multi-course meal; art provides an epicurean satisfaction in relation to the unthinking banality it opposes. Yet we are more than ever prepared to confront even the most obscure Beckett revival or challenging Mozart recital within the constellation of consumer choice – a dose of culture – which at the level of social status or perceived need affords a commodity-satisfaction above and beyond the intrinsic value of the experience. Through long training the ideological habits of consumerism increasingly attach to everything a phantom objective value. Reception is thus never innocent. Even the most evolved critical responses to high culture depend on reified conventions that the work of art is said to resist or withhold. The high cultural spectator may sublimate or repress boredom, laughter, or titillation as responses more appropriate to commercial entertainment. The alternative, however, likely is not some utopian form of contemplation but merely a more elevated consumer style. For the cultural pessimist, aesthetic production and reception in the modern period conspire to reify the artwork and facilitate its smooth digestion, as does the practice of the critic, who, at a second level, 'by making culture his object ... objectifies it once more.'[35] This gloomy state of affairs led critics like Adorno to conclude that the notion of culture is self-contradictory. A more organic or authentic cultural life would not be separated, named, and objectified, but rather would exist as a contiguous expression of community.

Betrayal intricately signals both reification and resistance. The play submits to the cultural marketplace but seeks to invert and disfigure its conventions. It violently destabilizes distinctions between high and low cultures by placing avant-garde and commercial tendencies in a protracted, off-putting embrace. Because of this aesthetic promiscuity – and together with its incongruous tone, style, structure, and subject matter – *Betrayal* has been regarded as a problem play in the Pinter canon. Formally, there seems a kind of ontological deceit in a work that relies so heavily on the conventional melodramatic realism one might encounter in the mass media. The claustrophobic spaces and malevolent objects of Pinter's earlier plays have given way to the referential transparency of television and film, a more familiar representational logic that significantly shapes a spectator's response. The play's problematic status also derives from discomfort with its subject matter and sketchy narrative. Formal worries are compounded by a commonsense perception that *Betrayal* is about 'a nasty little affair that really doesn't matter very much.'[36]

In gauging tensions between art and mass culture, however, this problem play is exemplary. The pleasures of conventional entertainment are rendered ambiguous in content as well as form. An odd, reflexive moment in the middle of the play underscores its unusual tone and the peculiar demands it makes on an audience. A well-off book publisher, Robert, and his wife, Emma, are in a hotel room on vacation in Venice. Emma is reading a novel, written by an acquaintance, which Robert had previously refused to publish. The novelist in question is a client of the couple's best friend, the literary agent Jerry. Robert is understandably somewhat perturbed, since he has just inadvertently received a letter from Jerry addressed to Emma, indicating that the two are engaged in a long-standing affair. Before confronting Emma, Robert begins the following conversation about the novel:

ROBERT: You think it's good, do you?
EMMA: Yes, I do. I'm enjoying it.
ROBERT: Jerry thinks it's good too. You should have lunch with us one day and chat about it.
EMMA: Is that absolutely necessary?
Pause.
It's not as good as all that.
ROBERT: You mean it's not good enough for you to have lunch with Jerry and me and chat about it?
EMMA: What the hell are you talking about?
ROBERT: I must read it again myself, now it's in hard covers.
EMMA: Again?
ROBERT: Jerry wanted us to publish it.
EMMA: Oh, really?
ROBERT: Well, naturally. Anyway, I turned it down.
EMMA: Why?

ROBERT: Oh ... not much more to say on that subject, really, is there?
EMMA: What do you consider the subject to be?
ROBERT: Betrayal.
EMMA: No, it isn't.
ROBERT: Isn't it? What is it then?
EMMA: I haven't finished it yet. I'll let you know.[37]

In symptomatic fashion, the ironies and subtexts in this exchange are more banal (and oddly, more self-conscious) than is typical in Pinter's plays. The nausea of words and objects in earlier works is here replaced by a pedestrian, if malevolent, human relationship. Tellingly, the title of the play does not stem from an object (*The Dumb Waiter*), an individual (*The Caretaker*), an event (*The Homecoming*), or a physical affliction (*A Slight Ache*). Betrayal is a lofty – indeed, hyperbolic – abstraction. Like the eponymous play, the notion of betrayal is contradictory, simultaneously significant and trivial. In modern usage, betrayal suggests the idiom of melodrama, with its longing for full emotional disclosure and transparency. The play's title taps this exhausted cultural vein, and the drama further erodes the grand cliché by dwelling on the triviality of betrayal's enactment.

Stranger still is the reflexive use of the title in the scene above. Towards the end of the exchange, it seems as if Pinter is speaking directly to the audience. We immediately question whether the subject of the play is betrayal, what Pinter 'considers the subject to be,' whether he has in fact 'finished it yet' and will let us know, and so forth. The entire enterprise quickly acquires a shopworn, defeated air. We feel as if there were indeed 'not much more to say on that subject,' yet the play perversely prolongs the motions. Moreover, there is nothing especially pleasant about the characters, the situation, or the mind games in which the play compels us to participate. The anomalous reflexivity is strangely apologetic, as though Pinter concurred with Emma: 'It's not as good as all that.' The arid concept of betrayal signals an analogous lack of richness in the play's language and socio-cultural raw materials. Further, the hermetic use of irony and self-reference in this scene encapsulates the play's authoritarian attitude towards its audience. Throughout, spectators are positioned not as active (if disoriented) readers of ambiguous situations, as in earlier Pinter writings, but as passive recipients of scripted ironies, as consumers of excessive information.

In contrast to the uncertainty in many of Pinter's other works,

Betrayal appears restrictive and overdetermined. The naturalistic settings, historically specified characters and locations, overabundant
plot, and familiar erotic triangle saturate the play's temporal, spatial,
and thematic dimensions. Strategies of enclosure rigidly structure audience response and effectively foreclose the possibility of outside associations. Further, there is an overarching bitterness to the drama that
directs us to the motives of its author. One is tempted to read *Betrayal*
biographically and ironically (Pinter's revenge against his social circle?) in order to clarify its uncharacteristic reflexivity. Yet the play's ironies are somehow ambient rather than anchored in a particular, stable
consciousness. *Betrayal* offers no secure cultural perspective or aesthetic
high ground. The structure and content offer themselves as melodramatic entertainment, but the grim protraction of melodrama engenders
a mounting distaste on which, by a kind of trickery, the audience is
made to choke. To complete the vicious circle – 'entertainment or art?'
could be *Betrayal*'s epigraph – anyone who wants to view this unpleasantness as biting satire must return to a play that is largely legible as a
piece of naïve, commercial realism (with one obviously crucial qualification). The stage version of *Betrayal* leads, predictably, to Jeremy Irons,
Ben Kingsley, and the earnest, cheerless film adaptation.[38]

The evolution of one critic's response encompasses both the play's
grayness and its self-consciousness, entwining the two suggestively.
Michael Billington, in his exhaustive *The Life and Work of Harold Pinter*
(1996), commends the play's portrayal of the 'corrosive complexity of
betrayal,' but only after admitting a change of heart. Billington quotes
his own 1978 opening-night review, in which he castigated the play for
its focus on a 'pitifully thin strip of human experience' and 'its obsession with the tiny ripples on the stagnant pond of bourgeois-affluent
life,' before concluding that 'Harold Pinter has betrayed his immense
talent by serving up this kind of high-class soap-opera.' What galva-
nizes and informs Billington's revised 1996 reading is a supplemental
second narrative – a personal one gleaned from interviews with the
principals – that makes clear *Betrayal*'s autobiographical basis. Evidently, the play's 'general chronology and specific incidents'[39] derive
from a real affair in Pinter's life. Biography is needed to embellish a
'thin' narrative, to transform 'soap-opera' into aesthetic 'complexity.'
This need underscores *Betrayal*'s 'problem' status, violating the modernist autonomy typical of Pinter's works by inviting the sort of external consumerist knowledge that popular culture requires to flesh out
and validate its bare-bones generic structures. In this respect Billing-

ton's revised reading ironically confirms his initial feelings about the storyline.

The plot centres on the squash-playing, martini-luncheon friendship of Robert, the publisher, and Jerry, the literary agent. In 1968 Jerry, who was best man at Robert's wedding, begins an affair with Robert's wife, Emma. The illicit couple takes a flat and continues their relationship for five years. In 1973, while on vacation, Robert discovers the affair and confronts Emma, who blithely concedes, 'We're lovers.' Robert's reaction is 'I've always liked Jerry. To be honest, I've always liked him rather more than I've liked you. Maybe I should have had an affair with him myself' (225). Immediately after the trip to Venice, Emma and Jerry meet at the flat, and Emma does not relate the fact that Robert knows about the affair. Similarly, Robert and Jerry later have lunch, exchanging unmemorable small talk while Robert fails to breathe a word.

Jerry, Robert, and Emma continue to socialize together, lending tension to their sublimated banter on stage. Finally, in 1975 Emma and Jerry call off the affair, disbanding their flat and agreeing 'It's not a home' (196). Things presumably revert to normal until 1977, when Jerry and Emma meet for a reunion drink. After some initial discomfort, Emma relates that she has begun a new affair, and that she and Robert are about to separate. This course of action was precipitated by a violent quarrel the night before, when Robert revealed that he had also been betraying Emma with other women for years. Emma tells Jerry that she communicated their betrayal to Robert, but insinuates that this confession happened only the previous night, not four years earlier. Jerry, shocked, goes to see Robert in an agitated state, only to find out that his close friend had known for years of his adulterous liaison, but had preferred to maintain their dubious friendship. Jerry is ultimately revealed to have been the victim of two betrayals of omission – to accompany his own extended commission – and the drama reaches its chronological end.

Anyone familiar with the play will know that there is a punchline to this synopsis, which I want to withhold temporarily in order to comment on the story in its present form. First, I want to suggest that at the levels of convention, structure, and theme, the play's ultimate preoccupation is with the problem of pleasure. The spectator is invited, often compelled, to adopt the familiar posture of a cultural consumer, to seek the enjoyments typical of conventional narrative. In various ways, however, *Betrayal* poisons this experience. The play dismantles its symbolic architecture to reveal a bare skeleton of convention, a pastiche of hackneyed forms, stereotypes, and clichés. Finally, in order to enjoy this self-deconstruction the spectator must acknowledge – even embrace – the ideological excess of cultural consumption, the frame of reference one assents to when consuming mass culture in whatever form. The play highlights this frame by breaking the spell of realism and identification that usually keeps spectators occupied. Instead, *Betrayal* projects back an image of one's own expectations, so that the price of gratification is a crude, unflattering reflection of oneself as a consumer.

To anyone expecting conventional entertainment the play must initially appear either sordid or overly abstract (or both). In what feels like overkill, the labyrinth of deceit seems both degraded and contrived. *Betrayal* imposes a formal self-consciousness that renders its tepid subject matter implausible. For its realist substance, the play draws from a barren set of social and cultural raw materials. The characters are taken from an imagined world of bloodless London literati. Almost immediately, realism begins to dissolve into conventional codes and clichés. As gallery owner, agent, and publisher, the three characters are functionaries of an official culture; they speak a familiar idiom and appear to be fully determined by their social roles. When not having business lunches or neglecting their children, the characters engage in the dispassionate infidelities and blithe trips to Venice that are by now a caricature of the leisure class. In this inverted world, the fictive 'betrayal' that Robert believes to be the subject of the novel ironically signals an emotional and moral depth unavailable in reality. Potentially, the play's subject matter might lend itself to reassuring social satire. But in *Betrayal*, the insularity of the scenario precludes the consolation of ironic distance; the audience is denied both contempt and identification.

Yet if one rejects satire as the drama's unifying perspective and attempts to look past the caricature for a human substance, the results are similarly discouraging. Even the most tentative expressions of human desire are either vulgar or elaborately repressive. During Emma's and Jerry's quarrel about whether their secret flat was 'for loving' or 'for fucking,' both options are equally unsavoury. Emma's next line is 'Well, there's not much of that left, is there?' (197), and the ambiguous use of the word 'that' conflates the two propositions. The debasement of desire is complemented by intricate sublimations and deferrals, underscoring the impossibility of fulfilment. For example, homoerotic desire between Robert and Jerry is centrally symbolized by an endlessly postponed game of squash. When Emma suggests that she watch the game and then take the two to lunch, Robert acidly responds: 'Well, to be brutally honest, we wouldn't actually want a woman around, would we, Jerry? I mean a game of squash isn't simply a game of squash, it's rather more than that. You see, first there's the game. And then there's the shower. And then there's the pint. And then there's lunch. After all, you've been at it. You've had your battle. What you want is your pint and your lunch. You really don't want a woman buying you lunch. You don't actually want a woman within a mile of the place, any of the places, really. You don't want her in the squash court, you don't want her in the shower, the pub, or the restaurant.' (209)

The double entendres here are certainly open to interpretation, yet in the context of the play this pastiche of camaraderie offers a shallow, compensating cleverness. The puns and sexual images refer back to a self-conscious author behind the scene. Whether we understand this 'author' to be Pinter or one of the characters remains an open question; all are enmeshed in an abstract, reflexive language that dehumanizes and represses. Indeed, the squash ritual is never consummated – whether understood sexually or literally is therefore irrelevant. Within the play's economy, squash is a mimesis of intimacy, one more fictive vignette of desire. For Robert, the evocation of male connection echoes his account of a day alone on the island of Torcello, after learning of the affair in Venice (a fact he neglects to tell Jerry). 'I was alone for hours, as a matter of fact, on the island. Highpoint, actually, of the whole trip,' he says, 'I sat on the grass and read Yeats.' Jerry intervenes, 'Yeats on Torcello?' Robert replies, 'they went well together' (247). This episode suggests a life performed (hammed up, really) rather than experienced. Sadness is poignant, pain operatic, loneliness literary.

Betrayal discourages the Archimedean detachment necessary for conventional satire, repels identification with characters, and punctures the aura of realism; the entertainment-seeker is thus obliged to find a different vantage point. With the refined aesthetic pleasures of irony and empathy unavailable, the spectator must descend one or two cultural rungs. In many respects *Betrayal* suggests a 'low' genre, one that solicits visceral sensations (as opposed to lofty sentiments) and encourages prurience, voyeurism, or the emotional hyperbole of melodrama. Indeed, *Betrayal* stretches these conventional responses to the point of self-deconstruction. The play creates dramatic irony and melodramatic pathos, but for the spectator these familiar pleasures quickly take on a sadistic, alienating tinge. Initially, contemplating the layers of ignorance and deception – knowing considerably more than the characters – can be both titillating and suspenseful. We relish the chilling effect of the over-literate, repressive idiom that insulates the characters from the blindness and dishonesty of their existence. The dialogue reminds us of the gap between inner life and the casual locutions by which desires are evaded or disguised.

These ironies have a pathetic quality reminiscent of melodrama, and the play's use of location and *mise en scène* is likewise consistent with the conventions of the genre. The succession of largely impersonal settings (pub, hotel, restaurant, rented love nest, etc.) further underscores the characters' alienation – a melodramatic approach to space that is developed in the film version of the play. The subject matter of *Betrayal* is well suited to the atmosphere of film melodrama, which Thomas Elsaesser describes as 'a sublimation of dramatic content into decor, color, gesture, and composition of frame, which in the best melodramas is perfectly thematized in terms of the characters' emotional and psychological predicaments.'[40] Indeed, the film of *Betrayal* is marked by pale colours, melancholy musical transitions, and an aura of claustrophobic intimacy and drabness in the composition of shots and the *mise en scène*. Moreover, in its evocation of city space, *Betrayal* assumes an ideological shape congruent with classical Hollywood melodrama. The play restages the cinema's leisurely approach to the selection of urban and suburban spaces as settings for the various elemental scenes. We drift between the bar, the restaurant, the love nest, the cocktail party, and the vacation spot. In pulp melodrama, this spatial promiscuity yields a libidinal thrill while mapping the film ideologically. The drama is stitched into a utopian conception of the modern city: a dynamic, erotically charged playground where the melodrama's social and sexual narratives unfold.

This melodramatic marking, however, masks an absence in both the play and the film. Like satire, *Betrayal* cannot maintain the formal and tonal stability necessary for genre coherence. It provides a conventional shell detached from the genre's cultural and ideological prerequisites. *Betrayal* lacks any empathic or erotic dimension. In conventional melodrama, the viewer is encouraged to re-experience his or her own traumas in the dramatized disjunction between inner life and social prohibition. The pleasure of melodrama depends on at least the possibility of fulfilment – sexual and emotional – an imaginary space outside societal constraints. For the fan of classical Hollywood melo-drama, the utopia of consummation persists in fantasy and memory, below the surface of the Hays Codes, beneath the mandatory restrictive attire, somewhere offscreen, just south of the frame. The pathos of melodrama rests on the recognition that outcomes might have been otherwise. Melodrama is presumably a redemptive (if ideological) enterprise, while *Betrayal* depicts an emotional wasteland in which inner life has been voided and social rituals have become parodies of connection. Moreover, the poignancy of deprivation, loss, and coura-geous sublimation ('forbidden love') associated with classical Holly-wood melodrama would have lacked teeth in the sexual climate of 1978. The cultural ground had shifted, yet the play solemnly repro-duces an ethos of deferral and repression without the supercharged, submerged libido that lent the genre its energy. The best melodrama is breathless and erotic, while *Betrayal* is clinical and gray.

Even if one were disposed to react earnestly to the play, it is hard to imagine an innocent approach to the dramatic situation. The human drama in *Betrayal* is to a large degree smothered by the weight of the sexual triangle as narrative form par excellence. Beginning with Oedi-pus and *The Iliad*, the sexual triangle opens twin pathways of hetero-sexual conquest and displaced homoeroticism, and its narratives are typically resolved in one way or another by the restitution of patriar-chal comradeship and the symbolic negation of the threat posed by the woman's desire. At least one interesting reading of this topic in *Betrayal* has been conducted; Katherine Burkman arrives at a quasi-feminist view of the men's homoerotic frustration and impotence, cou-pled with Emma's emergence as both victim and victor in a complex Oedipal drama.[41] I suggest only that *Betrayal* superimposes the sexual triangle on a network of structural, conceptual, and thematic determi-nations that together render the play opaque. Homoerotic and feminist interpretations certainly are available, but as a whole the play projects a mirage of deep meaning while turning the revelatory logic of Oedi-pal narrative inside-out (more on this below).

Given the play's devaluation of its subject matter, a disproportionate emphasis accrues to its form. Again, *Betrayal* is dialectical, simulta-neously creating and destroying a stable, pleasurable frame. The struc-ture is incompatible with the content, and considering the latter's debasement, it is tempting to align oneself with the former, to regard form as the play's ultimate point. The naïve mimetic realism of the episodes clashes with the self-conscious manner in which they are framed, and as good modernists we might expect to find in the frame a cogent critique of the mimesis, to read the play as a satire or some other form of coherent authorial statement. As I have suggested, however, *Betrayal* denies consistent perspective and distance; the meaning of the structure in relation to the content is at best complex, at worst opaque. The form and subject matter are mutually destructive; 'normal' cultural consumption begins to seem compulsive and pathological as the play proceeds radically against the grain.

To make matters more complex, the form of *Betrayal* itself is two-sided; the episodic structure works to domesticate as well as estrange. Indeed, given the play's critique of pleasure at the level of subject matter, it is odd that in one sense the form encourages pleasurable consumption. Despite its resistance to convention, the play is easily – perhaps oppressively – readable. *Betrayal* fluently speaks a reified language of stereotypes and clichés, and the narration has a similar picture-book quality. The action is arranged in nine short scenes, each with a small exposition, crisis, and denouement. Viewed charitably, this is a bold aesthetic experiment that blurs the lines between theatre and cinema. Enoch Brater, for example, argues that '*Betrayal* shows more clearly than any previous Pinter play the profound effect his work in the movies has had on his dramatic technique. And although *Betrayal* reads at times like a film-script, its real originality lies in the way it adapts certain cinematic strategies and makes them functional in terms of theatre.'[42]

For the spectator, however, the effect of these appropriated strategies is not entirely benign. The pleasures of cinematic epistemology are gradually compromised as the play deconstructs the ideological implications of this kind of spectatorship. If we take Brater at his word, *Betrayal* opens a large gap between narrative and narration, a disjunction that self-consciously refers back to the question of theatre vs film. This reflexivity further devalues the characters by positioning them in the crossfire between two mediums. Without the semiotic richness of the cinema or the ontological unity of Aristotelian drama, the play's hybrid aesthetic appears clinical and dehumanized. *Betrayal* renders lives in brusque shorthand. The episodic structure subjects the action to rigid chronological determination and reductively maps nine years of dismal existence in nine bleak scenes. These scenes effectively foreclose ambiguity and depth while creating the illusion of spatial and temporal fullness.

Examined carefully, the scenes of *Betrayal* are structurally and ideologically constituted as nearly indissoluble monads or units: miniature narrative commodities. The plot value of each scene can be summed up in a sentence or two, underscoring the violent compression involved in the play's technique. Emma's revelation in the Venice hotel figures as 'Robert discovers his wife has been having an affair with his best friend.' The scene between the three characters, including the squash debate, is something like 'Robert and Jerry engage in homo-erotic fantasy, while Robert ironically knows of the affair, and Emma knows he knows, but Jerry does not know Robert knows.' Robert's diffident 'Hullo' at the outset of scene seven signals and determines the subsequent sleepy enactment of Robert's ambivalence in the wake of Emma's revelation. We dutifully place the elemental narrative token within the broader chronology, and in this dubious transaction the value of the scene is largely exhausted.

All this is to say that *Betrayal* invites consumption rather than engagement. The crude instrumentality of the individual episodes reflects a commodity-logic that comes to define the narration as a whole. Given the predigested familiarity of the plot, one might argue that the play's structure is its most significant content. From a spectator's standpoint, process displaces substance, telling displaces tale. As theories of mass culture stress, however, commodified cultural texts convey an ideological perspective, a way of seeing, whatever their apparent substance. This is something like the play's ideological excess, the unwanted world view we ingest as we're playing the narrative guessing-game. In this sense, *Betrayal*'s devaluation of content renders more visible the dismal ideology that ghosts its form. What emerges is an extreme version of the way conventional mass cultural narrative regards and orders the world. Spatially, for example, the nine narrative monads collectively sketch an entire bourgeois topography. Moreover, this spatial coherence further eases our consumption of the episodes – aids digestion, as it were – by mapping the action on recognizable terrain. This is no longer the room of *The Dumb Waiter* (or *The Room*, for that matter), but is instead a hyper-modern cinematic cityscape, existentially unsuited to the more primitive forms of domestic life presupposed by earlier Pinter plays.

Thus, *Betrayal*'s structure, subject matter, temporality (more on this below), and spatial coordinates evoke an entire ideological formation, a cognitive map of a late-modern world. The play suggests that the comprehensibility of this alienated lifestyle increasingly depends on basic, formalized human relations indexically linked to a specified place: a dreary affair in an illicit flat, male bonding over a game of squash or business lunch, marital discord in a Venice hotel. The episodes of the play thus reflect a fragmented sense of place and a divided sense of self. The overall impression is of a stylized, scripted life that blurs the lines between existence and performance, space and *mise en scène*. *Betrayal* renders the relationship between self and world invariant and reified. Agency and freedom are violently curtailed, and topography emerges as an existential as well as a spatial necessity. Through the very act of following the drama, by making sense of it the audience admits familiarity with the play's mode of presentation and its ideological implications. We are drawn into the episodes, and, like the characters, we begin to cling to the episodic narrative logic that structures this life and makes possible the illusion of progress.

Ultimately, however, the very notion of progress is violently undercut. While my earlier synopsis was a reconstruction of linear plot, the most novel feature of *Betrayal* is the fact that it is told almost exclusively backwards. The narration inverts the story: the first scene is chronologically penultimate (1977), while the last scene is first (1968). The only exceptions to the regressive rule are scene two, Robert's revelation to Jerry that he has known for years of the affair, the last chronological event in the play; and scenes six and seven, which follow the Venice hotel episode with Emma and Jerry's reunion (she does not let on that Robert knows), and Jerry and Robert's subsequent lunch (Robert does not let on either). Scene eight is an intimate encounter between the adulterous couple in the flat in 1971, and scene nine details Jerry's first drunken schoolboy protestations of affection to Emma in 1968.

It is difficult to overstate the importance of this regressive structure to a distasteful drama that otherwise barely registers. Put crudely, the gap between plot and narration seems a gimmick, a *coup de théâtre*, a brash deployment of the cinematic flashback to a bizarre and egregious extent. The structure appears so brazenly that one feels obliged to read the entire play in its light. Enoch Brater writes that 'it is the arrangement of the scenes that makes ironies accumulate and the drama as a whole possible. It is not so much what we know but when we know it that is responsible for the real tension that bristles so ferociously beneath the contained surface of this work ... *Betrayal* makes us concerned with the unities and disunities of time, with deception and self-deception, with the past in the present and the present in the past.'[43] Logically speaking, however, the characters cannot learn these lessons (not in reverse), so the play is emphatically 'for us' insofar as its ironies do not arise from identification with a character's *anagnorisis* (recognition), as is typical in both realism and tragedy. Indeed, *Betrayal* short-circuits the causal energy that fuels conventional Aristotelian drama (in Brecht's sense), and its episodic structure embodies the narrative laxity of which Aristotle famously disapproved. Brater's analysis thus presupposes a non-traditional dramaturgy, a clinical approach that uses regressive structure to wring maximum irony from otherwise realistically drawn characters for the purpose of edifying (alienating? diverting? offending?) an audience. If it exists, this is irony of a dubious, purely dramatic variety: the sadistic/dramatic irony of watching rats in a maze. The value of the entire regressive conceit then depends on a spectator's satisfaction in knowing that the relationships are doomed, the anemic literati are shallow and conflicted, coupled with the pleasure of seeing, at the end, the flirtatious beginning in a profoundly ironic light. This is a difficult pleasure to quantify, and most of these recognitions would still occur – in some form – if the play were narrated chronologically.

I would argue that the regressive structure is excessive and gratuitous, particularly if irony is taken to be its ultimate purpose. In general, the play does not afford a pleasing vista on the characters' infidelities, nor does it provide a stable framework for ironic reflection. Rather, the most evident effect of the regression is to degrade the process and experience of conventional narration. In this sense, the medium is the message; the human drama is a pretext for an extreme formal exercise. The structure insinuates regression into a spectator's consumption of the melodramatic episodes. This is a violent gesture, since it seeks to interrupt a mode of cultural consumerism that is ostensibly progressive – in both a temporal and ideological sense – and to directly contradict the causal, teleological construction of the episodes. Regressive structure violates the habit of consumption that the episodes make a fetish. The technical device is familiar in modernism: the fragmentation of chronology and the reconstruction of detached, autonomous episodes. Yet the play does not succumb to the mischievous but finally bitter disinclination towards the world symbolized by the anecdote about Godard, who, when asked if one of his films had a beginning, a middle, and an end, replied, 'Yes, but not necessarily in that order.' Nor does *Betrayal* treat its subject matter as one might expect of parody or farce. The individual scenes are played straight, with a sense of fidelity to their hermetic, damaged world. Yet the love of ambiguity and phenomenological density that marks realist aesthetic practice is also absent from this play.

What remains is a series of well-made formal exercises that might serve an introductory acting class.

Against its will, the audience is forced to move forward through a story related in reverse. The perverse thrill of seeing backward is substituted for the pleasure of suspense. Since conventional closure is precluded by structural regression, narrative pleasure depends on identification of the play's structure and some libidinal investment in the fulfilment of its reverse teleology. This is an awkward position, to put it mildly. The play seems a devastating repudiation of Pinter's subtler examinations of conventional suspense in plays such as *The Dumb Waiter* and *The Homecoming*. Ben draws his gun, though he does not fire; Sam discloses his guilty secret, though the family greets the revelation with supreme indifference. The playful quality of these surprising denouements reflects a gentler satiric humour, one that retains some fondness for the conventions it is exposing. *Betrayal*, by contrast, is closer in tone to a radical critique of commodity culture. The play does not resist dramatic convention so much as explode in practice the ideological closure that cultural criticism unmasks in theory.

Whatever the play's value as a tour de force, it demands a high price from the spectator. Suspense – the exemplary instrumental structure of commercial narrative – is invoked but then deconstructed. In its violent and self-conscious arrangement of serial realist episodes, I can think of no better analogue to *Betrayal* than the daytime soap opera (albeit an analogue in reverse). In contrast to the mini-series or weekly series – which are structured by the expectation of episodic resolution, even where there is some unresolved problem across several episodes – Christine Geraghty writes that 'soap operas do not encourage such expectations and the longer they run the more impossible it seems to imagine them ending. Instead of narrative time being subordinate to the demands of the story, it dominates the narrative process and enables other formal structures to be brought into play. Time rather than action becomes the basis for organizing the narrative.'[44]

In *Love and Ideology in the Afternoon*, Laura Stempel Mumford largely concurs, with the qualification that all television is marked by the dialectic of repetition and variation, that is, seriality. She writes that 'soap operas can be distinguished from other programs that might air daily by the fact that they take serial form and are generally characterized by episodic nonclosure, which manifests itself through the postponement of individual storyline resolutions and the use of major and minor cliffhangers in place of the more definitive conclusions typical of traditional episodic television.'[45] Key, here, is the idea that soap opera spectators have a *different* cognitive relationship to narrative – presumably less instrumental, since the value of the experience no longer derives from its 'end' (in both senses) – as a result of the soap opera's radical approach to closure and form. Some feminist critics have argued that soaps subversively reconfigure desire itself in relation to popular culture; certain postmodernists contend that the soap opera is late-modern narrative par excellence. The analogy with *Betrayal* hinges on the privileging of narrative time and the subordination of dramatic action, though in Pinter's case, there are no 'other formal structures to be brought into play' beyond the mere fact of regression. *Betrayal* offers no alternative pleasure, save for the stark radicalism of its bitter experiment. The play subjects its atomized scenes to the iron law of regression as decisively as the soap opera imposes on its melodramatic episodes the rule of daily deferral. From opposite extremes, these negative forms call into question our insatiable thirst for cultural and ideological closure.

Writings on mass culture often emphasize surprising interpenetrations or resemblances between distinct cultural forms. In this vein, I think that *Betrayal*, of all Pinter's works, best argues the need to examine heterodox contexts and connections. The univocal 'Great Author' presupposed by some literary criticism of Pinter needs to be balanced by attention to antithetical notions such as the hybridity of his work, its links to popular culture, its pleasures and entertainment values. After all, high modernism and mass culture alike – despite obvious differences between the two modes of production – are historically connected to commodity reification and bourgeois capitalism. The consciousness of a consumer is also permeable, open to unexpected influences. An ostensibly unified text or performance may occasion contradictory associations or resistant modes of reception; no text fully determines its reader, and high and low cultures are not experienced as ontologically discontinuous realms. In this respect, however, Pinter's works seem nearer the closed forms of mass culture than the characteristic ambiguities of high modernism. On a scale of sheer intensity, Pinter's plays induce a response comparable to the most rapturous engagement with Hollywood film. Often, however, the intensity of response depends on passive submission rather than on what is commonly called audience participation. *Betrayal* creates strict parameters for the spectator, militating against the kind of active reading and critical distance often encouraged by the modernist text.

In writing about Pinter from the perspective of mass culture, one may start to feel that his work is more legible as entertainment than as art. Indeed, I think that the historical importance of his career partly lies in traversing these extremes, signalling a transition from the dialectic of modernism and mass culture to the greater cultural fluidity (or decay) of the postmodern. To give a concrete example that might be a starting point for the approach I have in mind: *Betrayal* inspired an episode of *Seinfeld*, also narrated in reverse.[46] One might initially understand this phenomenon in two ways, each suggestive of a broader attitude towards Pinter and mass culture in general. Either the *Seinfeld* adaptation is yet another sorry instance of high culture appropriated and degraded by commercial culture, or it is a perfectly appropriate tribute to the spirit of the play. I incline towards the latter view, partly because of my discomfort with those who see Pinter as a remote, intransigent high modernist – Beckett's direct descendant – and thus somehow above the popularity his works solicit and enjoy. As Pinter writes, 'In what way can one talk about one's work? I'm a writer, not a critic. When I use the word work I mean work. I regard myself as nothing more than a working man.'[47] As with many of Pinter's public pronouncements, this walks a line between the ingenuous and the disingenuous. His works strike a similarly delicate balance between mass culture and modernism, entertainment and art.

I regard Pinter as a popularizer of modernism or as a writer whose career demonstrates the theoretical problems – the internal contradictions – involved in making such a claim. Put crudely, his work occupies a historical and cultural territory somewhere between Beckett and *Seinfeld*; this intermediacy is both a defining enigma and a source of considerable appeal. Pinter's cultural status implies ambivalence with respect to the ambitions of the modern dramatist and the entertainer, the social functions of the artist and the 'working man.' *Betrayal* serves as a kind of meditation on this problematic, since it is the most commercial of Pinter's plays in substance yet one of the most radical in form. *Betrayal* encourages, then mutilates, a spectator's conventional expectations and even withholds the odd, yet (by 1978) recognizable pleasures of absurdist farce, comedy of menace, and other quasi-genres invented to familiarize the earlier Pinter.

Examined in the light of Pinter's career, the formal severity of *Betrayal* is extreme to the point of transformation. The play hints at a utopian content embedded in the regression it compels. In traditional psychoanalytic use, the concept of regression most often describes the movement, in the psychoanalytic process, from the developed self to more primitive experiences of dependence and desire. The idea is that regression allows a return to early life experiences that connect the divided self to its underlying truth or origin. An eminent psychoanalyst has recently argued against the notion that the regressed state necessarily constitutes the truth of the self. Stephen Mitchell writes that 'regression can be thought about more usefully not as movement down, into the heart of the self, but as a movement out, as an enrichment and overcoming of constraining self-organizations.'[48] In this sense, the utopian moment of *Betrayal* is not the invention of an ideologically pure form of theatrical entertainment, a return to some condition of cultural innocence. Nor does the play seek a modernist utopia, an autonomous aesthetic space radically disconnected from the marketplace. *Betrayal* sides with the revisionist understanding of regression. For Pinter as a writer and for the spectator as a cultural consumer, *Betrayal* suggests the value in overcoming 'constraining self-organizations,' a value that derives not from closure, familiarity, or resolution, but from difficult – perhaps endless – struggle.

To its final moments the struggle remains undecided, poised at a paralysing turning-point. As a kind of perverted lure, *Betrayal* ends with the mirage of pleasurable convention. As spectators, we are habitually directed to the closure of the final scene, even though we understand it to be chronologically first. When Jerry drunkenly declares his love for Emma at the party in 1968, she advises him, 'My husband is at the other side of that door.' Jerry stammers on: 'Everyone knows. The world knows. It knows. But they'll never know, they'll never know, they're in a different world. I adore you. I'm madly in love with you. I can't believe that what anyone is at this moment saying has ever happened has ever happened. Nothing has ever happened. Nothing. This is the only thing that has ever happened. Your eyes kill me. I'm lost. You're wonderful' (266–7). Few Hollywood melodramas boast such a saccharine monologue. Yet this remains one of the oddest, most pregnant moments in Pinter. Even knowing what we know about the ensuing catastrophe, this tableau, suffused with irony, still invites an exquisitely perverse shiver or thrill, as at the first blush of a new romance. To accept, to yield to the pull of convention, or to abandon the immediacy of feeling for the high ground of irony – this is the cultural predicament in which *Betrayal* entraps its audience.

CHAPTER THREE

Towards the Postmodern

After the high modernist period of 1958–65 it is tempting to divide
Pinter's plays into categories, though the pattern of development is
fluid and recursive rather than linear. There emerges an ensemble of
motifs and repeated concerns that circulate and recombine in various
ways as his career moves forward. Nonetheless, it would not be far off
to say that the two most important clusters of later works are the memory plays of the 1970s and the political plays of the 1980s and early
1990s. Though there are obvious differences between the two cycles,
they might be understood as components of a single process. What the
later works share is an aura of extremity and crisis, with rigorous antisocial withdrawal marking the first cycle and rigorous political
engagement marking the second. In retrospect, the opposition between
these diametric pulls appears dialectical. Indeed, issues of memory
and politics explored in Pinter's works of the 1970s and 1980s achieve
a kind of Hegelian synthesis in *Ashes to Ashes* (1996), to which I return
at the end of the chapter. In the light of this complex interplay of forces,
I think it is crucial to underscore the idea of *process*. As I have argued,
Pinter's career reflects an ongoing series of responses to the dilemmas
of late modernism. In the oscillating extremity of his later writings
Pinter shares the agitated spirit of British drama during the period,
though characteristically, he often seems to swim against the prevailing current. Yet Pinter and his contemporaries could be said to inhabit
the same postmodern moment, to the extent that there is in many quarters a growing self-consciousness about the problem of cultural production, an increasingly radical questioning of the relation of art to the
social world.

The postmodern moment is marked by aesthetic hybridity. With growing reflexivity, works advertise their own constructed-ness. Such postmodern works often come across as provisional and fragmentary; they openly cannibalize and reflect upon older forms and styles. With old bottles no longer adequate for the new wine, the artist must seek new vessels. *Form* becomes an increasingly central concern. In particular, the hermetic autonomy of the artwork, which the high modernist moment presupposed, is suddenly rendered problematic. The monolithic integrity and insularity of *The Homecoming* – the magisterial sense of an entire world willed into being – is transformed in Pinter's plays written after 1970. Instead, in a play like *No Man's Land* (1975), the autonomy of art is thematized as a morbid withdrawal from the world. The play depicts the artist as an old man, drinking away his last days in isolation. The utopian spark of modernist art – the negation of what exists that arises from the creation of alternative space – is here rendered as a kind of narrow, ineffectual solipsism. *No Man's Land* functions as a meditation on modernism, and the tone of elegy is again sounded, eighteen years later, in the postmodern *Moonlight* (1993), which was Pinter's first full-length play since *Betrayal* (1978). While *No Man's Land* dramatizes the death of hermetic art, *Moonlight* juxtaposes earlier formal and thematic preoccupations in a fractured postmodern pastiche. In between, of course, Pinter's work had rejected autonomous modernism in a different way, through the equivocal realism of the short political plays. These plays are essentially fragmentary. They function as local interventions, as quick jabs to society's midsection. They embrace a much different understanding of the social function of art than did the plays of Pinter's high modernist period.

Examined in this way, Pinter's career is uniquely well suited to tell us about the twilight of modernism. The modernity to which the phrase 'modern drama' refers is increasingly remote, and consequently historiography acquires a new urgency. The vocabulary of postmodernism suggests that the sands have shifted. The 'modern condition' is no longer self-evident; the old structures of feeling, to borrow Raymond Williams's phrase, no longer precisely obtain. Poised near the endpoint of the modern canon, Pinter's career provides an exemplary nexus for dramatic historiography. From this standpoint, the dialectic of memory and politics in the later plays is one of the most novel and valuable features of Pinter's work.

The memory plays: Pinter among the radicals

It is not the office of art to spotlight alternatives, but to resist by its form alone
the course of the world, which permanently puts a pistol to men's heads.

T.W. Adorno[1]

In a play littered with provocative formulations and epigrams – Pinter's
Old Times (1971) – it is easy to overlook one offhanded, suggestive
speech. Late in Act 1 the glib, increasingly desperate Deeley attempts to
impress his wife's old friend Anna: 'My work concerns itself with life all
over, you see, in every part of the globe. With people all over the globe.
I use the word globe because the word world possesses emotional political sociological and psychological pretensions and resonances which I
prefer as a matter of choice to do without, or shall I say to steer clear of,
or if you like to reject.'[2] In contrast to the play's most-quoted line –
Anna's 'There are some things one remembers even though they may
never have happened' (27–8), often considered an epigraph for Pinter's
memory plays in general – Deeley's speech might seem tangential. But
I would suggest that it provides a clue in deciphering the memory plays.
What is one to make of Pinter's inward turn in the 1970s, the decade in
which British theatre was being so noisily radicalized? There are certainly biographical explanations,[3] but we can also refer the question
back to Pinter's liminal modernism. What Deeley enunciates is a repudiation of social consciousness, a refusal of the public sphere. In mystifying fashion, the word 'globe' here stresses nature rather than history.
Just as a spinning globe can be enchanting – the magically self-given
Earth, the ant-like smallness of individual life, the reassuring sense of
universality – so too does Deeley's preference express ahistorical retreat.

'World,' by contrast, retains a sense of human agency, of struggle
and process. We might then understand the 'pretensions and resonances' that Deeley rejects as shorthand for politics itself. Similarly, I
think the memory plays need to be understood relationally in the context of British political theatre of the 1970s. What these plays refuse is
in some sense as significant as what they embrace. A play like *Old
Times* documents a crisis; it functions as a critique of socially committed art and also of meaning-making in general. Here, we return to the
idea of *negation* as a formative principle in Pinter's work. What is new
in the memory plays is what we might tentatively call an emergent

psychoanalytic dimension. We see Pinter centrally interested in problems of subjectivity, temporality, and human agency – the term 'memory,' I think, condenses these three areas of concern.

It would be a mistake, however, to overhastily segregate these works from Pinter's plays of the 1960s and 1980s; they should be not bracketed as purely subjectivist or exempted from social analysis. Just as the Freud of *Civilization and its Discontents* unexpectedly laid the blame for repression at the feet of society, I would argue that the memory plays retain a negative, critical relation to the social. In subtle ways, they anticipate the 1980s plays' more literal revelation of a key Pinter subject: the banality of barbarism and the barbarity of the banal (as mentioned above, *Ashes to Ashes* provides an interesting fusion of the memory and the political plays). The memory plays depict, first and foremost, a violence done to the experience of time, a temporal fragmentation that can be examined historically.

To approach the question of temporality obliquely, I think the first thing to notice about *Old Times* is its foregrounding of language and accompanying devaluation of space. Pinter's earlier works preserve a sense of temporal continuity – albeit often the empty temporality of waiting – by being anchored in densely particular spaces. In *Old Times*, by contrast, gone is the semiotically charged object-world of plays such as *The Caretaker* and *The Homecoming*. Instead, we are confronted with '*Spare modern furniture. Two sofas. An armchair*' (2). We are immediately aware of a principle of abstraction, a sense reinforced by the bedroom setting of Act 2, in which '*The divans and armchair are disposed in precisely the same relation to each other as the furniture in the first act, but in reversed positions*' (43). This is – to borrow a term from film studies[4] – a 'structural' play, whose specific subject-matter is refracted by formal experiment. The action, then, takes place in a kind of linguistic no-place, a space that feels abstract and schematic.

The minimalist, symmetrical settings form the ground of a recursive, fragmentary, contradictory narrative. A married couple, Deeley and Kate, receive a visit from Anna, an old friend of Kate whom she has not seen in twenty years. The three take turns rehashing the past in overlapping, often conflicting reminiscences. Deeley and Anna struggle to define the enigmatic and seemingly indifferent Kate, but finally, in a long, strange monologue, Kate appears to marginalize the others and reassert her identity. In circular fashion, the play concludes with a pantomime (Deeley lies across Kate's lap) that re-enacts an event the characters had remembered from twenty years earlier.

In Michael Billington's words, the play's ambiguity has 'led to end-less speculation among commentators. Is Anna really present or is she simply a figment of Deeley's and Kate's imaginations? Are Kate and Anna ... separate characters or dual aspects of the same woman? Are all three characters dead and merely re-experiencing some past meeting?'[5] This profusion of ontological questions suggests that we are dealing with a play constructed in accordance with what Freud calls 'primary process,' the bizarre combinatory logic of the unconscious in which 'cathexes can easily be completely transferred, displaced and con-densed.'[6] Similarly, there is an undigested, imagistic quality to *Old Times* that teasingly disobeys principles of truth and falsity, fact and contra-diction. Freud writes of dreams that the way in which they 'treat the cat-egory of contraries and contradictions is highly remarkable. It is simply disregarded. "No" seems not to exist so far as dreams are concerned.'[7] Likewise, as Anna indicates above, memory can also wilfully disregard contradiction. Memory is constructive rather than mimetic, and thus all versions of events in *Old Times* are marked as equally plausible.

To the extent that the play succeeds it does so not through narrative coherence but rather by engaging the spectator at the level of primary process. *Old Times* is a play about an elemental triadic structure, one rich in psychoanalytic associations. It dramatizes the problem of the 'third,' a person or psychic object that interferes with the desire for an unmediated relation between self and other. This desire mobilizes a regressive fantasy of return to the supposed unmediated plenitude of the relation between mother and infant. It is thus an Oedipal play, in the sense that it depicts the necessary splitting and frustration of desire that is the precondition of the formation of a 'normal,' that is, re-pressed, human subject. It is also a Lacanian play, insofar as the 'third' here is connected to the problem of language (which in Lacan is a cru-cial 'third' – the Law of the Father, the field of force that inaugurates the subject's movement from the comparative plenitude of the pre-linguistic into the alienating realm of the symbolic).

Indeed, I would suggest that the play is fundamentally about lan-guage, or what we might call the textuality of the remembered self. We are alerted to constructive power of language through the escalating verbal competition between Deeley and Anna, who engage in conver-sational struggle to fix meanings and to regulate the reticent Kate's identity. Often this struggle is conveyed through winking and light remarks, such as Deeley's reactions to Anna's use of mannered words like 'lest' ('Haven't heard it for a long time' [15]) and 'gaze' ('Don't hear it very often' [22]), and to her assertion that she finds England 'rather beguilingly' damp ('What the hell does she mean by that' [37]). Yet the light banter occasionally grows disturbing, as in their semi-competitive singing of lines from torch songs. Two or three well-chosen snatches of song can be suavely theatrical and ingratiating; on the other hand, eighteen ('Blue moon, I see you standing alone'/'The way you comb your hair'/'Oh no they can't take that away from me'/ etc. [22]) can begin to seem disconcertingly fragmentary.

The song lyrics are metonyms for the other small patches of language, image, and memory by which the text of the self is constructed. The singing acquires a mechanical, Ionesco-like quality. In post-structuralist terms, the words seem to speak the characters rather than the other way round. At one moment the quiet Kate, who is being remembered by Anna and Deeley, says 'You talk of me as if I were dead' (30), which underscores the morbidity of the self being 'spoken.' Kate turns the tables at the end of the play, when she effectively erases Anna by saying 'I remember you dead' (67) and by accusing Anna of stealing her 'little slow smile' (68). Kate's erasure of Anna culminates in the play's final lines: '[Deeley] asked me once, at about that time, who had slept in that [Anna's] bed before him. I told him no one. No one at all' (69). Anna – ostensibly the dominant partner in her relationship with Kate – turns out to be a kind of sponge, an appropriator of her friend's attributes. Kate's final speech causes Anna to adopt a deathly position by lying down and Deeley to sob and then act submissively towards Kate. Both Anna and Deeley ultimately appear spectral, their silence suggesting that language is a thin, inadequate veneer.

Indeed, though she appears in the strongest position at the conclusion, Kate is little more than a cipher herself. Though the credibility of the accounts is open to question, Kate is variously described as incurious, sleepy, and inward, a lover of solitary walks and long baths. She is prone to vacant pronouncements such as 'I was interested once in the arts, but I can't remember now which ones they were' (33). Given the ephemeral nature of all the characters, one is left to wonder whether the nostalgic evocation of bohemian post-war London is intended to convey an authentic ethos or whether we should regard it, instead, as a pastiche of cultural signifiers, a constructed faux memory mediated by cultural cliches.

Generalizing from all the textual fragments through which the characters negotiate their identities and relationships, one could say that the play functions as a critique of subjectivity. It underscores the degree to which the self is socially positioned as a subject through language and other cultural codes. Louis Althusser's term is 'interpellation,' which refers to the symbolic processes that falsely reassure us of our integral, meaningful relationship to the social totality.[8] Culture is a powerful force of integration, since it binds the individual to the social order in deep and often unconscious ways. Culture becomes a language through which we triangulate our relations to others and shore up our sense of self-coherence. The exchange of song lyrics demonstrates the imaginary nature of such relations, as do the spectral characters. The song lyrics lead us to suspect the many references to galleries, plays, poetry, locales, cafes, and films as so many meaningless cultural citations.

Set against the veneer of discourse and cultural signifiers are the play's many references to sexuality, which initially would seem to hold some promise of authentic human connection. On the basis of these references, one might be tempted to use sexuality to distinguish between a textual and an embodied self, the latter perhaps pointing a way past the play's reactionary stasis. But the play's portrait of sexuality likewise seems inauthentic, culturally mediated, and heavy with anxiety. One of the first details Kate recalls is that Anna used to steal her underwear. Over time, Kate encouraged her roommate to borrow from her underwear collection, and it is reported that Anna returned from social engagements to graphically recount her adventures in Kate's underwear. Extending this thread, Deeley later claims that he and Anna knew each other twenty years earlier, and he describes a party during which he looked up Anna's skirt. When Anna subsequently echoes this memory, she reveals that she was wearing Kate's underwear, which leads Deeley to say, 'Looking up *your* skirt in *her* underwear. Mmnn' (61).

How is one to interpret this chain of associations? The imagery suggests a stunted, adolescent, and prurient version of sexuality. The exchange of underwear reads like a young man's fantasy about the behaviour of female roommates, and likewise the play as a whole circles around lesbian desire without ever fully depicting it. It is as though the women's relationship had been partially rewritten by Deeley's unconscious, and the result is fraught with regressive aggression and anxiety. Underwear is, of course, a fctish-object par excellence, and the play's fixation on this item suggests that Deeley's look up Anna's skirt is a source of castration fear rather than actual desire. Similarly, the titillating banter between Deeley and Anna about Kate's love of long baths, towelling procedure, baby powder, and moisture is lascivious and crude. Moreover, the exchange remains all talk, since no physical contact with Kate takes place; again, language displaces the body. Ironically, the most erotic – as opposed to prurient – moment in the play is probably Kate's exclamation, 'Aaahh' (53), as she emerges from her bath.

This rather idealized suggestion of auto-eroticism might be interpreted as an alternative to the brutish, menacing conception of sexuality to which Deeley gives voice. Early in the play, recounting a trip to the cinema, he unexpectedly relates that 'there were two usherettes standing in the foyer and one of them was stroking her breasts and the other one was saying "dirty bitch" and the one stroking her breasts was saying "mmnnn" with a very sensual relish and smiling at her fellow usherette' (25). From the standpoint of primary process, the setting of this implausible fantasy in the foyer of a cinema is suggestive. The fantasy is the pornographic version of Deeley's conception of Kate and Anna's relationship, but like his preoccupation with underwear, the cinema fantasy rings false. The iconography of the fantasy seems borrowed from some adolescent's understanding of porn stereotypes. The swaggering 'dirtiness' of the anecdote expresses fear rather than machismo.

Michael Billington writes, 'Through the character of Deeley, who gradually disintegrates from a suave inquisitor into someone who is coarse, brutal and terrified, [*Old Times*] also becomes a play about the pathos of male insecurity.'[9] From Deeley's standpoint, we might say that the underwear, the usherettes, and Kate's bath fall on a single continuum, one marked by an inability to imagine female sexuality in other than fearful terms. In this sense, Kate's bath does not represent authentic female auto-eroticism, but rather is an idealization of female 'cleanliness' that compensates for the threatening 'dirtiness' of the usherettes. In any case, as a sexual paradigm, the auto-eroticism of the bath entails complete withdrawal from sexual contact with others to the point of monadic isolation. From the standpoint of the patriarchal unconscious, the bath represents a panicked, fantasized regression to pregenital sexuality, here overlaid with an idealization of the woman/ mother's body – scrupulously clean and purged (through Deeley's obsession with towelling) of all unwanted 'moisture.'

We begin to perceive the thoroughness and rigour of the play's negation, its unwillingness to mark any alternative conceptual space. Sexuality is implicated in the play's fundamental crisis, which I would say,

in psychoanalytic terms, is a crisis of relation. What begins as a dramatization of a couple's collective unconscious – the tissue of memory,
fantasy, and ideation that both binds and separates the dyad – comes to
resemble the clinical *mise en scène* of psychoanalysis and thus those primal relations that analysis seeks to restage. Anna, in this sense, could
be understood in the light of what Thomas Ogden calls the 'analytic
third.' Ogden writes that this term refers to 'a third subject, uncon-
sciously co-created by analyst and analysand, which seems to take on a
life of its own in the interpersonal field between analyst and patient.
This third subject stands in dialectical tension with the separate, individual subjectivities of analyst and analysand in such a way that the
individual subjectivities and the third create, negate, and preserve one
another.'[10]

The analytic scenario also provides a way of thinking about the
play's temporality. The stark, minimalist furniture begins to suggest an
analyst's office, an impression reinforced by the supine postures of
Deeley and Anna at the play's conclusion. Analytic time is not linear
time; analysis is often repetitive, recursive, regressive. *Old Times* manages to catch the sensation of this temporal mode by carefully eroding
the stability of the present tense. The play begins with Deeley and Kate
discussing Anna before her expected arrival, but disconcertingly, Anna
is already standing at the window, which suggests her perpetual presence. Twice, Anna and Kate begin to converse as their former selves,
and Kate's bath is an activity that belongs as much to the past as to the
present. In effect, *Old Times* functions as an extended psychoanalysis of
domestic drama, questioning this drama's faith in causality and linearity, grimly unearthing its sexual repressions, and exposing the tenu-
ousness of the identities on which it depends.

Beyond this psychoanalytic resonance, I would suggest that the
play's temporality has a social dimension as well. The final tableau is
strongly reminiscent of Sartre's *No Exit*, and *Old Times* seems touched
by the social world of 1971 just as Sartre's hell was ambiguously –
though palpably – shaped by the Paris of 1944. The connection is
admittedly faint in Pinter's case, but without some social commentary
it is difficult to explain the play's references to Carol Reed's film *Odd
Man Out* (1947). This detail is marked as a sort of key, since it is a lonely
point of explicit cultural reference. Reed's film, which contains an
uneasy mixture of character-driven melodrama, episodic naturalism,
and political intrigue, depicts the adventures of an escaped IRA operative (James Mason) on the run from the police. Whatever else the refer-

ence may signify, it functions as an allusion to a problematic, pseudo-political artwork. The film appropriates the politically charged context of Northern Ireland and the Irish Republican Army in service of an individualistic narrative heavy with psychological and allegorical overtones. Moreover, in the context of 1971 Britain, the film's political content is further estranged by historical distance.

Odd Man Out would seem to be a signifier of the impossibility of political art, or, to phrase it differently, of the usurpation of politics by culture. The reference to the film completes the veneer of cultural references and textuality by suggesting that the ability to know and to act upon society is undermined both by the psychoanalytic crisis of the subject and by the increasingly total veil of culture. This estrangement from social consciousness and action is compounded by the crisis in the experience of time, which – from Marx to Fredric Jameson – has been identified both as a symptom of capitalist society and as a force that inhibits political struggle and radical change. Writing in the 1920s, the Marxist philosopher Georg Lukács argued that under capitalism, 'time sheds its qualitative, variable, flowing nature; it freezes into an exactly delimited, quantifiable continuum filled with quantifiable "things" (the reified, mechanically objectified "performance" of the worker, wholly separated from his total human personality): in short, it becomes space.'[11]

What *Old Times* depicts is spatialized time, time congealed into *mise en scène*. Experience is reified as memory, as language, and as cultural fragment, and the resulting text is a frozen assemblage of parts rather than an organic, temporally unfolding sequence. One could then say that memory is the opposite of praxis, which presupposes a unity of action and thought. Memory is the disunity of action and thought, or more precisely the displacement of action by thought. In this sense we could say that aesthetically and philosophically, memory in Pinter works as an exact negation of the premises of political theatre, which seeks to link the aesthetic and the political and to merge intellectual and social activity.

Old Times reflects an extreme, crisis-ridden form of autonomous modernism, which makes for an instructive comparison with British socialist theatre of the 1970s. This comparison can be mapped against the dialectic of autonomy and commitment. Champions of autonomous art, such as Adorno, felt the aesthetic to be an oasis of comparative freedom besieged by a hostile reality principle. Art's necessary distance from the world is the source of its critical power but also of its marginality. Both the committed and autonomous tendencies can be understood as reactions to this predicament, the first seeking to annihilate the distance and the second to embrace it. In the epigraph above, Adorno argues that art should resist the social world 'by its form alone,' and though the memory plays comply with this directive, they do so in a self-critical manner.

A sense of cultural crisis infects both the memory plays and the socialist drama. The variety of British drama in the 1970s shows the antinomies of modernism at a symptomatic point of decay. Indeed, historically speaking, British theatre between 1956 and roughly 1980 constitutes one of the most vital periods in modern drama. Yet the analysis of this period sometimes resorts to narrow categories or single figures (socialist drama, the 'angry young man,' Pinter, Stoppard, etc.) instead of grappling with the heterogeneity of the situation. In particular, Pinter's evolution has often been held separate from the various working-class, then socialist, dramatic forms that emerged following John Osborne's *Look Back in Anger* in 1956. Pinter seems apart from a radical genealogy that extends from John Osborne to Edward Bond, John McGrath, Trevor Griffiths, David Hare, Howard Brenton, and Caryl Churchill. Yet the paucity of comparative analysis in itself does not establish a qualitative differentiation between, for example, the 1970s work of Pinter, Brenton, and Churchill. In the wake of Pinter's political cycle of the 1980s, the altered critical gaze cast on the politics of the earlier works suggests new ways of conceptualizing Pinter's relation to an increasingly politicized British theatre.

At first glance, one might think that such a comparison would yield a useful historical montage – what Walter Benjamin calls a 'dialectical image' – of radical culture and hermetic modernism interlocked in a time of political impasse. At first glance, a play like *No Man's Land* appears to embody a 'determinate negation' (Adorno's phrase for the process and power of autonomous works)[12] of the subject matter and formal proclivities of socialist drama. Under a microscope, however, the purity of the opposition is hard to maintain. In both the memory plays and socialist drama, committed and autonomous impulses circulate and combine in uneasy syntheses. The memory plays and their radical contemporaries are fraught with contradictions. On the one hand, *No Man's Land* can be read as a 'refusal' (to borrow a favoured 1960s term) of the public sphere and the tolerated radicalism of political theatre. Politically, however, this is an opaque gesture; what is refused is not the 'administered society' vilified by 1960s radicals but the institutionalized radical culture of the 1970s. Pinter taps the energies of autonomous modernism in order to resist this cultural situation. At the same time, one is obliged to recall the odd fact that this chill, distant play was one of Pinter's biggest popular successes. Despite its autonomous tendencies, No Man's Land subtly reaffirms the idea of art as a social fact.

At the other end of the spectrum, it is soon clear that the eruption of political drama in the 1970s was not a direct expression of dawning political consciousness but instead a noisy aesthetic withdrawal in the face of an encroaching and counter-revolutionary reality. The plays are sublimated political struggle, compensation for an abandoned fight. It is no coincidence that socialist theatre in England flourished not at the height of 1960s radicalism but during the decade of disintegration and decline in the aftermath of 1968. Thus, it is difficult to sustain any monolithic conception of British socialist theatre of the 1970s, since the 'movement' was in fact a patchwork of varied and sometimes opposed constituencies. Moreover, the apparent incommensurability of Pinter's work and the socialist paradigm reflects only the surface of a fluid cultural situation in which prominent figures frequently changed stripes.

The socialist theatre of this period radiates self-conscious disorder and heterodoxy. In a seminal essay, 'The Language of Crisis in British Theatre: The Drama of Cultural Pathology,' C.W.E. Bigsby frames the contradictions of political theatre as a crisis in language. Bigsby begins by reiterating the now-standard position that the social realism of the period 1956–68 was, in fact, naïvely mimetic, nostalgic, and even reactionary in character. 'Surely only in England,' he writes, 'could it be thought revolutionary to write about working-class characters in a naturalistic way.'[13] The real politicizing of British theatre occurs only between the late 1960s and the mid-1970s, by which time its utopian ambitions had proved unattainable. Even as it developed, the brief flowering of this drama acknowledged its own impermanence in relation to a larger cultural crisis. Within the Left, the ambivalent legacy of May 1968, images of brutal suppression in the Communist world, and the changing landscape of British politics all began to erode belief in the efficacy of political art.

Moreover, social and cultural contexts rendered political drama problematic during its brief renaissance. From the perspective of educational and class background, for example, most of the writers in this ostensibly new movement were members of the same Oxbridge intellectual elite that had dominated culture and politics in Britain for most of the century. Bigsby suggests that consciously or not, these Oxbridge alumni inherited a peculiarly British conception of literacy and self-articulation as the ideals of artistic expression, a cultural tendency with important political implications. In other words, British theatre was well prepared for a political art grounded in the belief that language can rationally document the realities of social decay; the result was an emergent 'drama of cultural pathology.' One consequence of the necessary faith in language is the diminution of ambiguity. Bigsby argues: '[socialist] playwrights require a transparent language, a clear glass through which to observe social realities. That this is a naive view of language matters less than the fact that it produces a denial of imaginative depth to experience ... Ambiguity is not a virtue, mystery has no place, an unconfident deconstructing art becomes a denial rather than an expression of human reality. Communication cannot be seen as problematic, since it is the *sine qua non* of committed art.'[14]

In practice, however, the 'clear glass' required by socialist drama leads to a number of contradictions associated with the committed tendency. Many plays seek to expose linguistic, social, and discursive instruments of repression and control – a conflicted gesture, in that a language deployed for purposes of domination can also, in the words of a properly motivated playwright, truthfully disclose the reality of this domination. A political reality enforced through discourse can be accurately illumined by discourse. Aesthetic mediations and transformations evaporate; art becomes indistinguishable from social or political knowledge. The notion that an unjust and coercive world can be fully decoded by rational analysis and that drama is an unproblematic venue for this analysis is an implicit article of faith. Caryl Churchill's *Softcops*, for example – written in 1978 but not produced until 1984 – reads like a primer for Foucault's *Discipline and Punish*, an influence Churchill acknowledges in an introductory note. The play, set in nineteenth-century Paris, focuses on new forms of policing and punishment. As Churchill writes: 'There is a constant attempt by governments to depoliticise illegal acts, to make criminals a separate class from the rest of society so that subversion will not be general, and part of this process is the invention of the detective and the criminal, the cop and the robber.' The play opens with Pierre, a liberal reformer, attempting a series of spectacular public executions as a means of inculcating moral responsibility. After a riot, however, Vidocq, a former criminal and archetype of the modern detective, argues: 'It's not what the punishment is ... it's knowing you're going to get it.'[15] The correct police method, according to Vidocq, is developing networks of informers, cataloging known offenders, infiltrating illegal organizations, and ensuring that criminals are caught.

The arc of the play is Pierre's conversion to Bentham's panopticon as the most efficient model of social organization. Punishment is superseded by the internalization of established norms through the constant fear that the unseen prison guard is watching. Following Foucault's famous analysis in *Discipline and Punish*, Churchill seems to regard the panopticon as an emblem of the linkage between power and knowledge in the modern state, where surveillance is an extension of instrumental reason to the control of human beings. Social phenomena are separated, classified, and restructured via disciplinary models until the social totality resembles an apparatus or machine. As a consequence, liberation in the play is only figured ironically in the image of the chain gang, whose physical enslavement frees them to dance together, berate their captors, and sing about breaking the chains. This utopian projection carries a hint of nostalgia for an era of visible, naked domination. The implication is that the fissures in the repressive social totality have long been sealed. It is increasingly difficult to know what or how to resist, since the machinery of 'soft' control is now ubiquitous and unseen.

In the present context, I would stress that in its biting critique of the irrationality of rational social engineering, the play uses a 'glass' that is demonstrably more coloured than the clear one that Bigsby describes. Churchill's use of transparent, discursive language gives way, at certain moments, to a more poetic sensibility. Here, one senses social reality striving towards full expression in a language that is transforming and artistic rather than conceptual. The naïve conception of reality that Bigsby views as the Achilles heel of socialist drama is unexpectedly complicated by the production of a new aesthetic value whose cognitive status is unclear but that the play nonetheless posits as a kind of social truth. Consider Pierre's description of the panoptic society: 'The criminals are supervised. The insane are cured. The sick are normalised. The workers are registered. The unemployed are educated. The ignorant are punished. No. I'll need to rehearse this a little. The ignorant are normalised. Right. The sick are punished. The insane are educated. The workers are cured. The criminals are cured. The unemployed are punished. The criminals are normalised. Something along those lines.'[16] In metonymic shorthand, the slips in who is to be educated, supervised, normalized, registered, punished, and cured gesture at the full evocation of an unfree world. Pierre's rhetoric serves as a crystallization of larger forces. Cognitively, this kind of knowledge depends on symbolic rather than logical operations. The speech is a form of parody anchored in socially committed dramaturgy, a modernist approach that emphasizes ironic distance rather than unproblematic mimesis. As any admirer of Churchill would point out, she is working in a different mode than the naïvely mimetic model of verbal theatre outlined in Bigsby's argument. In fact, this model is most useful in measuring degrees of variation; almost all the most notorious plays of the period openly diverge from or at least complicate the norm. In Bigsby's reading, such variations signal the emergence of a more equivocal sensibility, with a new insistence on ambiguity, contradiction, and the supple relationship between theatre and language. Undermining the rational, pedagogic gesture is a sense of dislocation, 'disintegration,' and 'the contingency ... and even destructively deceptive ... nature of language.'[17] For Bigsby, the demise of socialist drama was the result of the restrictive inadequacy of its linguistic model.

I would take Bigsby one step further and argue that a common, fundamental tension in socialist theatre is its reliance on imaginary resolutions of unresolved social contradictions, to modify a phrase from Fredric Jameson. As a kind of post-1968 despair settles over the theatrical Left, small utopian gestures are increasingly sewn into the rhetoric of the plays. The breakdown of earlier forms of mimetic rationalism documented by Bigsby often leads – via a grand displacement – to a vindication of individual style, artistic vision, and the formal power to project the aesthetic truth of objective social conditions that defy rational explanation. This gesture takes various forms, but it typically resorts to epigrams, bons mots, slogans, witty formulations, and at the other extreme, spectacle, imagery, utopianism, and moments of theatrical tour de force. Moreover, gestures that 'solve' social dilemmas by aesthetic means are late symptoms of the underlying conflict between committed and autonomous tendencies. In this sense, the socialist plays are consistent with the modernist realization that art can never fully square the social circle. Political art always functions as a commentary on the intractable problem of aesthetics and politics, even where it feigns resolution. Artistic commitment entails heightened consciousness of the distance between art and unwanted reality, a distance that the committed seek to annul by foregrounding the materiality of their art and equating performance with concrete social praxis. The social frames the aesthetic, not the other way round. Against this

backdrop, one notices the countervailing return in British socialist theatre to a poetic or spectacular sensibility that presents intermittent
flashes of aesthetic intensity as a kind of historical truth.

The importation of the ad hoc aesthetics of Situationism is a significant case in point. A small, primarily Continental subset of 1960s anar-
chism guided by the work of Guy Debord and others, Situationism
placed media society at the centre of the state's self-perpetuation.
Accordingly, disruptions at the site of cultural rather than capital production were taken as the most strategic form of resistance. This
emphasis on 'The Society of the Spectacle' (the title of Debord's 1967
book)[18] provided a fertile point of departure for British playwrights,
downplaying as it did the laborious business of mobilizing the prole-
tariat in favour of an aesthetic of spectacular disruption. The playwright David Edgar soberly writes: 'Revolutionary politics was seen as
being much less about the organisation of the working class at the
point of production, and much more about the disruption of bourgeois
ideology at the point of consumption,'[19] or, to quote the more titillating
title of a 1975 interview with Howard Brenton, 'Petrol Bombs through
the Proscenium Arch.'[20]

Situationism concedes, even embraces, the commingling of aesthetics and politics in the commodity world and from within this scenario
divines a revolutionary approach to both politics and art. This is a
postmodernist fantasy, an end to the tortuous mediations and
estrangements of modernism, which are magically superseded in the
false immediacy of a kind of counter-spectacle. Situationism answered
Sartre's question 'Why write?' in a manner appropriate to the television age. The dilemma of the committed writer's relation to reality
could be rewritten in purely aesthetic terms, since the ideological 'reality' of commercial culture itself was an aesthetic construction. The contradictions of this position are evident in its slogans. Brenton, whose
muscular epigrams are often taken as typical of the movement, said in
a 1975 interview that after the failure of alternative culture, committed
theatre must use the tools at hand, 'bloody and stained but realistic. I
mean communist tools. Not pleasant.'[21] Here, the invocation of realism
equates theatrical techniques with the ostensible authenticity of the
stained 'instruments' of the world, presumably borrowed from the
communist east. The final phrase, 'Not pleasant,' simultaneously indicts bourgeois theatre-going expectations and ominously suggests, by
understatement, that an unpleasant night at the theatre is akin to
bloody revolution. The figural form is extended promiscuous interplay

between the political and the aesthetic, with the final intercourse poeti-
cally promised yet deferred.

Gestures of this sort signal a dual crisis in the representation of politics and the politics of representation. Revolution becomes rhetoric;
wordplay displaces political struggle. Brenton's epigram expresses a
fantasized identity between theatre and world, an end to artistic distance in a society that insistently aestheticized the political. Similarly,
many socialist plays of the period are desperate, contradictory, self-
reflexive attempts to theorize and practice political art amid a cultural
situation that had collapsed the distance between art and politics. Revolutionary failure is a frequent motif, evoking a sense of obsolescence
that anticipates the political climate after 1980. Brenton's plays, for
example, are hybrids of politics and spectacle, will and resignation,
utopianism and despair. His *Weapons of Happiness* (1976) takes revolutionary struggle as an explicit theme by dramatizing the temporary
occupation of a potato-chip factory by a group of disaffected young
workers, and their subsequent flight to Wales. The key figure, however, is Frank, based on an actual Czech communist official who was
imprisoned and hanged for treason. Frank inhabits a physical and discursive space separate from his working-class English comrades. The
play opens with his address to the audience: 'I don't sleep. I walk
about London. So many people, sleeping. Around you. For miles. After
so many years, it is better to be tired. Not to think or remember. Ten
million, asleep, around you, is warm. The ignorant English, like a
warm overcoat. About me. It is better. While in the nightmare of the
dark all the dogs of Europe bark.'[22] After the monologue, the play
abruptly moves to more familiar ground: the discontented banter of
young workers on their lunch break in the factory yard. In the opening
minutes, two narratives begin. The first is the story of the historical
Frank, recounted in a series of flashbacks to his encounter with Stalin,
his time in prison, and his defiant death in front of a Russian tank in
Prague in 1968. The second, more realist narrative explores the relationship between Frank and Janice (the unofficial leader of the workers), the subsequent factory occupation, and finally, in another abrupt
shift of register, the flight to the countryside of Wales.

The two stories are linked by Frank, who is associated with ageing,
sickness, exhaustion, boils, bad breath, torture, and rotting refuse. In
the play's symbolic economy, his physical degeneration functions as an
imprint of violence but also as a source of wisdom and hope. Brenton
uses a poetics of the body to indicate both decay and transformation.

The unpleasant factory occupation, for example, is manifestly ineffective while serving as a kind of necessary political education. It is only after this period of suffering – vividly described in terms of urine, faeces, acne, potato-chip grease, sweat, and vomit – that the play is dislocated from repressive industrial London to the open-ended pastoral space of rural Wales. The dual aspect of Frank's bodily degradation is developed through his role as revolutionary educator. Superficially, his experience with the reality of the communist state is insistently juxtaposed with the political naïveté of the young revolutionaries. In this sense, Frank indicts the petty, anarchistic factory takeover by indicating a more properly Marxist conception of class struggle. Further, in contrast to the naïve workers, for whom 'there in't no history,'[23] Frank signifies historical guilt. He embodies the decay of present-day Britain, which remains hidden to the 'sleeping' English and the young revolutionaries, for whom decay is merely the symbol of advancing age. Finally, Frank reflects a fundamental ambivalence about the adequacy of 'communist tools,' as he offers visible evidence of the misery and failure of Stalinism.

Despite the misguided youthfulness that marks the factory occupation, the relationship of Janice and Frank hints at authentic radical consciousness and non-alienated experience. Initially Janice, who has 'read' Lenin, is presented as the most politically educated of the group. Clearly, however, she is drawn to communism as a sexy form of anarchist heroism, which provides a convenient and gratifying rationale for her own wilful, thrill-seeking behaviour. As the play develops, she is increasingly drawn to the sick, decaying figure of Frank, who remains physically repulsive to her comrades. Finally, she is willing to touch, kiss, and even copulate with Frank's body. It is only after this encounter that Janice attains the status of revolutionary. In Wales, in the play's final scene, she assumes control of the group, arguing that they should relocate to Manchester, because 'it's the city we know'; her last line, in response to the question of who Frank was, is to reply, without irony: 'He was a Communist.'[24] The implication is that communism is not a closed dogmatic system, but rather a philosophical style. For Janice, only when communism is disentangled from Leninist orthodoxy and anarchist adventure does the term acquire genuine, dialectical meaning.

The shortcomings of *Weapons of Happiness* are exemplary. The final tableau – a small, tentative collective, grasping at an uncertain future – is a familiar image in Brenton. The play imposes a false image of redemption, aware of its inadequacy, as a strategic gesture of frustration or defiance towards the unresolved contradictions of commitment. The tone is something like repressed hope, or, alternatively, utopian despair. The angst of imperfect revolution is characteristic of radical drama in the period. It is, ultimately, a sentimental gesture, which displaces anxieties about political struggle by immersion in a feeling-tone. Throughout the play, Brenton seeks to reinvent the terms of political debate in accordance with aesthetic principles. The body is a semiotic convenience expressing history, repression, immediacy, transformation, and recovery, depending on the point of view. The model of political education is also legible as conventional melodrama or coming-of-age narrative. Finally, the cryptic, melancholy treatment of Frank's communism is an aesthetic contrivance designed to evoke the spectre of 'real' political struggle by dubious recourse to a kind of Marxian pathos.

Brenton resurrects a modernist aesthetic in conflict with the realism that committed drama initially demanded. This return of the repressed in the radical theatre provides a useful point of return to Pinter's work. As socialist playwrights began to temper social analysis with ambiguity and reflexivity, Pinter continued to explore problems of indeterminacy in relation to the self, time, and human relationships. It is interesting that, though he had been a successful playwright since *The Caretaker* in 1960, Pinter's turn inward in the 1970s coincided with popular acclaim and his lionization as 'our best living playwright' in the words of the *Times*,[25] though such fulsome praise in fact masked considerable ambivalence. The incongruous circumstances surrounding Pinter's work in the 1970s raise a new set of questions concerning the politics of popular art. The polarized responses to *No Man's Land* are a useful illustration. Indeed, the play's popularity is perplexing, given the obscurity of its action. A renowned poet and critic, Hirst, after a chance encounter in Hampstead invites home a man named Spooner, who, now dissolute and middle aged, cleans tables in a Chalk Farm pub but also claims to have led a literary life. Oddly, it is Hirst who drinks himself into a stupor as Spooner pompously holds forth on lofty themes. As the night wears on, it becomes clear that Spooner is a supplicant seeking employment or some other benefit. Against Foster and Briggs – two thugs who serve as Hirst's secretaries, bodyguards, and possibly lovers – Spooner tries to insinuate himself into the role of Hirst's literary adjutant. Foster warns Spooner, as Hirst sits comatose in a chair: 'This man in this chair, he's a creative man. He's an artist. We make life possible for him ... Don't try to drive a wedge into a happy household ... Don't try to make a nonsense out of family life.'[26]

The next morning, Hirst, now brisk and sober, inexplicably mistakes Spooner for an old classmate named Charles. Spooner quickly adopts an appropriate rhetorical posture, and the two pass a pleasant fifteen minutes engaged in the chit-chat of affluent middle-aged English gentlemen. 'You did say you had a good war, didn't you?' Hirst asks. 'A rather good one, yes,' Spooner replies (129). They move on to rehash ancient love affairs with women, improbably named Stella and Arabella. Later, however, events take a sombre turn. After several whiskeys, Hirst enters a state of profound and frozen desolation. After a long, wheedling speech by Spooner and a protracted silence, Hirst says: 'Let us change the subject ... For the last time' (149). When Foster assures him the subject is now immutably fixed, Hirst asks: 'Is the subject winter?' Foster replies: 'The subject is now winter. So it'll therefore be winter forever' (150). After a few minutes of philosophical dickering, we reach the play's cryptic last lines:

> SPOONER: ... You are in no man's land. Which never moves, which never changes, which never grows older, but which remains forever, icy and silent.
> *Silence.*
> HIRST: I'll drink to that. (153)

The first thing to be said about *No Man's Land* is that it is simultaneously a repudiation of socially committed art and, crucially, a self-critical reflection on the morbidity of aesthetic autonomy. The play deconstructs the two extremes. The self-commentary on aesthetics harks back to the dialectic of mask and face, art and life, and fixity and flux in Pirandello. In plays such as *Henry IV* and *Six Characters in Search of an Author*, Pirandello chronicles the seductiveness of the mask – the alluring constancy and coherence of art compared with life – but also makes clear the morbid, life-denying aspect of such yearning. Thomas Adler detects a similar dualism in *No Man's Land*. The creative power of memory, Adler argues, is analogous to the flux of life. Death, then, is a kind of amnesia or impotence in memory: 'no longer can all times and events, both real and fictive, be present in the mind, but only one image will be fixed there permanently.' Spooner, he continues, is a figure of death come to call for Hirst. Adler traces Hirst's willingness to receive death before suggesting, 'If change is the essence of life, fixity is the property of art.' In this sense, the play can be taken as a reflexive meditation on the tension between the creative imagination of the art-

ist and the fixed symbolization of the artwork, with the latter representing a morbid and inhuman fixing of the former. 'For Pinter,' Adler
writes, 'life, with its flux and infinite variability, with its "becoming-
ness," is still preferable to art, just as life is preferable to death.'[27]

The tension is vividly dramatized in an exchange between Hirst and
Briggs in Act 2. Hirst offers to show Spooner his photograph album, and
he says of the portraits, 'Deeply, deeply, they wish to respond to your
touch, to your look, and when you smile, their joy ... is unbounded. And
so I say to you, tender the dead, as you would yourself be tendered,
now, in what you would describe as your life.' Briggs responds, 'They're
blank, mate, blank. The blank dead' (137). This is an elegant meta-
commentary on two views of art. Hirst voices a traditional belief in the
power of representation to redeem what is represented by acting as an
agent of genuine memory and even love. Art is thus humanizing and
ennobling. By contrast, the more Platonic Briggs seems to actively distrust mimesis. He brusquely counters by stressing the mortifying power
of the image, an image that in his view imprisons rather than liberates.
In this sense, the lyricism of Hirst's speech is made ironic, as from
Briggs's perspective poetic language might also be considered a 'blank'
prettification of the real. In this speech and throughout the play, Briggs
and Foster operate in a much different linguistic register, and his mono-
syllabic retort punctures the aura of Hirst's lofty sentiment.

This conflict leads us to a larger chain of oppositions that invite
structuralist analysis. On the one hand, this is certainly Pinter's most
'literary' play, the most allusive and self-consciously poetical. At the
same time, the poetic is systematically offset by the prosaic register of
Foster and Briggs. Indeed, these two characters are semi-familiar
Pinter thugs who might be more at home in *The Birthday Party* or *The
Dumb Waiter*. The opposition is generational as well. The older men
speak in a mannered, poetical idiom; Spooner, for example, begins Act
2 by saying, 'I have known this before. Morning. A locked door. A
house of silence and strangers' (117). On the other hand, Foster ends
Act 1 with a cryptic story about travelling in the outback, and Briggs
later spends a page describing the impenetrable maze of roads surrounding Bolsover street: 'I knew one or two people who'd been wandering up and down Bolsover street for years. They'd wasted their
bloody youth there' (120). One verbal register negates the other; a genuinely collective language seems inconceivable in the light of the fractured linguistic field. Ionesco once remarked that 'what separates us all
from one another is simply society itself,'[28] and *No Man's Land* creates a

similar impression. One might say that *No Man's Land* does to the cultural unconscious of the literati what *Old Times* did to the more prosaic cafes, cinemas, songs, and films of mainstream culture. Collectively, the two plays amount to a deconstruction and refusal of high and low culture, with both spheres represented as sources of mystification and estrangement. In the later play there is no cultural signifier as glaring and explicit as the reference to *Odd Man Out*, but its functional equivalent in *No Man's Land* is probably the extended banter about Oxford, the War, sexual infidelities, and literature. This exchange between Hirst and Spooner functions as a wicked send-up of pretensions associated with the privileged classes of the war generation. Somewhat later, in a desperate attempt to win a job, Spooner synthesizes these associations into a cultural pastiche: 'My cooking is not to be sneezed at. I lean towards French cuisine but food without frills is not beyond my competency. I have a keen eye for dust. My kitchen would be immaculate. I am tender towards objects. I would take good care of your silver. I play chess, billiards, and the piano. I could play Chopin for you. I could read the Bible to you. I am a good companion' (147).

Companionship in these terms is a commercial form of human relationship. Tenderness towards 'objects' sounds menacing when taken as a substitute for human compassion. Similarly, the ensemble of cultural signifiers reads like a shopping list. Whatever value Chopin or chess might have as discrete phenomena is degraded by their enforced association. The culture evoked here is what Brecht in another context called 'culinary'[29] – acquisitive and hedonistic – a sense reinforced by the explicit link to cooking. What this passage – and the memory plays in general – express is despair over the waning of art's capacity for negation. The plays testify to the waning of art's critical power, a power that Herbert Marcuse once described as 'the Great Refusal – the protest against that which is.' Writing in 1964, Marcuse argued: 'In the realm of culture, the new totalitarianism manifests itself precisely in a harmonizing pluralism, where the most contradictory works and truths peacefully coexist in indifference. Prior to the advent of this cultural reconciliation, literature and art were essentially alienation, sustaining and protecting the contradiction – the unhappy consciousness of the divided world, the defeated possibilities, the hopes unfulfilled, and the promises betrayed.'[30] The memory plays simultaneously embody and eulogize this principle of alienation.

We could summarize the foregoing discussion of *No Man's Land* with a rhetorical question: where is the social world? Surely there are few plays that create such a hermetic, withdrawn impression. The fragmentary bits of social mapping – references to Hampstead Heath, Jack Straw's Castle, Chalk Farm, Bolsover Street, Amsterdam, Bali, and Australia – are faint, ambiguous signals that might as well derive from another dimension. The process of antisocial retreat culminates with Hirst's lines, 'The light ... out there ... is gloomy ... hardly daylight at all. It is falling, rapidly. Distasteful. Let us close the curtains. Put the lamps on.' After Briggs closes the curtains, Hirst expresses satisfaction: 'Ah. What relief ... How happy it is' (144). The gesture powerfully evokes the death instinct – regressive desire for return to the stasis of the womb – and moreover implicates the theatre space and the audience in the chilling pleasure of this 'relief.'

The closing of the curtains suggestively points to larger questions of pleasure and audience response, which complicate assessment of the memory plays. One of the oddest things about these plays is surely the fact that they have succeeded as entertainment. In comparison to *Old Times*, *No Man's Land* deepens the aura of aesthetic crisis, yet it was also pointedly addressed to a broad popular audience. This is art about the impossibility of art, though it is also true, in Michael Billington's words, 'What gives the play its tension and energy is the constant switch between the opposite magnetic poles of paralysis and activity, resignation and resistance.'[31] This balancing act has precipitated ambivalent reactions. To some critics, it seemed that Pinter had developed a solipsistic drama of his own creative process during a time when theatre was increasingly concerned with social action and the public sphere. At the same time, however, the first production of *No Man's Land* represented a kind of apotheosis for Pinter. The first successful run at the Old Vic featured an exemplary production by Peter Hall and no less than Ralph Richardson and John Gielgud in the lead roles of Hirst and Spooner, respectively. Given this confluence of circumstances, the veiled bitterness of many reviews is especially surprising. The *Birmingham Post* noted: 'One has a suspicion, almost a certainty, that these plays, for all their top-dressing of style, are fast becoming clichés themselves.' For all its praise, the *Times* still admitted that 'the language is heavy, and straining towards wider significance. The feeling, in general, is that having located his territory and got to know its inhabitants, Pinter is now trying to extract meaning from them.' The *Observer* concurred, with the telling comment that 'Mr. Pinter's titles are a good index to the progress of his art: once they referred to characters, objects or events, now to abstractions.'[32]

Deep divisions between critics and audiences have marked Pinter's public reception since the bewilderment occasioned by *The Birthday Party* in 1958. It is only a slight exaggeration to say that one of Pinter's defining characteristics has been resistance to the interpretive efforts of professional critics coupled with a potent, visceral connection to audiences. Even the antisocial memory plays retain an embryonic populism through their perverse, determined entry into the public sphere. John Russell Taylor, author of the seminal *Anger and After*, has described Pinter's curious popularity as a kind of intractable social mystery: 'There was no question that his transition from being regarded as the *ne plus ultra* in obscurity, on the strength of *The Birthday Party* in 1958, to being one of the most commercially successful West End dramatists in 1960, as *The Caretaker* brought in coach parties from Macclesfield to the Duchess for some eighteen months, came about because of some shift in public taste, not from his having shamelessly set out to write a commercial play the second time around.'[33]

One way of addressing the problem of Pinter's social attitude is to envision the degree of his commitment to the 'coach parties from Macclesfield,' the inviolable, inexpressible character of this relation to middlebrow culture-tourists, which arouses the confusion of those other constituencies – journalists, academics, radicals – more directly invested in interpretation and usefulness. In this context, I want to focus on the closing of each of the two acts in *No Man's Land*, because the two curtain lines aspire to the kind of *coup de théâtre* that strikes a powerful relationship with audiences. These gestures of representational closure recall the socialists' aesthetic resolution of contradiction, the illusory union of representation and represented. At the end of the first act, Briggs has just escorted the drunken Hirst from the room, and Foster begins the following anecdote to Spooner: 'Do you know what I saw once in the desert, in the Australian desert? A man walking along carrying two umbrellas. Two umbrellas. In the outback' (114). After a pause, Spooner reasonably asks: 'Was it raining?' 'No,' Foster replies. 'It was a beautiful day. I nearly asked him what he was up to but I changed my mind.' 'Why?' Spooner wants to know.

> FOSTER: Well, I decided he must be some kind of lunatic. I thought he would only confuse me.
> FOSTER *walks about the room, stops at the door.*
> Listen. You know what it's like when you're in a room with the lights on and then suddenly the light goes out? I'll show you. It's like this.

He turns the light out.
BLACKOUT. (115)

One could plausibly say that this is a theatrical trick, a formalist weapon deployed to stimulate suspense and keep the audience anxiously brooding over their pints during the interval. There is a complicity established with the audience here – a violation of the fourth wall, to use conventional terms – a way of implicating the theatre in the logic of the room and the perversity of Foster's conduct. Pinter shows an affinity for the phenomenological nuances of David Storey's *The Contractor* (1969), a play that focuses on the erection of a real wedding tent by a crew of workmen. Does the tent signify 'tentness,' or, because of the 'real' canvas, poles, and stakes, does it radiate the recalcitrance of objective reality even more intensely because it is on stage? Are the actors playing workmen, or are they 'really' workmen because they install a real tent? Is acting work? Is performance labour? Is labour performance? Similarly, Pinter's technique telescopes the contrived image of the lunatic in the desert, which initially signals dream iconography or the creative transformations of memory, until the imaginary umbrellas are very nearly plunked in spectators' laps. But the imagery is so gratuitous, so wilfully obscure that it caricatures absurdity; the episode then acts as a meta-commentary on the potency and emptiness of dramatic spectacle, gently displacing what we might conventionally expect of this famous absurdist playwright. What lingers is only the few seconds of invisible collectivity, the moment when the stage and the auditorium become a single darkened room. That this is a grim parody, a photographic negative (blind, mute, static, obedient, unthinking, temporary) of genuine political community only underscores the crisis of representation in radical culture. In the final analysis, it is very difficult to classify this *coup de théâtre* as anything other than a small pleasure, an otherwise incomprehensible affirmation of relationship with the audience. For this reason, it is mainly ignored by critical interpretations of death, art, or any deeper theme. At the very least, however, the play insists on its relation to a public, through a moment of opaque, meaningless performativity that nonetheless functions as a primitive social contract.

The end of the play, quoted above, also fuses social engagement and negation in a single ambiguous gesture. Poised against the most poetical language in the play – Spooner's description of no man's land – is the insistent, banal lifeworld of the cocktail cabinet. 'I'll drink to that,'

Hirst says, and the line evokes a materialism of pubs, toasts, and sociality, opposed to lyricism, language, and abstract thought. But the toast is empty, void of context and significance; to what does 'that' refer? Throughout, Pinter obsessively uses alcohol as a refuge from meaning. In the analytic framework of structuralism, we might say that the play is organized around two opposing fields of force, one linguistic and the other corporeal. Just as sexuality in *Old Times* functions as an unfulfilled promise of experience outside discourse, so too does alcohol in *No Man's Land* constitute a horizon beyond speech. It's an open question whether this activity – simultaneously liberating and regressive – provides a viable alternative to the enervating stasis the play otherwise documents. Nearer substance than symbol, alcohol does not conveniently 'stand for' anything. Over time, and partly because of the dreary alternatives, drinking begins to signify a kind of purity, a construction that depends on a sense of alcohol's corporeality, its hostility to abstraction. Hirst's drinking, as the play proceeds, takes on a defiant air, as if it were a mode of resistance or recovery. Like the author of the memory plays, Hirst seems to be finished with activity, significance, and meaning. The conclusion of *No Man's Land* evokes the creative power of poetic imagination only to defuse it. Is this, on Pinter's part, a refusal or an affirmation? Hirst's decision to drink is, after all, a choice – a style of being in the world, however degraded. It is, finally, the gesture of a desolated art, animated only by tenuous connection to spectators. The 1970s Pinter has forsaken political will in favour of the reduced consolations of the popular. Like a moribund extension of Brenton's radicals, Hirst fulfils the ethos of revolutionary failure by *reductio ad absurdum*. Memory becomes action, drinking displaces social agency. Perversely, on such damaged terrain Hirst's decision to drink appears radical, almost revolutionary. It is difficult to figure redemption in an activity both social and antisocial, public and private, transgressive and defeated, and one that is furthermore explicitly tied to self-destruction. But this is the grim proposal that *No Man's Land* ultimately makes to the audience.

It does not seem coincidental that during the period of the memory plays Pinter was creating a theatre intricately opposed to both the commercial populism of the West End and the political populism of the socialists. These antisocial spectacles of inwardness, fixated on images of stasis and withdrawal, pointedly offered the mass audience emaciated pastiches of both low and high cultures and proposed to radical society a strict and extended refusal of the public sphere. In this sense, it is possible to read memory itself as an attenuated form of action or authorship that stands in these plays as a negative image of both art and social agency. The modernist dialectic of autonomous and committed art is here nakedly reduced, for the broadest possible audience, in an elaborate gesture of refusal. In this respect, at least, journalists and the theatrical Left might be united in their discomfort with the memory plays, though for different reasons. As we have seen, journalistic critics seemed uneasy with the perceived stagnation of a writer riding the crest of popular acclaim. The Left, certainly, would have every reason to be wary of a drama that regarded their stated agenda with such implicit hostility.

As epitomized by the two curtain lines, the use of spectacle in *No Man's Land* resists the kind of rhetorical closure that functions to aesthetically resolve social contradiction. As a point of comparison, consider the various theatrical coups in Howard Brenton's *The Romans in Britain* (1980), a play whose brazen mingling of politics and spectacle make it a fitting endnote to the 1970s. Briefly, the action takes place at three distinct historical moments: the Roman invasion of Britain in 54 B.C., the Saxon invasion in 515 A.D., and the British occupation in Northern Ireland in the late 1970s. The first act details the slaughter of a Celtic tribe by Caesar and the Roman army, including the graphic rape of a young priest. The act concludes with the shooting (!) of a fleeing slave girl. The Romans, unexpectedly, have been transformed into the modern British army, equipped with jeeps and helicopters, and the slave girl is now an unspecified figure in the Irish resistance. The second act alternates between the separate ordeals of two Celtic peasant women and the household of a Roman lady during the Saxon invasion, and the modern story of Chichester, a British intelligence agent assigned to assassinate a leader of the IRA in a field near the Irish border. Chichester, racked by guilt, confesses to the local IRA, who kill him without sentiment. The play's final scene is the meeting of the two peasant sisters, who have murdered their abusive father, and the two cooks who have been liberated from their Roman mistress, under 'brilliant moonlight.' A small collective is formed, and the motley band begins to speculate on the future. One of the cooks decides he will become a poet and imagines the legend of 'a King who never was.' According to the cook, when he died, the king and his court 'were mourned. And remembered. Bitterly. And thought of as a golden age, lost and yet to come.'[34]

The Romans in Britain completes the situationist tendencies in Brenton's work throughout the 1970s. The sudden appearance of modern weaponry in the context of the Roman occupation, for example, is intended to establish the essential similarity of colonial abuses through the use of spectacle. The intellectual value produced, however, is easily distilled in a sentence or two, and on the whole, the historical contrast is so sweeping and facile as to be nearly ahistorical in character. As one critic summarizes, Brenton's 'aim' is 'to suggest that England's treatment of Ireland is yet another example of that process of colonisation from which ... ironically, the English nation was itself created.'[35] But it is not at all clear that even this limited pedagogic aim met with any particular success. The other theatrical coup – the rape of the young priest and the noisome commentary of his attackers – effectively displaced any rational reflection on colonialism. Indeed, there is a dangerous spark of the irrational embedded in this gesture. The spectacle of the degraded, suffering body risks becoming a source of erotic or disciplinary pleasure (censoring the play was widely debated), beyond its power to shock or alienate. The general consensus is that the controversy surrounding the premiere at the National Theatre 'so eclipsed every other aspect of the play that the very title still carries an aura of notoriety among those who have neither seen nor read it.'[36]

In any case, the play's reliance on spectacle ultimately vindicates an aesthetic rather than a political vision. The final moonlit tableau is a utopian projection, immunized from criticism because set in an ill-defined, distant past. The cook's story of the 'King who never was,' with its plainly Arthurian associations, is intend to restore the progressive power of myth-making in the hands of an imaginary, non-alienated collective. Robert Gross takes the golden age myth as a paradigm for the progressive writer 'who creates self-deconstructing fictions that will resist being turned into fact and used as ideological weapons.'[37] This is a neat way of praising what is fundamentally a strategy of evasion. Gross is convincing in the sense that Brenton is at pains to emphasize the irony of the Celtic cook's invention of Arthur. Indeed, the assimilation of this Celtic myth to the imperialist domain of British mythology is preordained, thereby disarming attacks on Brenton's utopian fantasy in an aesthetic gesture that, as collateral damage, unfortunately renders the utopian moment opaque and meaningless. As Chichester, the British intelligence officer, remarks earlier: 'If King Arthur walked out of those trees, now – know what he'd look like to us? One more fucking mick.'[38] In circular fashion, the play's rhetoric undercuts political will in a way that makes it available only to the 'self-deconstructing' author: in this case, Brenton himself.

The double-edged blackout and Hirst's insensible toast in *No Man's Land*, by contrast, sabotage meaning and undercut the rhetorical authority of the author and his agents. Adorno wrote that the only hope in Kafka is 'tied to the salvation of things, of those which are no longer enmeshed in the network of guilt, those which are non-exchangeable, useless.'[39] Hirst's drinking resonates with this proposition. The 'useless' is an important category in analysing Pinter, particularly if one wishes to recover a utopian dimension from the typical ethos of cruelty and exploitation. Adorno is also emphasizing what we might call the politics of autonomous works. For Adorno, there was the grave question of whether art any longer had a right to exist. The only art worth the name, in his view, was something like the tremulous, devastated asceticism of Beckett, a rigorously separate art clinging to the world by a thread. This is an art that makes no statements, asserts no rights or privileges, but instead serves as a kind of negative image, a locus of memory, a testament. After 1980 Pinter appeared to abandon this course, and it is tempting to seize one section of his career as a lens with which to view the other. Pinter either awakened or fell into politics; the early plays are political or the political plays are aesthetically complex, depending on one's perspective. But this is to succumb to the postmodern truism that all culture is political and, in so doing, to negate a central, productive tension in Pinter's works and in modern drama generally. In retrospect, one of Pinter's most important contributions has been to model both the committed and autonomous tendencies, indeed to entwine the two so deeply that their dialectic is in some way preserved. Pinter's complex relationship to the new British drama offers a further opportunity to preserve historiographically what historical change is rendering obsolete. As British socialist drama moved from mimetic realism towards ambiguity, Pinter's interests shifted from abnegation to engagement with the political realities of torture and repression. Taken together, these reversals signal a late phase of modern drama amid the larger crisis of political art.

A poetics for thugs

The psychopath is not only a criminal; he is the embryonic Storm-Trooper; he is the disinherited, betrayed antagonist whose aggressions can be mobilized on the instant at which the properly-aimed and frustration-evoking formula is communicated by that leader under whose tinseled aegis license becomes law, secret and primitive desires become virtuous ambitions readily attained, and compulsive behavior formerly deemed punishable becomes the order of the day.

Robert Lindner[40]

These individuals are the most 'infantile' of all: they have thoroughly failed to 'develop,' have not been molded at all by civilization ... Here go the hoodlums and rowdies, plug-uglies, torturers, and all those who do the 'dirty work' of a fascist movement.

T.W. Adorno[41]

A brief, exemplary sequence in Alain Resnais's Holocaust documentary *Night and Fog* (1955) begins with the exterior of a comfortable villa, home to a Nazi commandant. The narrator reports that the residence was located near one of the concentration camps. Subsequently, three snapshots depict the wives of various commandants. One poses in the parlour, smiling, with a group of well-dressed visitors. Another sits beside her husband, a contented dog in her lap. The banality of these images is somehow intolerable. They evoke real but macabre domestic dramas performed in the shadows of the camps. Pinter's later plays explore similar convergences of horror and civility. In particular, *Party Time* (1991) enlarges the moral and political implications of Resnais's archival photographs, dramatizing a grotesque cocktail party for the ruling class during an evening of brutal military suppression. The play's political tenor and unspecified setting are consistent with three of Pinter's other works of the period: *The New World Order* (also 1991), *One for the Road* (1984), and *Mountain Language* (1988). At the same time, however, plays like *Party Time* and *One for the Road* reveal the summit of an authoritarian class structure whose foundations date much earlier. These works extend Pinter's previous treatments of criminality, adding a new branch to an evolving genealogy of thugs. The plutocrats, socialites, and functionaries of the later plays are affluent relations of the gangsters and sociopaths in *The Birthday Party* (1958), *The Dumb Waiter* (1960), and *The Homecoming* (1965). The glib prattling of the intelligentsia echoes the enigmatic chatter of the criminals. The privileged environments of the first group complement the uncertain, alienated spaces occupied by the latter. These diverse works compose Pinter's extended meditation on the proximity of civility and barbarism. Collectively, they develop a *mise en scène* in keeping with the villa, the dog, and the commandant.

From absurdist toughs to proletarian assassins, paranoid pimps, and neurotic inquisitors, Pinter's plays encompass a spectrum of authoritarians and criminals. These characters, I will argue, function as agents of a two-pronged critique of violence and its cultural representations. The terms of this critique can be outlined through the vehicle of the thug. For Pinter, the thug offers a dense, malleable cultural history, and this broad, iconic figure suggestively links the early gangsters with the torturers and functionaries of the anti-authoritarian cycle. Outwardly, however, Pinter's thugs coalesce in at least two distinct, seemingly incompatible groups. The first includes the dialogic, quasi-philosophical clowning of Gus, Ben, Goldberg, and McCann in the early plays, and the second is aligned with the monologic, eroticized self-narrations of Lenny in *The Homecoming* and Nicolas in *One for the Road*. Clearly, there is a sense of development in these characters – a shift from philosophical, comic menace to more inward, erotic modes of barbarity, from an absurd to a post-Freudian thug. Moreover, the late treatments of thuggery are distinguished by an enigmatic political realism. At the same time, however, the insidious dialogue between Des and Lionel in *The New World Order* is clearly indebted to the more comic interrogations of Goldberg and McCann in *The Birthday Party*, and in some obvious ways the political torturer, Nicolas, in *One for the Road* seems the offspring of Lenny, a small-time pimp in *The Homecoming*. In hindsight, Pinter himself has remarked on overlaps between the early works and subsequent political concerns. In 1988 he suggested that plays like *The Birthday Party* and *The Dumb Waiter* offer a critical look at 'authoritarian postures' and 'power used to undermine, if not destroy, the individual, or the questioning voice.'[42]

The representational genealogy of Pinter's thugs is thus enmeshed in larger questions about his politics. It is difficult to assess whether the 'political' plays of the 1980s and 1990s represent a qualitative shift or an organic development. For example, despite elements of realism, the anti-torture plays insist on historical indeterminacy and are less concerned with representing torture or violence than with implicating ostensibly benign linguistic, rhetorical, and social practices in murky offstage violence. Moreover, the anti-authoritarian cycle leads to the postmodern *Ashes to Ashes* (1996), a deeply ambiguous work mixing surreal Holocaust imagery, sexual thuggery reminiscent of Pinter's earlier domestic dramas, and violations of realism that recall the 1970s memory plays. Such gestures of equivocation and abstraction seem at odds with the notion of concrete political intervention. Jeanne Colleran argues that in *Mountain Language*, the 'dramatic situation ... is now grounded in a configuration that is at once political and ontological and which accords neither privilege,'[43] yet Pinter's comment, above, reflects a similar view of his earlier work. Indeed, in a previous interview, Pinter remarked of *The Birthday Party*: 'I don't think it is all that surrealistic and curious, because this thing, of people arriving at the door, has been happening in Europe for the last twenty years. Not only the last twenty years, the last two to three hundred.'[44]

Here, Pinter echoes Robert Lindner, who suggests that the psychopath is the embryonic storm trooper. In what follows, I contend that Pinter's modernist thugs 1958–91 reflect a coherent social philosophy. The later plays indicate that thuggery is political, but they retain an ontological violence derived from earlier absurdist variants. I end the chapter, and the book, with an extended discussion of the 1996 play *Ashes to Ashes*, which I consider an exemplary postmodern text, a concluding pastiche of authoritarianism and thugs. I will argue that collectively, Pinter's thugs express and endure a violence that is both ubiquitous and invisible. Assassins, gangsters, pimps, and torturers serve as equivocal links to a 'real' violence, which is then deferred and mediated in the plays. In symptomatic fashion, *The Dumb Waiter* concludes with a static tableau, deferring the resolution promised by Ben's pointed gun. The tension of this unspent bullet reverberates across Pinter's dramatic universe. Physical cruelty is typically consigned to anticipation, memory, or offstage space. His work is more centrally concerned with the sublimation of urges, the sedimentation of violence in posture, gesture, and speech, and the complicity of all such symbolic displacements with unrepresented barbarities. Hence, this preoccupation has often passed under the name of menace, or, more euphemistically, 'power.' But apart from superficial machinations lies an inarticulate suffering that cannot, or should not, be mimetically represented. For example, when Nicolas tells Victor in *One for the Road* that his son 'was a little prick,'[45] the mere shift of tense signals an inexpressible ending. The guilt of a language that commands, justifies, or obscures violence extends as well to the play's trappings of civility. The imagery oscillates between etiquette and barbarism, glib urbanity and abject terror, hors d'oeuvres and the 'rancid omelette,' cocktails and 'wet shit' (40). Even the title's inane, incongruous formality mocks the subject matter, positioning the play in a chasm between rhetoric and brutality, decomposed language and grisly reality, the visible and cruelty beyond figuring.

Of course, *One for the Road* is itself a sublimation: an aesthetic, nearly abstract rendering of presumed realities, a transformed piece of dramatic speech spoken on behalf of victims. As the play demonstrates, the power to describe and narrate both masks and enables real agency ('You're a lovely woman. Well, you were' [71]). In this sense, Pinter's theatrical critique of authoritarian politics constitutes his own artistic usurpation. Clearly, Pinter's theatre is alive to tensions between political and aesthetic speech, and his work resists imaginary resolutions of unresolved social contradictions, to modify a phrase from Fredric Jameson. Consider his response, in the late 1960s, to a journalist's question about politicians. 'I'll tell you what I really think about politicians. The other night I watched some politicians on television talking about Vietnam. I wanted very much to burst through the screen with a flame-thrower and burn their eyes out and their balls off and then inquire how they would assess this action from a political point of view.'[46] In juxtaposing rhetoric and brutality, Pinter ironically undercuts his own position as commentator. His expressed opinion concerns the noxious dissembling of politicians in their representations of Vietnam. However, this intervention is accomplished through the looking glass, as it were, making the literal images of violence seem fantastic while imparting violent overtones to the rhetorical emptiness of 'talking about Vietnam' or 'assess(ing) this action from a political point of view.' For all its nebulous influence, Vietnam itself lingers out of reach. This is not a facile resolution of the aesthetic and the political, but instead a complex rhetorical figure that Pinter offers in response to the question he chooses to answer, which is in this case less about Vietnam than about the relationship between representation and reality. His comment underlines the power of rhetoric to offer false reconciliations, for politicians *and* playwrights.

In 1953 Ionesco wondered: 'But how does one manage to represent the non-representable? How do you represent the non-representational and *not* represent the representational?'[47] Pinter's plays raise similar questions about the representation of violence. His emphasis on symbolic displacement rather than visibility indicates resistance to a culture saturated with violent imagery. Yet Pinter's thugs are also political and cultural constructions assembled from available models. To dramatize thuggery is always to confront prior incarnations; Pinter's thugs comment on their predecessors, and the dramas subtly engage the conventions by which social violence is coded and represented.

But the representational history of thuggery itself is notably complex.

The thug serves as a figure of collective fantasy, a symbolic negotiation of conflicting cultural attitudes towards violence, criminality, and social existence. For example, the thug's presumptive vocation is violence, yet the poignancy of thug narratives often depends on the sublimation of destructive urges. When juxtaposed with overt brutality, the hoodlum's love of his mother (*White Heat*), Beethoven (*A Clockwork Orange*), or even fresh produce (*The Godfather*) establishes contiguity between recognizable human attributes and insensible aggression. As a cultural icon, the thug embodies coherent social meanings beyond opaque, pathological otherness. The disturbing quality of a film like *Henry: Portrait of a Serial Killer* – with its coldly objective, naturalistic aesthetic – rests on the absence of any figure, voice, or code to make sense of the wanton killing. More typically, however, such representations simultaneously demystify and fetishize violence by mapping its unknowability on familiar iconographies. The thug's prohibited, recalcitrant deviancy enables collective fantasies around inverse questions of authority and submission. Yet an emphasis on violent closure and narrative coherence effectively orchestrates and represses potential transgressions; most often, deviance is contained.

In the two epigraphs above, Lindner and Adorno suggest that even from the thug's point of view, violence is not a consummation but a substitution, a symbolic, compensatory release of displaced aggression. The act matters less than the symbolic work it performs in relation to trauma, maladjustment, and fantasy, triggered by actual or perceived external provocation. Pinter's thugs, by contrast, are denied vocational fulfilment. They pursue the mechanics of barbarity detached from its physical culmination. This is a dual estrangement, encompassing both characters and audience. Pinter's crime dramas withhold crime, offering the formal shell of suspense without the release of violent spectacle. What remains is a gallery of authoritarian personalities rendered without the solace of visible horror. Through the very absence of conventional gratifications Pinter's work highlights our expectation of represented violence, and our veiled authoritarian sympathies.

The social symbolism of thuggery in Pinter's work is predominantly framed by popular narratives. His thugs operate within conventions of the crime story and the dominant form of suspense. In reshaping basic patterns in the cultural aesthetics of crime, Pinter exposes the repressive ideological sublimations at work in many crime narratives that contain (and sanction) violence by making it coherent and pleasurable.

Suspense usually entails the aesthetic organization of violence for purposes of pleasure, and suspense narratives typically impose strategies
of closure on the more broadly social, contradictory components of the
represented crimes. At the same time, suspense depends on anxiety
and fear – heightened by the deferral of narrative objectives and the
withholding of information – as the raw material of pleasurable resolution. Suspense narratives are dangerous, because the disturbing fantasies they seek to manage are socially and psychologically hazardous if
left uncontained. Pinter retools the conventions of crime narrative by
exploiting this dual aspect of suspense, re-figuring its ideological
shape in small, perverse fragments. His plays organize responses to
violence by deferring its final representation, thereby emphasizing patterns of dominance and submission in social and linguistic relationships and highlighting the psychosocial aggression that suspense both
encourages and conceals.

Popular narratives form one subtext of *The Birthday Party* (1958), a
play that jarringly mixes absurdist thugs with stereotypes derived
from domestic drama. In this work, Pinter parodies suspense conventions through violent generic mutation, yielding a curious hybrid of
music-hall comedy, absurdism, melodrama, and the crime thriller.
More radically, the play injects two otherwise gratuitous interrogations, fragmented and misplaced in the domestic context. Oddly, these
clichéd interrogation scenes constitute the theatrical and emotional
core of the play, though their alarming incongruity resists assimilation.
In seminal fashion, the interrogations inaugurate a number of characteristic tensions and displacements. Stanley, a former pianist of uncertain renown, has been living for some time in a strangely deserted
seaside boarding house run by a solemn man, Petey, and his flirtatious
wife, Meg, both of whom are in their sixties. One morning, on what
may or may not be Stanley's birthday, Meg announces that two men
have been enquiring about lodgings. Immediately suspicious, Stanley
avoids the two men, Goldberg and McCann, when they arrive. In the
evening, however, Goldberg and McCann confront Stanley, berating
him with nonsensical questions, finally inducing a semi-catatonic
silence. The next morning, they subject the unresponsive Stanley to a
second interrogation, then abduct him, explaining to Petey that 'He
needs special treatment.'[48]

The first interrogation begins with Goldberg and McCann forcing
Stanley into a chair, asking questions like 'Why did you leave the organization?' (48). The initial overtones of gangsterism and complicity are

juxtaposed with Stanley's escalating confusion and the woeful insufficiency of his responses. For example, when asked to defend his choice
of lodging, Stanley cryptically mentions a headache and Goldberg
presses him to describe his course of headache treatment. Stanley is
unable to recall the precise brand of fruit salts or definitively to assert
that he stirred them properly. 'Did they fizz?' Goldberg asks porten-
tously. 'Did they fizz or didn't they fizz?' (48).

After its conventional opening, the interrogation soon withdraws
from reassuring film noir or gangster clichés. Administering headache
remedies acquires the force of a categorical imperative. Even in the
mundane consumer space of using products and following directions,
the inability to stir 'properly' is taken as an index of some more universal guilt. As the interrogation proceeds, the initial gangsterism takes an
even more ominous shape. Goldberg and McCann enquire about the
political situation in Ireland, wicket-watering on a cricket pitch in Mel-
bourne, and 'the Albigensenist heresy.' They accuse Stanley of being a
traitor to the cloth, of soiling the sheet of his birth (after he admits that
he sleeps in the nude), before incongruously asking, 'Why did the
chicken cross the road?' When Stanley cannot satisfactorily respond,
they demand to know 'Chicken? Egg? Which came first?', which leads
Stanley to a wordless scream (51–2).

In compressed, economical fashion, the interrogation suggests a terrifying anxiety connected to even the most banal phenomena. The
frame of reference oscillates between one's sleeping habits and the
arcane tortures inflicted on heretics. Conventions, stereotypes, mundane references, and clichés enable a sense of familiarity, which is then
subjected to the most outrageous abuses and manipulations. Certainly,
there are a number of recognizable threads – religious, political, epistemological, social – woven into Goldberg and McCann's accusations.
Yet the structure of the interrogation is reminiscent of revue-sketch
comedy, with its furious rhythms, incongruous responses, and conceptual free association. For example, Stanley first suffers the acute social
embarrassment of not completing an ancient comic set-up with a thou-
sand possible punchlines (Why did the chicken cross the road?). Then,
in a metonymic displacement via the chicken, we arrive at the clichéd
recalcitrance of ontology itself (the chicken or the egg?). Thus Stanley
is very nearly being 'entertained' while he is humiliated, although, in
the manner of Don Rickles, Goldberg and McCann ridicule him when
he cannot keep pace, in what one might characterize as burlesque
inquisition.

Comedy, however, does not mesh comfortably with the manifest cruelty of these exchanges. With a toehold in a realist world, the interrogations refuse the consolation of a stable frame of reference – not only in relation to questions of fact, but also at the level of the generic sensibility informing the audience. The second interrogation, for example, undercuts even the limited stability of the first. At the conclusion of the second interrogation, Stanley has fully regressed to a prelinguistic gurgling. Goldberg and McCann now unexpectedly employ the rhetoric of restoration and cure. They assure Stanley that he will be reorientated, rich, adjusted, a mensch, and a success. Stanley is told that he will give orders and make decisions as a magnate and statesman with yachts and animals. Here, the earlier avenues of threat are unexpectedly transformed into the disembodied, sunny disposition of self-help advertising fantasy.

Taken together, the two interrogations transcode contradictory notions drawn from various social, philosophical, and commercial discourses. Goldberg and McCann represent an unnamed organization, and, as Raymond Williams contends, 'the fact that it is unnamed allows every effect at once: criminal, political, religious, metaphysical.' The broad ambiguity of menace miniaturizes suspense. Language, freed from the burdens of referential realism, is purely instrumentalized towards domination, and the deferral of physical violence effectively insinuates coercion into the naked power of speech, independent of meaning or content. This extreme, perverted form of conversation is, in turn, reflected on the skeletal banalities littered throughout the play, evoking what Williams terms 'the dead strangeness and menace of a drifting, routine-haunted, available common life.'[49]

In a purer form, Pinter's *The Dumb Waiter* (1960) presses the conventions of suspense narrative, evoking the imprint of violence on the symbolic parameters of social and cultural life. *The Dumb Waiter* clearly owes a debt to existing iconographies, engaging these traditions in complex ways. Yet the play – with its absurdist thugs, endless digressions, and final paralysis – again is concerned with symbolic crimes, with representational displacements of violence. The plot concerns a pair of ostensible assassins, Gus and Ben, who bide time in the basement of what may once have been a restaurant, waiting for instructions on their next hit. After much desultory and occasionally malevolent conversation on a variety of topics, the disused dumbwaiter in the back wall springs to life, issuing written demands for increasingly bizarre and exotic meals. Finally, Gus leaves to get a glass of water. Ben receives instructions from the heretofore silent speaking tube, indicating that the target is on the way. Gus re-enters, dishevelled. Ben, his pistol drawn, stares at Gus in a final tableau.

The play's opening foregrounds the problem of represented cruelty and suffering. Ben disgustedly reads two newspaper stories aloud, while Gus intermittently responds with astonishment: 'He what?' 'No?' 'Go on!' 'Get away.' 'It's unbelievable.' This extended theatrical business subtly indicates the remote barbarity of an unknowable world – a gratuitous, generalized violence that permeates the apparent safety of the basement. The first newspaper story concerns an old man who unwisely tried to cross a road in a traffic jam by crawling under a stationary lorry, which then proceeded to run over him. Ben concludes, 'It's enough to make you want to puke,' but concedes, incredulously: 'It's down here in black and white.'[50] The second, somewhat more Freudian story centres on an eight year-old girl who allegedly killed a cat, while her brother, aged eleven, viewed the incident from the toolshed. Regarding this unpleasant scenario, Ben can only manage, 'That's bloody ridiculous' (88).

In this first interchange, familiar expectations for suspense narrative are both established and undercut. Identification, humour, and incipient suspense are troubled by an uneasy, regressive logic behind the seemingly coherent illusion. At the level of character, one might initially detect a reassuring and comprehensible dualism, drawn from the constellation of passive/aggressive, servant/master, straight-man/comedian, id/ego types. Ben, it would seem, is the more assertive and misanthropic, while Gus is a bit of a credulous 'ponce.' This distinction, however, is undermined by the reciprocity of their strangeness, as though the two were halves of a singular and all-encompassing 'personality,' in the abstract and alienated sense of the word. Further, the manifest silliness of the news items and the snorting, exaggerated indignation of the responses are certainly funny, yet Ben's declaration 'It's bloody ridiculous' is not a punchline. Instead, it betrays a symptomatic failure of the definitive insight and perspectival closure essential to ironic or sarcastic humour.

At the outset, *The Dumb Waiter* presents alienated, languishing killers who read reports of violent incidents that escalate in Freudian perversity in inverse proportion to their apparent seriousness. Violence – as an index of reality beyond the play's claustrophobic codes and conventions – is available only through filters of unreliable reportage, narrative, and representation. The fulfilment of visible killing, expected, ironically, by both killers and audience, is immediately displaced by symbolic aggressions embedded in the newspaper. Indeed, taken together, the two newspaper items gravitate towards a gnawing unpleasantness. In regressive fashion, the cat-killing suggests a more trivial yet somehow more grisly and dismal sensibility than the faux tragedy of the old man, which appears increasingly incommensurable and incongruous in the light of the anecdote that succeeds it.

As the action progresses, aggression circulates around the ostensibly innocent newspaper, a mundane object that eventually divides the characters. *The Dumb Waiter* plays with the contradictory feelings aroused by newspaper-reading as emblem of healthy populism and good citizenship, a triumphant ratification of the social contract, coupled with the familiar chill of seeing another person immersed in a newspaper across the now fully demarcated territories of human separation. A torso and face concealed by a newspaper engender a kind of suppressed loathing for that inviolable spectacle of self-absorption on the other side of the breakfast table or living room, eerily summed up by Gus's petulant question – 'How many times have you read that paper?' (102).

The unexpected malevolence of the play's opening suggests that Pinter is less concerned with suspense as the pleasurable organization of violence than with a suspense that frustrates precisely those conventions. Aggression resides in the sphere of banal small talk and domestic objects (the newspaper, the malfunctioning toilet, the dumb waiter itself), which now function as disturbing ideograms of a violent history. I would argue, moreover, that Pinter distill suspense to an extreme manifestation, so that it no longer constitutes a narrative category in the broad sense of plot or event, but rather expresses the ill-fated microscopic impulses towards closure in the silences amid disconnected dialogue, the implied foundational uncertainty of subjects and their relationships, and the phenomenological dislocation between subject and world. These deferred, prolonged transactions and the continual move to complete them are the engine of Pinter's narrative (such as it is), at the level of the episode and the play as a whole.

As an illustration, consider the apparently semantic debate between Gus and Ben on the subject of making tea. The exchange begins with Ben directing Gus to light the kettle and Gus insisting that lighting the gas is the proper figure of speech. The argument continues to escalate, nearly precipitating a physical altercation, before Gus concludes, 'I bet my mother used to say it,' an assertion that Ben cryptically challenges: 'Your mother? When did you last see your mother?' (97–8). The scene recapitulates the play's familiar pattern of suspenseful escalation to the brink of physical violence, simultaneously enabled and deferred by innocuous, though aggressive, verbal gestures. The sublimating functions of language as a system for negotiating desires and resolving disputes, together with the symbolic civility of English tea, are here indicted as specious reconciliations. Further, the digressive triviality of the scene, the regressive movement from 'Go and light it' to 'your mother,' suspends the causal strictures of narrative expectation. Like the play's final tableau, the kettle digression inhabits 'dynamic' instrumentalized narrative only to boil it down to an elemental stasis. Suspense – as the expectation of resolution and as a figure of eternal waiting – is held like a gun to the audience's head.

In these early plays, Pinter's critique of suspense is expressed dialogically: through a polyphony of caricatured thugs trapped in regressive micro-narratives, who still can be disavowed as types, clowns, or tokens of a larger parody. In later works, however, the thug evolves from comedic cipher to post-Freudian subject, and the problem of narrative refers not only to conventional dramatic forms but also to self-narration, to inner libidinal violence documented in self-dramatizing monologues. Nicolas, in *One for the Road*, is perhaps the central example. His two scenes with Victor are dominated by narcissistic, wheedling self-disclosures. Here, regressive gestures in dialogue are to some degree superseded by monologic digression, by the intermittent substitution of self-narration for dramatic suspense. This is a complex shift with several new points of emphasis. The appeal of represented violence partly rests on the symbolic fulfilment of prohibited aggressions and desires. For thugs, real violence likewise plays a symbolic role. In the absence of violent consummation, the thug's frustrated, digressive monologues mirror the spectator's analogous lack of fulfilment. Watching Pinter's post-Freudian thugs, the spectator's expectations are disturbingly aligned with the characters' elaborate pathologies, encouraging and highlighting unwanted identifications. The monologic mode gradually negates even the small pleasures of dialogue, plurality, and conventional suspense, and the remaining drama rests on the unpleasant spectacle of self-disclosure.

As we have seen, even the early works dramatize generalized aggression without visible violence, a suspension that refuses to pleasurably display its grisly referent. The new political emphasis introduces a new problem; it is difficult to represent the lived reality of political violence without perpetrating a second, artistic injustice. Pinter's late plays negotiate a line between critique and exploitation; they increasingly stress psychopathic interiority and the corollary aesthetic form of monologue. This approach explores the authoritarian implications of the single, coercive voice, and the links between erotic fantasy, social ideology, and political violence. The monologic mode also interrupts the causal, interpersonal logic of popular narratives, subtly resisting the rendering of violence in conventional, entertaining forms.

Again, the thug acts as a crucial instrument of transformation. Lenny, the misanthropic racketeer of *The Homecoming* (1965), is a key transitional figure in the development of the late Pinter. His seemingly gratuitous speeches to Ruth in Act I assume importance by virtue of their exceptional length, strangeness, and misogyny, but also by their eerie reminiscence of the cat-killing recounted in *The Dumb Waiter*. We are later given to believe that Lenny is a mid-level pimp, though the final, ludicrous schemes concerning Ruth suggest a deranged, delusional underling. In any case, the erotic component of his thuggery is clear, and the confluence of frustrated sexuality, violence, and guilty confession in these two speeches underlines the complicity between pleasure and aggression in the psyche of the thug.

In contrast to earlier conventions of the soliloquy, Kristin Morrison argues that 'now the telling of a story allows characters that quintessentially "modern," Freudian opportunity to reveal deep and difficult thoughts and feelings while at the same time concealing them as fiction or at least distancing them as narration.'[51] In Pinter, self-representations function as verbal symptoms. The thug's monologues simultaneously repress, enact, and reveal. Lenny's anecdotes compress narcissism, exhibitionism, aggression, and sexual anxiety in a single gesture. Shortly after meeting his visiting sister-in-law Ruth for the first time, Lenny's brother Teddy having gone to bed, Lenny incongruously asks if he can hold her hand. 'Why?' she asks, and Lenny proceeds to tell the rambling story of a sexually aggressive, pox-ridden woman accosting him one night near the docks. Scandalized by the woman's indecent proposals, Lenny beats her and even entertains thoughts of murder, but decides against getting himself into 'a state of tension,' opting instead to give her 'another belt in the nose and a couple of turns of the boot.'[52]

Ruth is unimpressed by this account, and Lenny unhesitatingly launches into an even stranger anecdote, which opens on a winter morning when, feeling civic minded, he volunteers to shovel snow in the neighbourhood. He spends several enjoyable hours at this task before being rudely interrupted by an old woman during his mid-morning tea. The woman enlists Lenny's help in moving an iron mangle inconsiderately left in the wrong room by her brother-in-law. Unfortunately, Lenny can't move the mangle because 'It must have weighed about half a ton.' Heroically struggling with the mangle, 'risking a rupture,' Lenny is nonplussed by the woman's failure to assist him, precipitating the rhetorical question, 'why don't you stuff this iron mangle up your arse?' Lenny is tempted to give her a 'workover,' but considering his good mood, he settles for 'a short-arm jab to the belly' (49).

On the one hand, Lenny's monologues document a litany of sexual abnormalities, including fetishism, sadism, and masochistic exhibitionism. Despite desperate attempts to indicate mastery, he appears regressed, childish, polymorphously perverse. At the same time, Lenny evinces a deep, neurotic disgust with the pox-ridden 'liberties' of sexuality and a consequent inability to consummate the symbolic murder and by implication the sexual act. His anxiety when confronted with Ruth's subsequent overtures confirms the sexual panic concealed in the anecdotes. Further, his crude substitution of 'clumping,' 'belts,' and 'jabs' for intercourse suggests that the deferred 'murder' may stand for a terrifying, disavowed orgasm. These displacements speak to a catastrophic repression. Self-destructive sexuality is externalized through violent fantasies directed against the other.

Pinter's eroticized thug exists at the borderline of psychosis and neurosis, a space between the fantasized omnipotence described by Lindner and Adorno and the tremulous displacement of sexual and violent urges. More disturbingly, Pinter aligns the authoritarian pathology of the thug with the psychology of the spectator. He unexpectedly joins violent, sexual, and narrative desires in a single uneasy suspense. The unwanted 'state of tension' that Lenny associates with murder is an apt image for the digressions, deferrals, and repressive sublimations experienced by the viewer. Fantasy images that perplex the characters become metaphors for an artistic process that implicates the audience. For example, 'mangle,' a noun, signifies a primitive, vaguely monstrous laundry apparatus ('they're out of date, you want to get a spin drier' [49]), while 'mangle,' a verb, implies mutilating disfigurement. This single image intimates archaic, repressed memories, a

pronounced castration threat, and the condensed or displaced 'disfig-
urements' necessary to symbolic representation. The mangle's resonance with Freudian dream imagery is surely not gratuitous. Pinter's
late thugs function as social and psychological surrogates, monologists
of collective, authoritarian fantasy.

Pinter's expectation that we identify with post-Freudian thuggery is
evident in the plays' latent psychic and social pathology. In the absence
of narrative containment, closure, or violent resolution, this disturbing
dynamic remains unsublimated. The question of pleasure, de-eroti-
cized in the early suspenseful narratives, is here externalized as a poly-
morphous sexuality coupled with violence and aggression. This
sexualized violence, incipient in *The Homecoming*, finds almost pure
expression in *One for the Road* (1984), a play centred on the erotics of
torture. Indeed, Lenny's descendant Nicolas, the high-ranking thug of
the latter play, nakedly embodies both tendencies. *One for the Road* consists of four short scenes in which Nicolas separately interrogates a
father, mother, and son. Two encounters – between Nicolas and the
father, Victor – open and close the play. In the first, Victor, brutalized,
pleads for his own execution; in the second, prior to his release, Victor
learns of the repeated rape of his wife, Gila, and the murder of his son.

One for the Road projects an alluring yet intensely problematic aura of
resolution in the light of Pinter's career. Its disturbing, topical subject
matter encourages the retrospective impression that the play is a kind
of ur-text for Pinter's thugs. It is indeed tempting to read the play as a
regression from the clownish, innocent early thugs to a grim political
violence at their origin. But this teleological reading is troubled by
Pinter's conflicted gesture. Like other plays in the anti-authoritarian
cycle, the setting of *One for the Road* is left ambiguous. Disclosure of the
thug's secret, political meaning is balanced by mystification of historical context. This play about 'real' torture retains a curious degree of
abstraction. Moreover, *One for the Road* refrains from depicting torture
and focuses instead on purposeless, digressive conversations at torture's periphery. Despite its apparent realism, the play's links to real
violence remain equivocal. Again, Pinter's subject is the representation
of violence; the play exposes aggressions inscribed in speech, intima-
tions of violence deprived of spurious visible consummation.

As a verbal rather than physical torturer, Nicolas conjoins erotic and
political violence in the language of fantasy. Throughout the play, his
obsessive identification with father figures is mirrored by his excoriat-

ing hatred of Gila and preoccupation with the actual and symbolic rape of the guilty maternal figure. His intermittently wheedling, seductive monologues to Victor sharply contrast the inane, dialogic interrogation of Gila, who embodies an intolerable threat first confronted then disavowed. The erratic, contradictory quality of such symbolic manoeuvres signals psychic instability, an impression deepened through many verbal slips. For example, an attempt at thuggish menace leads Nicolas to mention castration as an antidote to Victor's despair, but the monologic form suggests that the anxious fantasy belongs to the speaker. Similarly, Nicolas's perverse questions to Nicky about parental love echo his own half-joking maternal reference, 'Do you think I'm mad? My mother did' (33). Finally, the repellent 'joke' concerning Gila's sexuality is so poorly told, riddled with pauses, and punctuated by 'wild' laughter that Nicolas feels compelled to explain it. Again, attempted intimidation yields to uncontained sexual anxiety, and the frantic explication reflects a desire to discipline the joke's unruliness.

More broadly, *One for the Road* centres on pathologies embedded in language. In the play's representational sphere, the civilities and sublimations of speech share reciprocal guilt with the imagined violence offstage. Nicolas's polite frankness at the outset introduces respectable discourse, and subsequent civil locutions are arrayed against the boot, castration, and 'the death of others' (45) as reminders of the ineluctable suffering that rhetorical civility disguises and enables. 'One has to be so scrupulous about language' (40), Nicolas remarks, and *One for the Road* blurs the boundaries between torture and the coercive power of rhetoric. For victims, speech is a luxury, and when Nicolas taunts the silent Victor with the latter's reputed fondness for 'the cut and thrust of debate' (45), the context mocks the liberal ideal and the colourful image points to unsublimated realities lurking beyond the metaphor. Nor is the audience left innocent. On the one hand, the spectator is aligned with Victor, a passive, silenced victim of the narrator-as-torturer. Yet the comfort of a safe, privileged distance, the ideology of the cultural spectator, is unavailable or denied to victims, and this complicity extends to neutrally dissecting the play after the performance. To quiescently attend *One for the Road* is in some way to countenance it, which is, I think, what Pinter intends.

Indeed, what distinguishes *One for the Road* is its perverse, insistent theatricality, an aesthetic rendering of torture that presupposes an audience. In this sense, Nicolas functions as both narrator and *metteur en scène*. His florid images, melodramatic ruminations, rhetorical posturing, psychological disclosures, and wild shifts in substance and tone, coupled with the nearly mathematical variation in monologic and dialogic modes of expression, the manipulated verbal rhythm of each distinct scene, the fully orchestrated permutations of standing and sitting figures, and the contrived erotics and politics of space – all conspire to render the interrogation as spectacle. Psychologically, Nicolas bears resemblance to psychoanalyst Christopher Bollas's description of a particular form of hysteria, hysterical psychosis, which is marked by the patient's tendency to perform for the analyst, to trap the analyst in a mutually destructive dramatization of the self: 'Hysterical psychosis presents undigested images, visual scenes that defy meaning ... Clinicians working with the psychotic actions of the hysteric do indeed find them very hard to think about, precisely because the hysteric has presented himself or herself in a grotesquely vivid manner. This is a kind of sexual psychosis, as the patient wraps these scenes in sexual lining, all too often driving the analyst into further bewilderment by an erotism gone awry ... For this is a psychosis that represents sexuality. Sexuality that drives the self mad.'[53]

Emanating from one of the higher-ranking thugs in the Pinter canon, Nicolas's hysterical psychosis provides a psychic foundation for authoritarian violence, condensing aggression and sexuality in a single figure. At a second level, if one substitutes 'author' for 'hysteric' and 'spectator' for 'clinician,' Bollas offers a fair description of Pinter's creative process. The hysterical psychotic's performances are resistant and undigested, symptomatic rather than transparent. The dramatist requires similar displacements in representing social violence, and Pinter's thugs are thus better read as symptoms than mimetic imitations. Indeed, considered realistically, Nicolas provides an easy target. Marked by his profession, visibly attached to institutional torture, the character elicits immediate and satisfying outrage. The true horror of *One for the Road* inheres less in Nicolas than in the audience's untenable relation to the spectacle. In the broad context of Pinter's work, Nicolas functions as the symptom of deeper pathologies. In the ultimate hierarchy of thugs, he ranks no higher than functionary.

Compared with its predecessors, *Ashes to Ashes* (1996) gives thuggery a postmodern form. The plays discussed thus far could be mapped on a single spectrum. Their thugs embrace an equivocal realism, with one foot in ontological absurdism and one in political reality (to modify Colleran's phrase, above). Like *Moonlight* (1993), discussed in the introduction to this book, *Ashes to Ashes*, I will argue, represents a provocative and open-ended turn. In one unbroken act, a middle-aged couple spends an early evening talking in the sitting room of an English country house. As the play opens, Rebecca is describing to Devlin (her current husband or lover) a sadomasochistic ritual prac- tised with a former lover. This unnamed lover would ask Rebecca to kiss his fist as he put his other hand around her throat; she would kiss his palm as he guided her into a submissive sexual posture. 'My body went back,' Rebecca says, 'slowly but truly.'[54] The remainder of the play consists of Devlin's inquisitions and diatribes concerning Rebecca's memories of her lover and the odd vignettes that these mem- ories trigger. At the play's end, Devlin assumes the sadistic posture described at the beginning, and Rebecca delivers a fragmentary mono- logue punctuated by an echo. From even this brief synopsis it is clear that *Ashes to Ashes* significantly diverges from other plays in its repre- sentation of thuggery. The violations of realistic convention are unlike the earlier anti-authoritarian cycle; the play's concluding echo and its expressive, metaphoric controlling gesture (the ritual of fist and throat) suggest a striving towards meanings incommunicable by other means. This is a new and difficult sort of ambiguity, a poeticized politics that stands in contrast to the politicized poetics of the early plays and the equivocal realism of the other political works.

   Ashes to Ashes looks back on the dialectic of civilization and barbar- ism I introduced in relation to *Night and Fog*, but its symbolization here is disintegrating and unstable; placed side by side with *One for the Road*, the later play seems less an allegory than a pastiche. The topics and motifs of *Ashes to Ashes* are certainly heterogeneous and hybrid, and in a further sense the play fits recent postmodernist criticism.[55] Lately, much writing on Pinter has focused on the intricate relation between the personal and the political, and *Ashes to Ashes* incarnates this relation in an unsettling way. The play blurs the boundaries between marriage and interrogation. It dramatizes the ephemeral tis- sue of memories, beliefs, and understandings on which relationships rest – a couple's necessary collective unconscious. But it also gestures at the world's hard edges, at horizons of action and victimization that mock the fuzzy self-indulgence of domestic navel-gazing. The domes- tic discontent of plays like *A Slight Ache* and *The Lover* is uncomfortably fused with the verbal torture of *One for the Road*. Ironically, the title here comes from Devlin and Rebecca taking turns singing lines of a song, a rare episode of human connection that also harks back to the dialogic mode of earlier Pinter plays. But like *One for the Road*, this is centrally a drama about monologue, about the will to narrate and the political implications of univocal semantic power.

One can begin to outline a poetics of this verbal power by looking at the title more closely. *Ashes to Ashes*, like *One for the Road*, is in one sense a metonymy. It originates in the song Devlin and Rebecca sing together (as 'one for the road' is Nicolas's inane tag line) and both titles thus are interior fragments used to stand for the respective plays. On the other hand the use of 'ashes to ashes' is also metaphorical insofar as it imposes a heavy allusive weight, inviting us to equate the phrase and its prior symbolic associations with the ultimate meaning of the play. Metaphor and metonymy have been subjected to many complex meta-commentaries. Roman Jakobson, for example, considered these two master-tropes as distinct poles of any discourse; among many other applications, Jakobson identified metonymy with narrative (a moving, interconnected sequence, existing in time) and metaphor with poetry (a forged unity of disparate elements, outside temporal and spatial relation or contingency).[56] In a later influential account, Peter Brooks uses the two tropes, along with psychoanalytic theory, to out-line a theory of narrative. Narrative depends on a complex interplay of metonymy and metaphor, the former associated with the pleasure principle (desiring, playing, moving the story along) and the latter with the death drive (the metaphoric equivalence of beginning and end, which, outside time, enclose and terminate the plot's metonymic sequence).[57]

Reasoning from Pinter's work, one might say that metonymy and metaphor are often political. Metonymy is premised on interconnec-tion and interdependence, on respect for the 'local detail,' in Austin Quigley's phrase.[58] In Pinter's universe, metaphor, by contrast, could be understood as a kind of identity-thinking. Metaphor solicits and expresses a lust to fix and control, to determine what a thing is by forcibly equating it with something it is not. In a number of ways, metaphor might be considered authoritarian. Metaphor glorifies the creativity of assertion while disguising its violence; rips things from their contexts and forces them into contrived relation; stands outside time and history; denies the complexity of relations and determina-tions; and expresses an absolutist desire for fullness, transparency, and the absence of contradiction.

Seen in this light, *Ashes to Ashes* is a sparring session between meta-phor and metonymy against the horizon of a history whose guilt – measured by flickering images of barbarity and violence – stains the making and imposing of meanings. In general, Rebecca is metonymic, Devlin metaphoric. Devlin says of Rebecca's lover, 'It would mean a great deal to me if you could define him more clearly' (11). This reflects an authoritarian wish, a desire to dominate. He wants to give the lover a 'concrete shape' (12), to neutralize a threat by subjecting it to examination and turning it into knowledge. Devlin is hostile to metonymy: 'all you can talk of are his hands ... There must be more to him than hands. What about eyes?' (13). Devlin's fondness for terms of endearment contains a more sinister identity thinking as well. He calls Rebecca 'darling,' and when she says, 'I'm not your darling,' he replies ominously, 'Yes you are' (15). To say You Are My Darling is to say that you are first and foremost my darling; you are coextensive with what I mean by my darling; all those elements of you that do not conform to the phrase, to darling-ness and all it implies, are herewith excluded from what you are. It is therefore not surprising that Rebecca says, 'I'm nobody's darling' (17).

By contrast, Rebecca's speech and thought tend towards the metonymic pole. While Devlin is preoccupied with the big picture, with assimilating memories and perceptions to a body of information, Rebecca stubbornly sticks to particular images and details. She alights on a hand, a cap, a siren, a pen, coats, bags, gravy, mud, a rigid spectator, suitcases, and finally, a bundled baby. In a familiar Pinter idiom, Devlin expresses a love of big metaphors, life lessons, civic sentiments, philosophical postulates. 'You know what it will be like, such a vacuum?' he asks, repulsed by Rebecca's evocation of a godless world, 'It'll be like England playing Brazil at Wembley and not a soul in the stadium' (40). For Devlin, the consequence of this lack of authority is social paralysis: 'A world without a winner' (41). The absence of a synthesizing, authoritative eye – a metaphoric eye – leads to a world without master narratives, without political order.

At moments, *Ashes to Ashes* itself aspires to metaphor, and on this basis we can begin to reflect on the complex politics of the work as a whole. Drew Milne suggests that the play can be taken as an elaboration of the (metaphoric) significance of a single suggestive image: a woman kissing a man's fist as he tightens a hand around her throat.[59] By contrast, Pinter has argued that *One for the Road* is not a metaphor, implying that it is a kind of fact.[60] The earlier political plays derive force by establishing a realist foundation but subtly abstracting it so that the claim to reality becomes equivocal. This crucial tension is altered in *Ashes to Ashes*. How are we to respond to the central image and the final echoed narration? They are invested with a spectacular sensibility almost non-existent elsewhere in Pinter; the gestures seem earnest, devoid of irony. One could argue that *Ashes to Ashes* succumbs to the lure of metaphoric synthesis, that it attempts an aesthetic integration of irreconcilable realities. In his critique of Pinter's sexual politics, Milne cites Michael Billington's suggestion that the kissed fist summarizes a kind of 'sexual Fascism.'[61] This phrase seems a good description of one of the play's aspirations, but at the same time the kissed fist seems reductive and inadequate as an account of either fascism or patriarchy, much less the relationship between them.

If the fist is an ambiguous controlling image, the play's interior discourse develops an entire political symbolism that also cuts in various ways. In measured, rhythmic fashion, Rebecca introduces a number of crypto-fascist imagistic fragments, and this evolving iconography provides the counterpoint to a skeletal melodramatic pastiche made of sporadic and incomplete references to suburban life, infidelity, family visits, and trips to the movies. Something essential about the play's politics resides in the structural interplay of these two fields of force. The political fragments are variations on a theme. Rebecca's lover, she initially recalls, was a sort of 'guide' (21) with a travel agency, but she then recounts a trip she made with him to a factory where he was greeted by adoring workers wearing caps, who respected him because 'he ran a really tight ship' and because of his 'purity' and 'conviction' (25). He claimed the workers would follow him over a cliff. Later, jarringly, Rebecca says that her lover's job as a guide involved tearing babies from their screaming mothers on a railway platform (27).

In a subsequent vignette, Rebecca remembers looking out a Dorset window on a beautiful day and seeing a number of people carrying bags, being led by guides through the woods and into the sea. 'The tide covered them slowly,' she says; 'Their bags bobbed about in the waves' (49). At the play's conclusion, she describes seeing a little boy and an old man holding hands and dragging suitcases down an icy street, followed by a woman carrying a baby. She then abruptly shifts to the first person – 'I held her to me. She was breathing' (73) – whereupon Devlin approaches, puts one hand round her neck, and asks her to kiss his fist. Rebecca refuses and instead speaks a series of short phrases – each met with an echo – describing how her baby, bundled in a shawl, was torn from her arms on a railway platform. Asked by another woman about her baby, Rebecca responded: 'what baby?' 'I don't have a baby,' and 'I don't know of any baby' (83–4).

I would suggest that the political symbolism in *Ashes to Ashes* can be interpreted in opposing ways, and that this tension is symptomatic of the fluid cultural politics of postmodernism. In the modernist *Night and Fog*, Resnais uses montage to fuse two realisms whose intolerable juxtaposition underscores the barbarity of an irreconcilable and fractured reality. The vignettes in *Ashes to Ashes*, by contrast, could be read as conscious attempts to create a surrealist authoritarian iconography, a sort of image gallery of synthesized political atrocities. The strands of the vignettes have been ripped from particular contexts and recombined; historical realities have been filtered through an imaginative, transforming process, and thus aestheticized. One might argue that the dignity of what the vignettes represent is compromised because its specificity is attenuated; the iconography is simultaneously too symbolic and too literal. By contrast, the interrogations of Stanley in *The Birthday Party* create a self-alienating representation of political thuggery that implicates the audience by entertaining it. Such alienated representation preserves a tension between the reality of torture and the obscenity of a culture that has masked and enabled atrocity – sometimes by sentimentalizing it, by fashioning a distance from which atrocity can be condemned, lamented, and disavowed. The politicized images in *Ashes to Ashes* have a troubling earnestness; one senses they are meant to 'stand for' something.

At the same time, one could plausibly see these images of historical atrocity as symptoms of a process of abstraction, codification, and disintegration that pervades the play, rendering it an indeterminate mix of conflicting signifiers. A capacity to generate diametrically opposed but equally persuasive readings is a good indicator of a text poised between allegory and pastiche; politically, *Ashes to Ashes* has been taken to embody both progressive utopianism and reactionary incoherence. Mireia Aragay speaks approvingly of the play's ability to evoke a 'shared sense of subjectivity' and awareness of 'responsibility for the suffering of others' that moves beyond postmodernist political resignation.[62] From Drew Milne's reading, on the other hand, emerges a play that inappropriately conflates fascism and sexual violence: 'The imaginative juxtaposition of holocaust "memories" with female desire for misogynist authoritarianism nevertheless leaves political responsibility disturbingly ambiguous.' Milne concludes that the play 'remains prismatic, a generator of politically indeterminate interpretations.'[63]

At moments even Aragay's analysis grows equivocal. For example, she concludes that Rebecca's final monologue creates a redemptive sense of shared responsibility 'and also, paradoxically, the human capacity for resigning that responsibility.' Do these mixed messages not negate each other, making the monologue opaque? Elsewhere in Aragay's account, there emerges a sense of semiotic entropy threatening the play's coherence. She alludes to the 'biblical echo'[64] of Rebecca's three ultimate denials of the baby's suffering, but, while this interpretation has a certain plausibility, it also points to a symbolically overstuffed, overdetermined text that strains its bounds (how can a biblical allusion be integrated with the play's other registers?).

Ultimately, one could contend that the play's politics are unreadable. Aragay makes much of Rebecca's speech lamenting the fading police siren – 'as the siren faded away in my ears I knew it was becoming louder and louder for someone else' (29) – as evidence of shared subjectivity and social connectedness. But Rebecca (ironically? earnestly?) continues by saying of the siren: 'I hate it echoing away. I hate it leaving me. I hate losing it. I want it to be mine, all the time. It's such a beautiful sound' (31). This leads in turn to Devlin's chilling speech about the police, which stands in some sense unrefuted: 'There isn't one minute of the day when they're not charging around one corner or another in the world, in their police cars, ringing their sirens. So you can take comfort from that, at least. Can't you? You'll never be lonely again. You'll never be without a police siren. I promise you' (33). What is one to make of this exchange? Even the muted utopianism of 'shared subjectivity' and collective responsibility here is lampooned as a deadly mirage. The glue of society turns out to be nothing more than the exposure and permeability of every nook and corner of the social order to potentially brutal state power. One gets a depressing sense that every species of liberalism, including that intermittently voiced by Rebecca, is contingent on a certain faith and libidinal investment in law and order, and thus is a kind of masochism (cf. the play's governing image).

Ashes to Ashes extends the cultural imaginary of thuggery across a postmodern line. One becomes aware, through this play, of the extent to which Pinter's drama has steadily and systematically amassed an available symbolism of authoritarianism in all its guises – social, sexual, political. *Ashes to Ashes* fuses several familiar elements in an unexpected combination, both provocative and problematic. Pinter's authorial voice here is allied with the 'eclectic mingling' that Austin Quigley identifies with postmodernism.[65] The husband is now interrogator verging on torturer; the openly political thug is (perhaps) a former lover; the civilized world of leafy suburbia, family visits, train stations, and movie houses is invested with a surrealist dimension in which people are marched to extermination and babies are torn from mothers. Like Pinter's earlier dramatizations of thuggery, visible violence is carefully withheld, but it is here driven underground, made part of the unconscious collective memory as so many fictionalized images and scenes. The play aestheticizes authoritarian violence in tableaus, familiar signifiers (the march, the stolen baby, the hand on throat) distilled from the great mediator and enabler of violence: culture. Whether Rebecca has 'really' experienced what she describes or whether, as a kind of psychic sponge, she has absorbed it from films, television, history books, and other forms of cultural representation – this calculated ambiguity is a key part of the play's point. Her horror, and her pathology, is to have realized that representation, like memory and fantasy, is a phenomenon of distance, of working through symbolically rather than actually, and is thus a form of non-intervention.

Freud's key essay 'A Child Is Being Beaten'[66] underscores the complex fluidity of sexual fantasy, and Jean Laplanche and Jean-Bertrand Pontalis suggest that fantasy is a shifting *mise en scène* rather than a fixed form: 'Fantasy is not the object of desire, but its setting.'[67] Pinter's treatments of thuggery shift and recombine an ensemble of positions and roles to make clear, through the mechanism of fantasy, how pleasure, sexuality, and violence are intimately linked. Father, husband, lover, wife, mother, daughter – these positions circulate and crystallize relations of dominance and submission (although, as Milne and others have shown, Pinter's treatment of gender is far from unproblematic). A key function of cultural representations of violence is to create a space of collective fantasy, to mobilize and contain sadomasochistic desires by repetition of basic scenarios and structures, and to turn these fantasy exercises into a source of pleasure. As Pinter's plays suggest, such representations are ways of countenancing the real violence of power – political power, economic power, cultural power – whose invisibility is guaranteed by the ecstatic visibility of so much graphic violence.

Ashes to Ashes takes this critique to an extreme, nearly schizophrenic level, and some of the political hazards of 'eclectic mingling' are dramatized by this postmodern play. Past a certain point, the distillation and combination of authoritarian signifiers may suggest that they are *only* codes, and the work as a whole may be processed as a large-scale aestheticization, as a pastiche that sublimates political will into a kind of aesthetic appreciation. The idea of mediation, central to the modernist plays, presupposes the real, even as it grants its non-identity with the image. Goldberg and McCann, I have argued, derive their power from still receiving the historical signal of fascism and the Holocaust, however faintly; Lenny and Nicolas, collectively, link authoritarian violence to a credible, disturbing psychopathology. *Ashes to Ashes*, by contrast, is the by-product of a postmodern fragmentation. Like *Moonlight*, *Ashes to Ashes* jumbles together thematic concerns from other periods of Pinter's career. The play's final tableau, the closing monologue and echo, are reminiscent of the memory plays and their interest in ambiguities of time and subjectivity. The difference is that *Ashes to Ashes* refers to historical atrocities, and its ending uneasily joins an earlier aesthetic with a new and indeterminate form of political assertion.

In a holistic appraisal of Pinter's career, however, I believe *Ashes to Ashes* can be recuperated as part of an ongoing, if deeply equivocal, political realism. Like Nicolas in *One for the Road*, Devlin and the unnamed lover rank no higher than authoritarian middle-management. Real authority hides; power is made visible in symbols, sirens, institutions, doctrines, beliefs, codes – forms in which it can be exercised and obeyed without being threatened. In Pinter's canon the insidious thugs have purged all outward signs of thuggery and delegated the dirty work to adjutants. Insulated and invisible, the true *metteurs en scène* carouse while their militias cleanse the streets. This is the scenario of *Party Time*, the highest rung on the thug's ladder. Both the proletarian sphere of the early modernist plays and the disintegrating post-bourgeois world of *Ashes to Ashes* circle an unseen centre. The upper echelons of thuggery wage a campaign of symbolic terror, manipulating cultural signifiers, stigmatizing the undesirable. Cloaked in respectability, the sanitized thug enters and then propagates the cultural mainstream. In a popular culture steeped in violent imagery, violent realities are effectively displaced. The brutality of this culture lies less in what it depicts than in what it conceals.

Notes

Introduction

1 Jameson, *Postmodernism*, 16–17.
2 Huyssen, *After the Great Divide*.
3 The two are Raby, *Cambridge Companion*, and Lois Gordon, *Pinter at Seventy*. Both are discussed below.
4 Cronin, *Samuel Beckett*.
5 Raymond Williams's famous phrase; see his *Marxism and Literature*.
6 Bottoms, *Theatre of Sam Shepard*, 4, 9.
7 See 'On Adaptation.'
8 Wollen, 'The *Auteur* Theory,' 528, 532.
9 Raby, Introduction, *Cambridge Companion*, 3.
10 Pinter, Introduction, *Complete Works: Four*, x.
11 See Merritt, *Pinter in Play*.
12 Williams, *Drama from Ibsen to Brecht*, 19.
13 Raby, Introduction, *Cambridge Companion*, 3.
14 Quoted in Dukore, *Harold Pinter*, 7.
15 Shklovsky, 'Art as Technique,' 12.
16 Ibid., 18.
17 Pinter, *The Homecoming*, 33.
18 Quigley, *The Pinter Problem*, 18, 275.
19 Ibid., 276–7, 28.
20 Adorno, 'Commitment,' 179.
21 Quoted in Brandt, *Modern Theories of Drama*, 210.
22 Adorno, 'Commitment,' 187, 180.
23 Adorno, 'Autonomy of Art,' 242.
24 Marcuse, *One-Dimensional Man*, 76.

25 Sartre, *What Is Literature?* 284–5.
26 Adorno, 'Commitment,' 182.
27 Pinter, *One for the Road*, 33, 40.
28 Adorno, 'Commitment,' 190–1, 191.
29 Peacock, *Harold Pinter and the New British Theatre*, 134.
30 For a commentary on this 'authorial revisionism,' see Drew Milne, 'Pinter's Sexual Politics,' 196–7.
31 Quoted in Merritt, 'Pinter and Politics,' 133.
32 Austin Quigley writes that Pinter has careened between 'undervaluing and overvaluing the political,' in his essay 'Pinter, Politics, and Postmodernism (1),' 9.
33 Aragay, 'Postmodernism (2),' 246.
34 See Silverstein, *Harold Pinter*.
35 Foucault, *Discipline and Punish*, 26.
36 Aragay, 'Postmodernism (2),' 252.
37 Quigley, 'Postmodernism (1),' 11, 7.
38 Quigley borrows this phrase from Pinter; see ibid., 14.
39 Ibid., 23, 10, 12.
40 Ibid., 12.
41 See Adorno, *Minima Moralia*.
42 Adorno, 'Commitment,' 191.
43 See Lois Gordon's excellent 'Chronology' in *Pinter at Seventy*, xliii–lxv.
44 King, 'Harold Pinter's Achievement,' 247.
45 See the collected essays in Gale, *Films of Harold Pinter*.
46 I am thinking here particularly of Adolphe Appia's and Gordon Craig's calls for a director-centred theatre focused on lighting, bodies, and other plastic elements of performance; of Antonin Artaud's 'theatre of cruelty,' with its reliance on spectacle and hostility to language; and Jerzy Grotowski's idea of a 'poor theatre' that avoids borrowing from the aesthetics of other mediums and instead focuses on the actor-audience relation.
47 See Williams, 'Film Bodies,' 701–15. Williams is borrowing the phrase 'body genres' from Clover, 'Her Body, Himself.'
48 Beckett, *Endgame*, 32.
49 Vernet, '*Film Noir*.' Copjec (New York: Verso, 1993) 1.
50 Pinter, *The Homecoming*, 44.
51 Lenny, in *The Homecoming*, 68.
52 Huyssen, *Great Divide*, ix.
53 Adorno, 'Notes on Kafka,' 245.
54 Adorno, 'Cultural Criticism,' 208.
55 Quigley, 'Postmodernism (1),' 7.

56 Adorno, 'Essay as Form,' 98, 98, 99, 101.
57 Jameson discusses the Van Gogh painting in *Postmodernism*, 7–9.
58 Horkheimer and Adorno, 'Culture Industry,' 155.
59 Jameson, *Postmodernism*, 305.
60 Frith, 'The Good, the Bad, and the Indifferent,' 353–5.
61 Ibid., 353.
62 See Rebellato, *1956 And All That*, 18–25.
63 Stokes, 'Pinter and the 1950s.'
64 See Stuart Hall's account of the history of British cultural studies in 'Cultural Studies.'
65 Pinter, *Moonlight*, 10.
66 Ibid., 73–5.
67 Horkheimer and Adorno, *Dialectic of Enlightenment*, 125.

1: The Politics of Negation

 1 Marcuse, *The Aesthetic Dimension*, 72–3.
 2 For a discussion of the tension between fact and metaphor in Pinter's political drama, see Milne, 'Pinter's Sexual Politics.'
 3 Benjamin, 'Reflections on Kafka,' 114.
 4 Pinter, *The Homecoming*, 21.
 5 See 'Kenneth Tynan and Eugene Ionesco, "The London Controversy,"' in Brandt, *Modern Theories of Drama*, 208–14.
 6 See the last sentence of Benjamin, 'Work of Art,' 242.
 7 Quoted in Evans and Evans, eds., *Plays in Review*, 64–5.
 8 Ibid., 65.
 9 Pinter, *The Birthday Party*, 20. Subsequent page citations are given parenthetically in the text.
10 Williams, '*The Birthday Party*,' 22, 19.
11 Quoted in Evans and Evans, *Play in Review*, 64.
12 Bloom, Introduction, *Harold Pinter*, 1.
13 Quoted in Billington, *Life and Work*, 128.
14 Pinter, *The Caretaker*, 17–18. Subsequent page citations are given parenthetically in the text.
15 Stokes, 'Pinter and the 1950s,' 36.
16 Ibid., 35.
17 Sontag, 'Godard,' 165.
18 Jameson, *Marxism and Form*, 407–8.
19 Stokes, 'Pinter and the 1950s,' 31, 30.
20 Milne, 'Pinter's Sexual Politics,' 195.

21 Quoted in Evans and Evans, *Plays in Review*, 64.
22 Zarhy-Levo, 'Pinter and the Critics,' 215.
23 Ibid.
24 Ibid.
25 King, 'Pinter's Achievement,' 253.
26 Esslin, *Theatre of the Absurd*, 293, 316.
27 Ibid., 213.
28 Adorno, 'Commitment,' 191.
29 Jameson, *Postmodernism*, 7, 8.
30 Ibid., 8.
31 Ibid., 9.
32 Dyer writes that entertainment does not present fully realized utopian worlds, but rather conveys a sense of what utopia 'would feel like'; see 'Entertainment and Utopia,' 17–34.
33 Forte, 'Realism,' 20, 20–1.
34 Ibid., 21.
35 Billington, *Life and Work*, 162–77.
36 Pinter, *The Homecoming*, 37. Subsequent page references are given parenthetically in the text.
37 Hansberry, *Raisin in the Sun*, 151.
38 Quoted in Stokes, 'Pinter and the 1950s,' 32.
39 Silverstein, *Harold Pinter*, 81, 86.
40 Freud, *Introduction*, 324, 322, 323.
41 Freud, 'Fetishism,' trans. James Strachey et al., *The Standard Edition of the Complete Psychological Works of Sigmund Freud*, ed. James Strachey (London: Hogarth P and the Institute of Psycho-Analysis, 1961), vol. 21, 132–3.
42 Freud, *Introduction*, 323.
43 Laplanche and Pontalis, 'Fantasy,' 26.
44 Foucault, *Introduction*, 17.
45 Freud, *Introduction*, 324.
46 Freud, *Totem and Taboo*, 499, 500–1.
47 Ibid., 501.
48 Miller, *Death of a Salesman*, 12.

2: The Modernist as Populist

1 Benjamin, 'Author as Producer,' 236.
2 Quigley, *Pinter Problem*, 23.
3 Diamond, *Pinter's Comic Play*, 90; also Bloom quote, 90.
4 See Borges, 'Pierre Menard.'

5 Quoted in States, 'Attitude,' 374.
6 See, in particular, States, 'Attitude' and *Great Reckonings*.
7 States, 'Attitude,' 370.
8 Diamond, *Printer's Comic Play*, 89, 90, 91.
9 Ibid., 91, 92, 95, 108–9.
10 See Frank Krutnik's thorough and readable overview, *In A Lonely Street*.
11 For an updated genealogy of the private eye in film see Cawelti, 'China-town.'
12 See Vernet, '*Film Noir.*'
13 See Jameson, 'Reification.'
14 Billington, *Life and Work*, 90.
15 See Jameson, 'Cognitive Mapping,' 277–87.
16 Pinter, *The Dumb Waiter*, 129–30, 131–2. Subsequent page citations are given parenthetically in the text.
17 Diamond, *Pinter's Comic Play*, 108.
18 Benjamin (quoting himself anonymously), 'Author as Producer,' 224–5.
19 See, for example, Martin Esslin's treatment in *Pinter*, which advances both interpretations.
20 Quigley, *Pinter Problem*, 62.
21 In the United States, I have been able to locate a 1976 Chicago production in the Library of Congress.
22 Esslin, *Pinter*, 87.
23 Guralnick, *Sight Unseen*, x, 101.
24 Harold Pinter, *A Slight Ache*, 169–70. Subsequent page citations are given parenthetically in the text.
25 Adorno, 'Popular Music,' 205.
26 See Crisell, *Understanding Radio*, 17–41, 14.
27 Brecht, *Brecht on Theatre*, 51.
28 See David Cook, *A History of Narrative Film* (New York: Norton, 1990), 5–6.
29 Jameson, 'Synoptic Chandler,' 36.
30 Chandler, *Farewell, My Lovely*, 4. See also Jameson, 'Synoptic Chandler,' 37.
31 Phillips, *Terrors and Experts*, 103.
32 This pessimistic approach to mass culture is usually associated with the critique of the 'culture industry' advanced by members of the Frankfurt School and developed by subsequent Marxist critics, and it should be distinguished from the more celebratory, populist (or 'culturalist') analyses derived from British critics such as Raymond Williams and E.P. Thompson, and from the structuralist-Marxist tradition following the work of Louis Althusser. For a seminal discussion of reification, see Lukács, *History and Class Consciousness*. For a critique of rationalization, see Max Weber, *From*

Max Weber, and for the seminal application of reification to an analysis of bourgeois culture see Horkheimer and Adorno, *Dialectic of Enlightenment.* The Frankfurt School tradition was famously extended to other arenas of modern society by Herbert Marcuse in books such as *One-Dimensional Man* and to contemporary media culture by Fredric Jameson in works such as *Signatures of the Visible.*

33 Jameson, 'Reification,' 9–10.

34 Ibid., 11–12.

35 Adorno, 'Cultural Criticism,' 22.

36 Fehsenfeld, 'That first last look ...,' 125.

37 Pinter, *Betrayal*, 215–16. Subsequent page citations are given parenthetically in the text.

38 See *Betrayal* (film).

39 Billington, *Life and Work*, 261, 258, 257.

40 Quoted in Geraghty, *Women and Soap Opera*, 30.

41 See Burkman, 'Pinter's *Betrayal*,' 142–56.

42 Brater, 'Cinematic Fidelity,' 110.

43 Ibid., 109.

44 Geraghty, *Women and Soap Opera*, 11.

45 Mumford, *Love and Ideology*, 38.

46 According to www.sonypictures.com – the website of Sony Pictures, which owns syndication rights to the show – this is Episode 908, 'The Betrayal,' first aired in November 1997. The episode begins with *Seinfeld*'s end credits (!) and then depicts the acrimonious aftermath of a trip to a wedding in India. Entwined farcical mini-melodramas are recounted backwards, introduced by titles such as 'One day earlier,' 'Fifteen minutes earlier,' and so on. For good measure, the groom is named 'Pinter Ranawat.'

47 Pinter, Introduction, ix.

48 Mitchell, *Hope and Dread*, 141.

3: Towards the Postmodern

1 Adorno, 'Commitment,' 180.

2 Pinter, *Old Times*, 36–7. Subsequent page citations are given parenthetically in the text.

3 For a brief account of the circumstances surrounding Pinter's inward turn, see Billington, *Life and Work*, 179–81.

4 'Structural film' is P. Adams Sitney's term for avant-garde films of the late 1960s and 1970s in which form is marked as primary and determining; see 'Structural Film.'

5 Billington, *Life and Work*, 212.
6 Freud, *Beyond the Pleasure Principle*, 40.
7 Freud, *Interpretation of Dreams*, 353.
8 See Althusser, 'Ideology,' 127–86.
9 Billington, *Life and Work*, 219.
10 Ogden, 'Analytic Third,' 487.
11 Lukács, *History*, 90.
12 See Adorno, 'Autonomy of Art,' 245.
13 Bigsby, 'Language of Crisis,' 13.
14 Ibid., 35.
15 Churchill, *Softcops*, 3, 17.
16 Ibid., 49.
17 Bigsby, 'Language of Crisis,' 50.
18 See Debord, *Society of the Spectacle*.
19 Quoted in Bull, *New British Political Dramatists*, 13.
20 See Brenton, 'Petrol Bombs,' 4–20.
21 Ibid., 11.
22 Brenton, *Weapons of Happiness*, 183.
23 Ibid., 232.
24 Ibid., 209, 253.
25 Quoted in Evans and Evans, *Plays in Review*, 218.
26 Pinter, *No Man's Land*, 112. Subsequent page citations are given parenthetically in the text.
27 Adler, 'Flux to Fixity,' 136–7, 138, 139.
28 See 'Kenneth Tynan and Eugene Ionesco, "The London Controversy,"' in Brandt, *Modern Theories of Drama*, 211.
29 Brecht, *Brecht on Theatre*, 35.
30 Marcuse, *One-Dimensional Man*, 63, 61.
31 Billington, *Life and Work*, 246.
32 Quoted in Evans and Evans, *Plays in Review*, 215, 218, 216.
33 Taylor, 'Art and Commerce,' 178.
34 Brenton, *Romans*, 101, 105.
35 Peacock, *Radical Stages*, 128.
36 Gross, 'Romans in Britain,' 76.
37 Ibid., 81.
38 Brenton, *Romans*, 77.
39 Adorno, 'Notes on Kafka,' 271.
40 Lindner, *Rebel without a Cause* (New York: Grune, 1944); quoted in Adorno et al., *Authoritarian Personality*, 764. *Note*: The title of this section was suggested by Stanley Elkin's short story 'A Poetics for Bullies.'

41 Adorno et al., *The Authoritarian Personality*, 763.

42 Quoted in Page, *File on Pinter*, 106.

43 Colleran, 'Disjuncture,' 58.

44 Quoted in Esslin, *Pinter*, 36.

45 Pinter, *One for the Road*, 79. Subsequent page references are given parenthetically in the text.

46 Quoted in States, 'Pinter's *The Homecoming*,' 13.

47 Ionesco, 'Notes on the Theatre,' 53.

48 Pinter, *The Birthday Party* and *The Room*, 85. Subsequent page references are given parenthetically in the text.

49 Williams, *Drama*, 324, 325.

50 Pinter, *The Caretaker* and *The Dumb Waiter*, 86. Subsequent page references are given parenthetically in the text.

51 Morrison, *Cantors and Chronicles*, 3.

52 Pinter, *The Homecoming*, 47. Subsequent page references are given parenthetically in the text.

53 Bollas, *Hysteria*, 143.

54 Pinter, *Ashes to Ashes*, 7. Subsequent page references are given parenthetically in the text.

55 See the syntheses of postmodernist theory and political analyses in Quigley, 'Postmodernism (1)' and Aragay, 'Postmodernism (2),' 7–27; 246–59.

56 This analysis was introduced in Jakobson's essay 'Two Aspects of Language,' 55–82. See the explanation, commentary, and application of Jakobson's model in Lodge, *Modes of Modern Writing*, 73–124.

57 See Brooks, *Reading for the Plot*.

58 Quigley, 'Postmodernism (1),' 7.

59 See Milne, 'Pinter's Sexual Politics,' 207.

60 Pinter, 'A Play and Its Politics,' 7–8. Pinter's claim is cited in ibid., 196.

61 Billington, *Life and Work*, 377. Quoted in Milne, 'Pinter's Sexual Politics,' 209.

62 Aragay, 'Postmodernism (2),' 255.

63 Milne, 'Printer's Sexual Politics,' 209.

64 Aragay, 'Postmodernism (2),' 255.

65 Quigley, 'Postmodernism (1),' 12.

66 Freud, '"A Child Is Being Beaten."'

67 Laplanche and Pontalis, 'Fantasy,' 26.

Works Cited

Adler, Thomas. 'From Flux to Fixity: Art and Death in Pinter's *No Man's Land.*' *Critical Essays on Harold Pinter.* Ed. Steven H. Gale. Boston: Hall, 1990. 136–41.

Adorno, T.W. 'The Autonomy of Art.' *The Adorno Reader.* Ed. Brian O'Connor. Trans. C. Lenhardt. Oxford and Malden, MA: Blackwell, 2000. 239–63.

– 'Commitment.' Trans. Francis McDonagh. *Aesthetics and Politics.* Trans. ed. Ronald Taylor. London: NLB, 1977. 177–95.

– 'Cultural Criticism and Society.' *Prisms.* Trans. Samuel and Shierry Weber. Cambridge: MIT P, 1990, 17–34.

– 'The Essay as Form.' Trans. Bob Hullot-Kentor and Fredric Will. *The Adorno Reader.* Ed. Brian O'Connor. Trans. C. Lenhardt. Oxford and Malden, MA: Blackwell, 2000. 91–111.

– *Minima Moralia: Reflections from Damaged Life.* Trans. E.F.N. Jephcott. London: New Left, 1974.

– 'Notes on Kafka.' *Prisms.* Trans. Samuel and Shierry Weber. Cambridge: MIT P, 1990. 243–71.

– 'On Popular Music.' *Cultural Theory and Popular Culture: A Reader.* Ed. John Storey. Athens: U of Georgia P, 1998. 197–209.

Adorno, T.W., et al. *The Authoritarian Personality.* New York: Harper, 1950.

Althusser, Louis. 'Ideology and Ideological State Apparatuses: Notes towards an Investigation.' *Lenin and Philosophy and Other Essays.* Trans. Ben Brewster. London: New Left, 1971. 127–86.

Aragay, Mireia. 'Pinter, Politics, and Postmodernism (2).' *The Cambridge Companion to Harold Pinter.* Ed. Peter Raby. Cambridge: CUP, 2001. 246–59.

Beckett, Samuel. *Endgame.* New York: Grove P, 1958.

Begley, Varun. 'On Adaptation, David Mamet and Hollywood.' *Essays in Theatre* 16.2 (1998): 165–76.

Benjamin, Walter. 'The Author as Producer.' Trans. Edmund Jephcott. *Reflections*. Ed. Peter Demetz. New York: Schocken, 1978. 220–38.
– 'Some Reflections on Kafka.' Trans. Harry Zohn. *Illuminations*. Ed. Hannah Arendt. New York: Schocken, 1968. 141–5.
– 'The Work of Art in the Age of Mechanical Reproduction.' Trans. Harry Zohn. *Illuminations*. Ed. Hannah Arendt. New York: Schocken, 1968. 217–51.
Betrayal. Dir. David Jones. Screenplay Harold Pinter from his play. Perf. Jeremy Irons, Ben Kingsley, and Patricia Hodge. London: Horizon, 1992.
Bigsby, C.W.E. 'The Language of Crisis in British Theatre: The Drama of Cultural Pathology.' *Contemporary English Drama*. Ed. C.W.E. Bigsby and Malcolm Bradbury. New York: Holmes, 1981. 11–51.
Billington, Michael. *The Life and Work of Harold Pinter*. London: Faber, 1996.
Bloom, Harold. 'Introduction.' *Harold Pinter*. Ed. Harold Bloom. New York: Chelsea, 1987. 1–6.
Bollas, Christopher. *Hysteria*. London and New York: Routledge, 2000.
Borges, Jorge Luis. 'Pierre Menard, Author of the *Quixote*.' Trans. James E. Irby. *Labyrinths*. Ed. James E. Irby and Donald A. Yates. New York: New Directions, 1988. 36–44.
Bottoms, Stephen J. *The Theatre of Sam Shepard: States of Crisis*. Cambridge: CUP, 1998.
Brandt, George W., ed. *Modern Theories of Drama: A Selection of Writings on Drama and Theatre, 1850–1990*. Oxford: Clarendon P, 1998.
Brater, Enoch. 'Cinematic Fidelity and the Forms of Pinter's *Betrayal*.' *Harold Pinter*. Ed. Harold Bloom. New York: Chelsea, 1987. 105–16.
Brecht, Bertolt. *Brecht on Theatre*. Ed. John Willet. London: Methuen, 1978.
Brenton, Howard. 'Petrol Bombs through the Proscenium Arch.' *Theatre Quarterly* 17, March 1975.
– *The Romans in Britain*. London: Methuen, 1980.
– *Weapons of Happiness*. *Plays: One*. London: Methuen, 1986.
Brooks, Peter. *Reading for the Plot: Design and Intention in Narrative*. New York: Knopf, 1984.
Bull, John. *New British Political Dramatists*. London: Macmillan, 1984.
Burkman, Katherine. 'Harold Pinter's *Betrayal*: Life before Death – and After.' *Critical Essays on Harold Pinter*. Ed. Steven Gale. Boston: Hall, 1990. 142–56.
Cawelti, John G. '*Chinatown* and Generic Transformation in Recent American Films.' *Film Genre Reader II*. Ed. Barry Keith Grant. Austin: UTP, 1995. 227–45.
Chandler, Raymond. *Farewell, My Lovely*. New York: Vintage, 1992.
Churchill, Caryl. *Softcops*. *Plays: Two*. London: Methuen, 1990.

Clover, Carol. 'Her Body, Himself: Gender in the Slasher Film.' *Representations*, 20 (Fall 1987): 187–228.

Colleran, Jeanne. 'Disjuncture as Theatrical and Postmodern Practice in Griselda Gambaro's *The Camp* and Harold Pinter's *Mountain Language*.' *Pinter at Sixty*. Ed. Katherine H. Burkman and John Kundert-Gibbs. Bloomington: IUP, 1993. 49–63.

Cook, David. *A History of Narrative Film*. New York: Norton, 1990.

Crisell, Andrew. *Understanding Radio*. London and New York: Routledge, 1994.

Cronin, Anthony. *Samuel Beckett: The Last Modernist*. New York: HarperCollins, 1997.

Debord, Guy. *The Society of the Spectacle*. Trans. Donald Nicholson-Smith. New York: Zone, 1994.

Diamond, Elin. *Pinter's Comic Play*. Lewisburg, PA: Bucknell UP, 1985.

Dukore, Bernard. *Harold Pinter*. London: Macmillan, 1988.

Dyer, Richard. 'Entertainment and Utopia.' *Only Entertainment*. London: Routledge, 1992. 17–34.

Elkin, Stanley. 'A Poetics for Bullies.' *Criers & Kibitzers, Kibitzers & Criers*. New York: Thunder's Mouth P., 1990. 197–217.

Esslin, Martin. *Pinter: A Study of His Plays*. New York: Norton, 1976.

– *The Theatre of the Absurd*. Garden City, NY: Anchor, 1961.

Evans, Gareth, and Barbara Lloyd Evans, eds. *Plays in Review, 1956–1980: British Drama and the Critics*. New York: Methuen, 1985.

Fehsenfeld, Martha. 'That first last look ...' *Pinter at Sixty*. Ed. Katherine Burkman and John L. Kundert-Gibbs. Bloomington: IUP, 1993. 125–8.

Forte, Jeanie. 'Realism, Narrative, and the Feminist Playwright: A Problem of Reception.' *Feminist Theatre and Theory*. New York: St Martin's P, 1996. 19–34.

Foucault, Michel. *Discipline and Punish: The Birth of the Prison*. Trans. Alan Sheridan. New York: Vintage, 1995.

– *An Introduction*. Trans. Robert Hurley. New York: Random, 1978. Vol. 1 of *The History of Sexuality*.

Freud, Sigmund. *Beyond the Pleasure Principle*. Trans. James Strachey et al. New York and London: Norton, 1961.

– '"A Child is Being Beaten": A Contribution to the Study of the Origin of Sexual Perversion.' Trans. James Strachey. *Freud on Women: A Reader*. Ed. Elisabeth Young-Bruehl. New York and London: Norton, 1990. 215–40.

– *A General Introduction to Psychoanalysis*. Trans. Joane Riviere. Garden City, NY: Garden City Publishing, 1943.

– *The Interpretation of Dreams*. Trans. James Strachey. New York: Avon, 1965.

– *Totem and Taboo* (excerpt). Trans. James Strachey et al. *The Freud Reader*. Ed. Peter Gay. New York and London: Norton, 1989. 481–513.

Frith, Simon. 'The Good, the Bad, and the Indifferent: Defending Popular
    Culture from the Populists.' *A Cultural Studies Reader: History, Theory, Prac-
    tice.* Ed. Jessica Munns and Gita Rajan. London and New York: Longman,
    1996. 352–66.

Gale, Steven H., ed. *The Films of Harold Pinter.* Albany: State of New York P,
    2001.

Geraghty, Christine. *Women and Soap Opera: A Study of Prime Time Soaps.*
    Cambridge: Polity P, 1991.

Gordon, Lois. 'Chronology.' *Pinter at Seventy: A Casebook.* Ed. Lois Gordon.
    New York and London: Routledge, 2001. xliii–lxv.

Gross, Robert. 'The Romans in Britain.' *Howard Brenton: A Casebook.* Ed. Ann
    Wilson. New York and London: Garland, 1992. 71–84.

Guralnick, Elissa. *Sight Unseen: Beckett, Pinter, Stoppard, and Other Contemporary
    Dramatists on Radio.* Athens, OH: OUP, 1986.

Hall, Stuart. 'Cultural Studies: Two Paradigms.' *A Cultural Studies Reader:
    History, Theory, Practice.* Ed. Jessica Munns and Gita Rajan. London and New
    York: Longman, 1996. 194–205.

Hansberry, Lorraine. *A Raisin in the Sun.* New York: Vintage, 1994.

Horkheimer, Max, and T.W. Adorno. *Dialectic of Enlightenment.* Trans. John
    Cumming. New York: Continuum, 1991.

Huyssen, Andreas. *After the Great Divide: Modernism, Mass Culture, Postmodern-
    ism.* Bloomington and Indianapolis: IUP, 1986.

Ionesco, Eugene. 'Notes on the Theatre.' Trans. Donald Watson. *Twentieth-
    Century Theatre: A Sourcebook.* Ed. Richard Drain. London and New York:
    Routledge, 1995, 53–5.

Jakobson, Roman. 'Two Aspects of Language and Two Types of Aphasic
    Disturbances.' *Fundamentals of Language.* By Roman Jakobson and Morris
    Halle. The Hague: Mouton, 1956. 55–82.

Jameson, Fredric. 'Cognitive Mapping.' *The Jameson Reader.* Ed. Michael
    Hardt and Kathi Weeks. Oxford and Malden, MA: Blackwell, 2000. 277–
    87.

– *Marxism and Form: Twentieth-Century Dialectical Theories of Literature.*
    Princeton: Princeton UP, 1971.

– *Postmodernism, or, the Cultural Logic of Late Capitalism.* Durham, NC: Duke UP,
    1999.

– 'Reification and Utopia in Mass Culture.' *Signatures of the Visible.* New York:
    Routledge, 1990. 9–34.

– 'The Synoptic Chandler.' *Shades of Noir.* Ed. Joan Copjec. New York: Verso,
    1993. 33–56.

King, Kimball, assist. Marti Greene. 'Harold Pinter's Achievement and

Modern Drama.' *Pinter at Seventy: A Casebook*. Ed. Lois Gordon. New York and London: Routledge, 2001. 243–56.

Krutnik, Frank. *In a Lonely Street: Film Noir, Genre, Masculinity*. New York: Routledge, 1991.

Laplanche, Jean, and Jean-Bertrand Pontalis. 'Fantasy and the Origins of Sexuality.' *Formations of Fantasy*. Ed. Victor Burgin, James Donald, and Cora Kaplan. London: Methuen, 1986, 5–34.

Lodge, David. *The Modes of Modern Writing: Metaphor, Metonymy, and the Typology of Modern Literature*. Ithaca: Cornell UP, 1977.

Lukács, Georg. *History and Class Consciousness*. Trans. Rodney Livingstone. Cambridge: MIT P, 1971.

Marcuse, Herbert. *The Aesthetic Dimension: Toward a Critique of Marxist Aesthetics*. Boston: Beacon P, 1978.

– *One-Dimensional Man: Studies in the Ideology of Advanced Industrial Society*. Boston: Beacon P, 1964.

Merritt, Susan Hollis. *Pinter in Play: Critical Strategies and the Plays of Harold Pinter*. Durham, NC: Duke UP, 1990.

– 'Pinter and Politics.' *Pinter at Seventy: A Casebook*. Ed. Lois Gordon. New York and London: Routledge, 2001. 129–60.

Miller, Arthur. *Death of a Salesman*. New York: Penguin, 1976.

Milne, Drew. 'Pinter's Sexual Politics.' *The Cambridge Companion to Harold Pinter*. Ed. Peter Raby. Cambridge: CUP, 2001. 195–211.

Mitchell, Stephen. *Hope and Dread in Psychoanalysis*. New York: Basic Books, 1993.

Morrison, Kristin. *Cantors and Chronicles: The Use of Narrative in the Plays of Samuel Beckett and Harold Pinter*. Chicago: UCP, 1983.

Mumford, Laura Stempel. *Love and Ideology in the Afternoon: Soap Opera, Women, and Television Genre*. Bloomington: IUP, 1995.

Ogden, Thomas. 'The Analytic Third: An Overview.' In *Relational Psychoanalysis: The Emergence of a Tradition*. Ed. S. Mitchell and L. Aron. Hillsdale, NJ: Analytic P, 1999. 487–92.

O'Neill, Eugene. *Long Day's Journey into Night*. New Haven and London: Yale UP, 2002.

Page, Malcolm. *File on Pinter*. London: Methuen, 1993.

Peacock, D. Keith. *Harold Pinter and the New British Theatre*. London: Greenwood P, 1997.

– *Radical Stages: Alternative History in Modern British Drama*. London and New York: Greenwood P, 1991.

Phillips, Adam. *Terrors and Experts*. Cambridge: Harvard UP, 1996.

Pinter, Harold. *Ashes to Ashes*. New York: Grove P, 1996.

- *Betrayal. Complete Works: Four.* New York: Grove P, 1981.
- *The Birthday Party* and *The Room.* New York: Grove P, 1968.
- *The Birthday Party. Complete Works: One.* New York: Grove P, 1976.
- *The Caretaker. Complete Works: Two.* New York: Grove P, 1977.
- *The Caretaker* and *The Dumb Waiter.* New York: Grove P, 1988.
- *The Dumb Waiter. Complete Works: One.* New York: Grove P, 1976.
- *The Homecoming. Complete Works: Three.* New York: Grove P, 1978.
- Introduction. *Complete Works: Four,* New York: Grove P, 1981.
- *Moonlight.* New York: Grove P, 1993.
- *No Man's Land. Complete Works: Four.* New York: Grove P, 1981.
- *Old Times. Complete Works: Four.* New York: Grove P, 1981.
- *One for the Road.* London: Methuen, 1985.
- *A Slight Ache. Complete Works: One.* New York: Grove P, 1976.

Quigley, Austin. 'Pinter, Politics, and Postmodernism (1).' *The Cambridge Companion to Harold Pinter.* Ed. Peter Raby. Cambridge: CUP, 2001. 7–27.
- *The Pinter Problem.* Princeton: Princeton UP, 1975.

Raby, Peter, ed. Introduction. *The Cambridge Companion to Harold Pinter.* Cambridge: CUP, 2001. 1–3.

Rebellato, Dan. *1956 and All That: The Making of Modern British Drama.* London and New York: Routledge, 1999.

Sartre, Jean-Paul. *What Is Literature?* Trans. Bernard Frechtman. New York: Philosophical Library, 1949.

Shklovsky, Victor. 'Art as Technique.' *Russian Formalist Criticism: Four Essays.* Ed. and trans. Lee T. Lemon and Marion J. Reis. Lincoln: U of Nebraska P, 1965. 3–24.

Silverstein, Marc. *Harold Pinter and the Language of Cultural Power.* Lewisburg, PA: Bucknell UP, 1993.

Sitney, P. Adams. 'Structural Film.' *Visionary Film.* Oxford and New York: OUP, 1979. 369–97.

Sontag, Susan. 'Godard.' *Styles of Radical Will.* New York: Farrar, 1969. 147–89.

States, Bert O. *Great Reckonings in Little Rooms: On the Phenomenology of Performance.* Berkeley: U of Cal. P, 1995.
- 'The Phenomenological Attitude.' *Critical Theory and Performance.* Ed. Janelle Reinelt and Joseph Roach. Ann Arbor: U of Mich. P, 1992. 369–80.
- 'Pinter's *The Homecoming*: The Shock of Nonrecognition.' *Harold Pinter.* Ed. Harold Bloom. New York: Chelsea, 1987. 7–18.

Stokes, John. 'Pinter and the 1950s.' *The Cambridge Companion to Harold Pinter.* Ed. Peter Raby. Cambridge: CUP, 2001. 28–43.

Taylor, John Russell. 'Art and Commerce: The New Drama in the West End

Marketplace.' *Contemporary English Drama*. Ed. C.W.E. Bigsby and Malcolm Bradbury. New York: Holmes, 1981. 177–88.

Vernet, Marc. '*Film Noir* on the Edge of Doom.' *Shades of Noir*. Ed. Joan Copjec. New York: Verso, 1993. 1–32.

Weber, Max. *From Max Weber: Essays in Sociology.* Ed. and trans. H.H. Gerth and C. Wright Mills. New York: OUP, 1949.

Williams, Linda. 'Film Bodies: Gender, Genre, and Excess.' In *Film Theory and Criticism: Introductory Readings*. Ed. Leo Braudy and Marshall Cohen. New York and Oxford: OUP, 1999. 701–15.

Williams, Raymond. '*The Birthday Party.*' *Harold Pinter*. Ed. Harold Bloom. New York: Chelsea, 1987. 19–22.

– *Drama from Ibsen to Brecht*. London: Chatto and Windus, 1968.

– *Marxism and Literature*. Oxford and New York: OUP, 1977.

Wollen, Peter. 'The *Auteur* Theory.' Rpt. *Film Theory and Criticism: Introductory Readings*. Ed. Leo Braudy and Marshall Cohen. New York and Oxford: OUP, 1999. 519–35.

Zarhy-Levo, Yael. 'Pinter and the Critics.' *The Cambridge Companion to Harold Pinter*. Ed. Peter Raby. Cambridge: CUP, 2001. 212–29.

Index

absurdism, 57–8
Adler, Thomas, 152–3
Adorno, T.W.: autonomous art, 3, 14–17, 36, 40, 58, 135, 142–3; on Beckett, 17–18, 21, 40, 161; commitment, 14–17, 40; 'culture industry,' 191–2n32; on details, 36; essay as form, 25; fascism, 28, 40, 162, 166, 174; immanent criticism, 25–6; on Kafka, 25–6, 161; negation, 21; on popular music, 103
Althusser, Louis, 139, 191n32
Appia, Adolphe, 188n46
Aragay, Mireia, 19, 182–3, 194n55
Arden, John, 48–9
Artaud, Antonin, 97, 188n46
Ashes to Ashes, 17, 133, 163, 164, 177–85; metaphor and metonymy, 179–80; political imagery, 181–2, 184; politics of, 17, 180–3; and postmodernism, 6, 177–8, 183–5
auteur theory, 7–8
authorship, 4–5, 6–10, 112, 114, 130
autonomous art, 14–18, 26, 142–4, 152, 161. *See also* Adorno, T.W; commitment

Beckett, Samuel, 6, 17–18, 21, 40, 51–2, 131, 161; *Endgame*, 23
Belsey, Catherine, 64
Benjamin, Walter, 38, 79, 89–90
Bentley, Eric, 83
Betrayal, 113–14, 116–32; and autobiography, 119–20; and melodrama, 123–4; narrative form, 124–6, 127–30; narrative pleasure, 120, 122–4, 128–30; and popular culture, 22, 113–14, 116–17, 119, 125–6, 130–2; as problem play, 116–17, 119–20; reflexivity, 118–19, 122; regression, 131–2; sexual triangle in, 124; and soap opera, 129–30; subject matter, 118–19, 121–2, 126–7
Bigsby, C.W.E., 144–5, 147
Billington, Michael, 4–5, 65, 85, 119–20, 137, 140, 155, 181, 192n3
Birmingham School, 30–1
Birthday Party, The, 40–8, 167–9; and dramatic form, 42–5, 46–7, 167–9; fascism, 39, 47–8, 164; interrogations, 44–5, 167–8; politics of, 46–8; premiere of, 18, 41
Bloom, Harold, 47; *The Anxiety of Influence*, 80